COLLECTED POEMS 1959-1999

Also by Andrew Waterman

Living Room
From the Other Country
Over the Wall
Out for the Elements
Selected Poems
In the Planetarium
The End of the Pier Show

The Poetry of Chess [Editor]

Andrew Waterman

COLLECTED POEMS 1959-1999

CARCANET

First published in 2000 by
Carcanet Press Limited
4th Floor, Conavon Court
12-16 Blackfriars Street
Manchester M3 5BQ

A CIP catalogue record for this book
is available from the British Library
ISBN 1 85754 409 9

The publisher acknowledges financial assistance
from the Arts Council of England

Funded by THE ARTS COUNCIL OF ENGLAND

Set in 10pt Ehrhardt by Bryan Williamson, Frome
Printed and bound in England by SRP Ltd, Exeter

Author's Note

This is not a *Complete Poems*, but a *Collected* containing the poems written through forty years up to 1999 that I wish to preserve. An author is on perilous territory if allowing present perspectives to tamper with past vision and stances; but there is no other reason why he should not change things, and to suppose the fact that he has at some point been content to publish a poem a bar to its further consideration is to attribute an irrational mystique to print. I have omitted previously published poems which seem undeserving on literary grounds: some mortally flawed in execution; others perhaps serving their moment but of no larger interest, or which approximate too closely to something done better elsewhere; others again which seem simply not doing enough, or vitally enough. Likewise on aesthetic grounds, I have made revisions to many poems: most a small change of phrase or punctuation. In a few cases where a worthwhile notion seemed salvageable from defects, I have rewritten more radically. My long poem *Out for the Elements* has been streamlined where the original seemed too much running-on-the-spot, and revised throughout.

I have included previously uncollected poems, indicated as such on the Contents page by italic titles. These include several poems from the years up to 1967 when the earliest in my first book was written, and also recent poems since my last collection.

The *Collected Poems* are arranged in chronological order of their completed composition. Through the decades of their writing, life has carried me from my native London, via the English East Midlands to thirty years of living in Northern Ireland, and for the last year back in England on the Norfolk coast. While by no means all one's poems are immediately autobiographical in content, and those which are are not enslaved to fact, all are perforce of a piece with one's temperament and vision of things, and a story, a quest, unfolds through the whole.

Contents

Titles of previously uncollected poems are in *italics*.

Early Poems 1959–1967

Sunday on the Housing Estate

A drab, blustery day:
canopy-blinds creak in a breeze
whirling scraps by the telephone-kiosk,
wresting Sunday-paper racks
in shop doors, and blowing smoke
clean off roofs, flat back
past telegraph-poles and trees
pencilled upon grey sky,

and over the lighted prefabs
from each of which as you pass
floats the same TV-programme sound.
Not many people about:
on the lustreless March grass
at the edge of the Council Estate
a couple of football clubs
are chasing a ball around.

The shop-fronts' glassy sweep
ends at enormous structure
of comprehensive school
factory-shaped, painted blue.
Beyond, like a contour map,
the golf course spreads away;
slack in Sunday sweaters
golfers swing and stroll.

A column of motor-bikes rips
down the curve of the bypass, turns
past monstrous boxes of flats
to enter the blue-tarred streets

Early Poems 1959–1967

Sunday on the Housing Estate

A drab, limited day.
Shop-blinds creak in a breeze
whirling scraps by the telephone-box,
twisting Sunday-paper racks
in shop doors, and blowing smoke
clean off roofs, flat back
past telegraph-poles and trees
pencilled upon grey sky,

and over the lighted prefabs,
from each of which, as you pass,
floats the same TV-programme sound.
Not many people about;
on the lustreless March grass
at the edge of the Council Estate
a couple of football clubs
are chasing a ball around.

The shop-fronts' glassy sweep
ends at enormous structure
of comprehensive school,
factory-shaped, painted blue.
Beyond, like a contour map,
the golf course spreads away;
slack in Sunday sweater,
golfers swing and stroll.

A column of motor-bikes rips
down the curve of the bypass, turns
past monstrous boxes of flats
to enter the blue-tarred streets.

Anonymous boys in black leather
scintillating with zips,
they shatter the quiet tones
of the streets and the grass and the weather.

And an ice-cream van chimes and waits
among these streets that bear
the names of prominent poets
(Keats Crescent, Chaucer Way);
dotted among them are
little identical greens
(on each, a notice warns:
Children must not play.)

Three o'clock teapots are cold
but dining-room tables are laid,
eggs poach in pans, kettles pant,
and toast-fingers with fishpaste are spread.
Mum shakes a strawberry jelly
from rabbit-shaped animal-mould,
calls Dad in from the front
in time for tea and telly.

The Delegates

The room was hot, a fly buzzed in a pane.
Here, every day, the delegates conferred,
made subtle points, took notes, sometimes concurred
on details, smoked to ease the nervous strain.
The clock ticked like the quiet talk; withdrawn,
each gazed into the table. At weekends
they joked, were snapped together on the lawn.
The newsreels showed they were the best of friends.
A mile away, five thousand men parade
outside the Court. Police fire on the crowd.
A woman shrieks. More shots. A truck is burned.
The street is cleared. A few arrests are made.
The sun shines on white walls; high up, one cloud
loiters like Murder to drench the ground.

Cautionary Tale

To the boy, the wide sky was ecstatic with light,
the birds in the trees sang that life was all right,
and thousands of streetlamps illumined the night.

So he booted a football exuberantly
about the park grass; exhausted lay
balancing the sun on a nonchalant knee.

But they told him: *Concentrate on your exams*;
made him write for employment on permanent terms
to a random selection of banking firms.

One of the millions the Underground spews,
a shine on his suit and dust in his shoes,
there were worlds to be won, and nothing to lose.

In a softly-lit cellar, soft twittered guitar,
but he left the crowd boozing, went out past the bar:
deep in the night burned an intimate star.

He flung wide his window, heard traffic hum
down the bypass, spring air foamed into the room;
vivid burst the green buds on black boughs lopped last autumn.

Pack the job in, pack a case up; he watched steam drift by
the train window, then terminus, dark customs shed, quay:
his cigarette-butt arced into the sea.

So he picked a spry living through holiday isles;
but above each thin roof, melancholy gulls
mocked him with dissonant vocables.

You can't reach life down like a bottle of scotch,
whisky and logic will not charm the latch,
time is worth more than is shown on a watch;

the universe is merely a huge currant bun,
the earth, it is due to drop into the sun,
the stars, so they say, will burn out one by one.

Old tramps who stand singing in subways know
no questions are answered, there's nowhere to go.
Emptiness weighted his shoulders like snow.

Back in the City, he sat on his arse
at a desk in an office; owns houses, shares, cars;
and passes time waiting for time to pass.

Once Upon a Time

Jack's parents were poor, but honest, runs the tale:
his father a woodcutter by trade, his mother
died at his birth, since when her spinning-wheel

has never revolved. Jack's father took another
wife, as beautiful as she was cruel,
who hated Jaaack (the usual bad stepmother),

and made him sweat his guts for crusts and gruel
scrubbing the kitchen floor, or chopping wood,
and burned his picture-books. To gather fuel

she took Jack one day deep into the wood
and threw him down a well, left him to shout.
Tough. However, after dusk the good

dumb creatures of the forest lugged him out,
fed him nuts and honey, led him thence
to their friend the hermit's mud-and-sticks hideout.

A rustic life preserved his innocence:
he never visited the city whores,
or smoked, or swore; was vowed to temperance.

Content, he kept the hermit's pigs for years
(the very word sounds like a yawn), until
one day he left the forest: gazed in fierce

sunlight upon the city on its hill.
The walls' high glitter symbolised success
and beckoned him; but more intriguing still

the Palace tower, where languished in distress
the cruel King's fair daughter. And Jack ran
to its foot to his heartbeat's rhythm. The Princess

signalled coy endearments with her fan.
He was resolved. Although the wall was decked
with ivy's slow extensions offering an

authentic model of the circumspect,
he climbed the drainpipe, took her in his arms,
and when the King surprised them, stood erect,

and promised to perform, to win her charms,
the ritual feats: so, sallying forth, cut off
some dragon's head, and slew the giant worms

guarding the ancient treasure, and with one puff
sank the rebel fleet. He'd earned his marriage.
It seemed the usual princess-swineherd stuff.

He studied etiquette, waved from his carriage
to loyal citizens who smiled and cheered,
put up with caviare, but still preferred porridge.

And lived in pomp that bored, pleasures that tired,
paced below battlements that circumscribed
the sky; in dull abstraction never cared

that his vile wife hit the bottle, nagged and gibed,
ignored their children, formed a debauched liaison
(all the Palace servants could be bribed

to keep things from the King) with the Court magician,
an ageing, disreputable voluptuary.
Jack climbed forgotten stairways of decision

and lit out for a province far away.
The small-town streets were graceless and unswept,
but lower rooftops meant a wider sky.

The King fumed savagely, his good Queen wept.
They shrank from scandal, and the papers would
play hell with this. Indeed, they never slept

until the soldiers brought Jack back for good.
His life was snapped with variegated pains
(they put it out he'd died from too much food).

So much for Jack (chars swab off the bloodstains);
his body dumped for jackals in the wood,
his beard a pull-through for the Palace drains.

Late-Night Final

Sex killer loose in Potters Bar –
Bridegroom burnt to death in car –
Smart set storm suburban Tube –
New credit squeeze: the bankers boob –
British girls are eating more –
Inside: Fashion Special for
the Fuller Figure – In Bengal
rice failure thousands starve – Shares fall –
Spaniards slaughtered 7-0 –
Official error: bomb-tests kill
nomadic tribe who could not read
warning leaflets – Reds succeed
in sending rockets into sun –
Prime Minister hits hole in one –
Surgeon heals afflicted heart –
Kissless Marriage: couple part –
Clerk claims call-girl cheated twice –
Evening X exposes vice
(details Page 3) – Six Africans
shot dead in street – Strike Peace Talk plans
falter again – Defective door

delays delegate – Stand by for
new boom in babies – in Bangkok
fishing boat unloads in dock
thousands of radio-active fish –
Queen has cold, feels feverish –
Package factory explodes –
More deaths this month on Britain's roads –
Paris fashion house decree
hitched hem above the knee.
Latest forecast: visibil-
ity is sinking fast to nil,
depression spreading, outlook rain
and fog. The sun won't shine again.

Walking to School

Round the corner the cold wind blows;
face clenched, I lean forward onto my toes;

wind sings through my ears and furrows my hair,
and scatters the birds all over the air.

The shops on the Green are all shuttered and dead;
and conkers rattle down on the roof of a shed

that lifts and rebounds. Light, blown with the breeze,
charges over the grass, and swarms all the trees.

Each night I lie reading by torchlight in bed:
they told me: *Your eyes will drop into your head,*

it happened to your Aunt Jane, they said,
who wears dark glasses. Uncle Jack, who's dead,

was insolent like you, until
one Christmas he was given a lump of coal

and nothing else. Gates bang in the wind,
and hordes of dead leaves swarm like redskins behind.

Last night I dreamed I stayed out late
on the playing fields back of the Council Estate,

when all the clouds melted like froth, with no sound,
and the goalposts slid like worms underground,

the sky went smooth as slate, and dark,
and silence drummed on in my heart,

and from under each bush as it floated away
a man and a girl ran shrieking away.

Across the brown and grassless plain
ranks of crabs moved towards me. I ran

and ran. The distant rooftop line
dwindled away. I looked round, and the line

of jointed feelers and ponderous claws,
and hooked, half-hid, misshapen jaws

gained steadily. I could not breathe,
from air like clay I chewed each breath,

stumbled and fell, under black sky that
flapped and gibbered like a bat,

hung, grimaced, swooped . . . And I woke in bed,
sunshine filling the room. But by my head

the roses on the curtains wore
crueller faces than before.

School has warm smells of ink, milk, desk, chalk;
twigs tap on the window and join in our talk.

When I grow up, I'll do as I choose;
sit in my office decoding all clues;

and as tall oaks that overcast
the sky, my wishes shall grow vast.

December Song

A jammed-on car-horn blares to drown
loudspeakered carols drifting down
the empty decorated street;
in cold, slabbed butchers' windows, meat

hangs skewered; and on left and right,
flagrant lanterns in the night,
church and pub, each bulged with strong
dogmatic and affirming song;

and brilliant shop windows show
gifts set on imitation snow.
Now, follow the strung streetlamps where
light tunnels through the night, the flare

obliterating sky and stars.
Boughs dipped in golden light disperse
black beams of shadow, splayed across
on houses set in copious

gardens; and lit panes disclose,
detached from larger contexts, those
so-human gestures: arm aslant
a green dress, laughter, argument,

impersonal as ballet or
a tableau, lovers on a floor.
A party's noise and actions spill
their rhythms from an open sill

on half-seen flowers free to move
in measures only winds approve.
Then leave the road to burrow through
its night, and bring the night in view.

Walk up the frailly lifting town's
last lane reclined on tilting downs,
whose gentle curves accommodate
emotions that will not abate.

Violent violet the night
above South London on the right;
across the valley, tracts of black,
intractable, stare blankly back,

until the passing clouds allow
the lucid moon to form below
with fluent light a calmness, real,
eternal and ephemeral.

The Last of Summer

(Richmond Park, 1962)

Sun splayed through elm-tops falls, to light
up leaves or faces, and ignite
slivers of pond. Across calm sky
pass slow clouds, great blooms of white,
immune from challenge. You and I

lie side by side, deep in grass shoots.
A bird loops round the the sun, then loots
the earth, tears worms from the pond's beach;
and the great tree beyond has roots
in earth and sky, locks each to each.

The sky's rim seals round a world here
complete, self-validating. Deer
glimpsed among trunks like shafts of light
inviolable beauty wear;
this day's sheer benediction might,

its greens, blues, hum of summer, stun
receptive minds, so almost one
might not admit that all that made
it so must end it, and the sun
sink to dissolve its world in shade.

Appearances bely the storm
gestating in what it will deform.
We know the pageantry these trees
wear as we wear out love will warm
no winter boughs, but rot and freeze.

And down promiscuous pavements roll
the tampering images, that cajole,
and finger thoughts we would ignore;
in the doorways of the soul
temptation lounges like a whore.

Sunset. And now the ponds drain light
from earth, trees, sky; and left and right
wind froths the grass; torn paper bags
shift crabwise up the slope; the white
clouds are slowly burned to rags.

But as dusk links, blends, purifies
the park of dapple, dazzle, dyes
the whole a deeper tone, may we
who leave its summer for what lies
ahead, compound to unity.

Intimations of Revolt Working in a London Bookshop

'Well, Waterman, you're back again. No joy?
Oh, out of stock at Batsford's, is it? Well,
we'll pick it up at retail price at Foyle's.
No profit for us, but we must keep well
in with Sir James – he's calling back at four.
Next, we'll get these books delivered down
Pall Mall, shall we? Debrett's *Peerage* for
the Athenaeum. Oh, if we have no joy
at Foyle's, try elsewhere. Right, then, off to Foyle's.
What seems to be the trouble? . . . Put that down!'

'So, *we* shall take these books then, shall *we*, down
the Strand, eh, hand in hand? That should be joy.
Then sell Sir James the book we've bought at Foyle's? –
we mustn't lose his custom to, say, Foyle's.
Then on to the Athenaeum: I'll stop for
a piss on all the clubland steps, as well
as shambling drunkenly through each entrance. Well,
glad this *Peerage* is handy, useful for
a bludgeon, don't we think? Serves very well . . .
What seems to be the trouble? Fallen down
your basement stairs? We're radiant with joy.'

High Tide at Richmond

A gold tide floods up the evening river
compounded of sunset and water. The populous
riverside beer-lawns are festive with colours;
radio songs yearn for summer for ever.

A motor launch rides the compliant water,
ablaze like a fireship with jazz and laughter.
Today is for ever, there's no morning after.
Lissom the light alive on the water,

startling idling yachts to alertness,
lifting the boughs of the suppliant willows,
delighting the bathers it drenches or pillows
in swathes or cascades of cordial brightness.

The affluent river floods its creeks, empties
its pockets of oodles of glittering silver.
I walk down the towpath past lovers in clover,
and the noise of boys running with armfuls of empties.

Like a lyric, the suburbs adorning the river:
Kingston, Kew, Twickenham, Hampton; all summer
all windows open, receptive to summer;
expanding like stanzas adoring the river,

tennis balls soaring and shadows relaxing
in small parks like teatrays laden with picnics;
enclasping a landscape embroidered by traffic,
bus-stops among foliage, life's impulse flexing.

The Reject

He was born in a city of boxes
of flats like broiler houses,
broken upon the wheel
of ponderous institutions
that examined and processed and channelled him
to a desk in a cubical striplit
office where he would contribute
most to National Production:
backslapping, handshaking, they told him,
You're making the grade, doing well.

Howling escalators
dragged him daily down
congested gloomy circuits
of the Underground.
Follow the coloured lights,
the porter muttered; dim figures
gibbered of sales, stocks, markets,
figures; gusts ripped dropped news-sheets
to shreds, his voice rang in despair:
Tell me, why am I here?

And they stopped, shocked, but replied.
The scientists spoke algebra,
the bankers gave tips about shares,
dons sent him definitive books
on life from their padded chairs.
Beaming priests intoned, *Abracadabra!*
You can get on HP, admen lied,
the dream life everyone seeks;
while politicians bawled, *Vote*
for more of all you've got!

Which was not what he sought.
So he flung off his ready-made suit
one morning, just sauntered away.
His parents said he'd gone mad,
his friends that he'd always seemed queer;
neighbours gossiped, *Oh, he was a bad
lot, a drifter, a ne'er-do-well*;
his Firm warned, *You've thrown away
security, prospects, we all
thought you cut out for this career.*

And he pitched a low tent by the river,
under the suppliant willow,
with no nets to fish for tomorrow.
And they shook their heads in sorrow,
passing; *Life's passed you over,
O pick your wits from the gutter.
Paupers get no girls.
See, leaves fall already, the gales
of winter will smash your frail shelter.*

Devon Interlude

Leaves in the sunlight waving, gentleness:
nudged down by thicket to the river's edge
we waded where bright water wound
among slopes lush with pure green silence,

my jeans rolled, your skirt hitched.
How delicately each bared leg advancing
sliced cool water, sluicing light
through reeds to lift fronds trailing from slant trees.

Only our toes groping the riverbed, sifting
shifting sand, met subsidence, so
plunging, for safety we clasped hands;
and saw, imaged in water, black sleeve linked to white.

While butterflies embroidered their effortless peace
on the simply perfect day. But round the shining
final riverbend, the valley opened upon
the world's ways, all the roads leading

back to the city, and the vague years
of confusion, attrition. And no doubt all
must have come to parting: we failed to manage complexities
blurred in memory now, where dream-clear

endures that image of linked tenderness
fixed in water moving
moving past leaves in the sunlight waving,
past banked greenness, and reeds nodding.

Commuter Country

The unresisting downland sprawls, soft curves
bound by chains of road and tons of brick,
what rivers there are, irresolute,
discursive, wandering miles from a lost sea.

No sign now of torsion or stress,
of whatever earthsplitting violence once rucked
this land up into rugged folds, bared rock.
The tension is lapsed now, the worn stumps smothered.

The earth is cropped and prosperous,
sectioned into cornland, pasture, sportsgrounds, gardens,
overruled by concrete, wire and fence,
and sliced in portions by electric trains.

Delivered home each night, the rising young
executives from monster city blocks
mutter of 'a hard day at the office'
but have forgotten how they once loathed their jobs.

The mortgage is almost paid off on the roof that shelters
the roomsful he's worked for, built-in wardrobes are stuffed,
chairs settle into the fitted carpets.
Hot waterpipes whisper, gentle but unconsoling.

Upstart ambitions that his young mind bred
died of neglect; shame buried them. And now
the junk is cleared from the attic, his student journals
smoke from the garden incinerator,

while his children play on the lawn, their costly toys
ignored or broken. The fathers lounge at ease
in padded lives, swap small-talk or their wives,
passionate only over bills, cars, tennis.

Only sometimes, surrounded in the night
by banks where their balances are silently rising
through their lives like rising damp,
do they catch themselves wondering if all they have

is all they should, or once meant; and to what
grim reckoning they drift unballasted;
what end no friends can join them in like drinks,
or clerks be set the routine bits to do.

Because I'm a Londoner

Your restlessness is centripetal. Trains converge
ceaselessly into your railway terminuses
to shake fresh faces down from the branches of childhoods
rooted in small parks in suburbs

where you are a glow to the north at night, generating
rumour and myth to heat armchaired families.

And multiple, dazzling, incorrigibly promiscuous,
stripteasing in neon, setting heads spinning,
accosting, perfumed, expensive to enjoy,
you captivate your footloose young,
who pay you to tell them lies and, lonely,
wipe their tears away in your dirty corners;
are entranced by the casual necklace of river you dangle,
and hang round your crookedest smile, rotting tenements
where like gold fillings gleam evenings of girls and laughter;
and when the cinema-title's lettering glows
a more conspicuous red through thickening twilight,
and starlings descend with dusk on your grey roofs twittering,
and you whisper from doors, and music trickles from gratings
to swell into estuaries of exquisite sadness,
surrender to you completely.

All is demanded, they yield to your fertile waste,
and ageing, recognise in your progeny,
in so many hands crawling between ruled margins
of ledgers, manacled by white cuffs,
in so many ashtrays heaped with distress and boredom,
in faces clenched shut against something like fists,
in such litter of promises broken,
the unmistakable image of all they are.

And too late they hate the old whore you were always,
gone at the waist, breath stinking, varicose-veined,
battening on them, querulous, money-tongued, nagging
behind the golden girls on the Underground posters,
sprawling uncaring, unmadeup.

Yet when in soft rain falling past the streetlights
you comb down your golden hair,
or when, brooding in fog, your great buildings stand
marooned in dreams of all they set out to be,
we turn again to embrace you.
Seduced once more by the terrible glamour of failure.

Room for Living

Flowers disintegrating wetly on
the cemetery graves in autumn. You
pronounced contemptuously, 'They must be mad,
those people who put flowers out on graves,
they think their being there comforts dead souls' –
which I'd not known, but – 'Bloody superstition!
It wouldn't matter in a country with
room for its dead, but it's plain criminal
in England, where we need all space to live,
were I the government, I'd see no one
was buried, all cremated, smother all
existing graveyards deep in concrete and
build flats for decent living' – somehow all
this angered me, although I don't pretend
to know of souls as things surviving death,
nor fail to see cremating's more hygienic,
and that it's how one lingers in the minds
of those one's loved that matters, not a corpse.
For I'd hope, if I'm buried, to be buried
in a world with some room for its dead.
Amenities don't seem to help us love,
graves may for some, and love's what's most worth living.
But, eclipsing talk, exact response
came as six women walking up the hill
towards us, old, and no doubt superstitious,
with fresh flowers to replace some withered ones,
or maybe just for some grave so far bare.
You dare not tell them what they ought to want;
nor, should you, would they listen, for all they
care is that something wants replenishing.

Outsider

In a public bar
pint mugs and glasses
filled with light
or dark, a glistening
placidness, slowly
emptying, held
steadily, shifted
on wooden tables
surely in known
moves of a closed world
and never spilled,
trouble my mind.
I push back my chair
and travel on.

Living Room (1974)

A Landscape for Edward Thomas

Journeying often across the heart of England,
Oxford to Leicester, I watched winter
exacting a frankness as it stripped a landscape
rain-sodden in early-failing light:
iron ploughland glinting, sheep
shorn of complacency, the air absorbing
colour or dazzle, sopping up all contrast.

Sad November trees scattered along
the level fields fling bare branches entreating
nothing, for nothing particular,
no gift of bud or birdsong on one bough
could signify: joy in this grey season
would be disease. Austerely all
endures until some general change of climate,
astonishing, perhaps to come, but not
absolving from responsibility
to what exists, is possible, today.
Pools sprawled down long troughs in fields reflect
blankly the sky's wide openness.

The unforgotten pretensions summer flourished,
its foliate rhetoric, saturated, numbed
with richness, certainties. But this meagre landscape
could draw a scrutiny that refuses
the accomplishement of gesture to reach through
submission to the strictness of what is
the finest truths there resonant, alert

to chips of flint, splashes of dung
feigning white flowers of spring, even
when it is spring, in solitude
drenched clean as earth by rain, still travelling on
down green roads, disused possibilities
long overgrown that yield an intimate
voice hinting from past the edge of the world
inhuman harmonies throng a bird's song,
seeking beyond where it could last turn back.

The Spirit Within the Shape

After the gowned ceremony and pomp
and Latin peroration, all exalting
the graduands gathered here in Congregation
to a community of scholars, a drift back
across the campus, under a bloody great
fang of reinforced concrete that perhaps
symbolises Science Surging Forward,
and past the rest of the architectural junk
put up to accommodate expanding numbers,
to the old main building, once a lunatic
asylum, bought up forty years ago
by a local self-made bigwig, given the city
that its young might have a chance he'd never had,
its thick redbrick's now ivied, almost mellow;
and fronting it, a small, well-tended lawn,
a tablet of pure graciousness doled out
from the original groves of Academe.

And here, digesting still the Chancellor's words,
'The spirit within the shape of education'.
fathers click cameras and chaff each other,
and their prinked wives in long white gloves reveal
severities or double chins as yet
concealed within the profiles of bright daughters
never seen here not wearing jeans before.

Happiest, fullest of it, a labouring man
stiff in best suit, who'll tell his mates one day,
'My missus were in tears that day we saw
our Rita get her cap and gown. And when
she went up on the stage, well all the robes,
the mace and stuff, and all that foreign Roman,
fair got me. Aye, I ached with pride myself.
Her mam and gran went into mill from school.
She's in London now, writes ads, married a Systems
Analyst. No kids. Huge house. We went there
once. It's wonderful, an education.'

Betrayal

'If you think that of me, you do not know me.'
'No, I do not know you.'
Each turned away. He heard
her cry a little, muffled in a pillow,
and risked, 'Please, darling, let us try
again.' But could not reach his arm across.
'Again? To try again again?' He shrank.
And so, apart, both slept.

And wake to find their bodies are entwined
familiarly in warmth, and disengage
retreating to the bed's cold edges,
embarrassed that unwilled flesh should betray
the separation of true minds.

Only Connect

Loose-wire emotions
spark pain
kicking at contact,
slamming down snobs
and fools, the petty

or muddled, the cared-for
who forget and compromise.
Too fierce a caring
blows frail connections.
Or slowly burns
through manageable
decent lives only
a track left empty
and edged with darkness.

Living Room

Once, a bare room, a sill
to lean from. Easy when spring
took the streets with a simmer of blossom
and roofgutter sparrows wrung
from themselves ever fresher song
to pack up and go.

Now seasonable lusts,
regrets, again infest
the blood like viruses,
I keep indoors, although
out on the common, grass
bursts through dumped chairs, stoves, cars.

Freedom to thrust like that
through all I've dumped into
a bare life since first bareness
seemed failure forfeited
by each act that furnished it,
I dwell here claimed by what
I've chosen: living room
that by the more it holds
feels less my home.

What Remains

In what remains is most pain of the loss:
letters in a shoebox, pebbles gathered
at margins facing seaward; photographs
through the bowed redbrick arch
of the little bridge you lean against, the canal
quivers fixing Leicestershire greenness.

Shelves stay uncleared. I do not
take down your prints. A powder compact rests,
mirror broken, on the bathroom sill.

We meet by arrangement now. Wearing the same
red dress in which you once cried out beneath me,
you tell your news. To let hurt show, then check
the lovers' quarrel we have disclaimed now wrenches
bones of a love worn down to only bones.

Back in rooms half in them jars to home,
I hang away the tie you gave me, pour
down the sink the undrunk daily pint of milk
uncancelled still, on the margin of our bed
turn single to the wall.

Railway Poems

I TAKEN ON

Rain from the roadbridge girder irregularly dripping
spatters flooded tarpaulins, barrels full
of frozen mutton blackly glistening,
abandoned trailers by a shattered hut,
stacked sleepers, rusting chains,
littered disconnected things. A haze
steams from the widening wilderness of rails.

'Here's where you'd work. Just lifting things.
Place is run down now, not like it was.
There's no shift on this time of day. Those sheds,
they built to last in them days, but they're half-
empty now, not suitable.' Beyond
a broken lamp and standing trucks they bulk
through rain, marooned in dreams
of all the Railway Age set out to be.

But SIMO LOADED THIS chalked on a van,
hats set on dummy-elephant collection boxes
awaiting delivery, a cast-off door
across two oildrums, nail for coat, JOCK'S OFFICE
DO NOT DISTURB ON BUSINESS above, a lantern
storing balls of twine, bald brooms, a barrow's
handles worn to a shine – all seemed
touched by usage to an almost-glow
of harmony, as then a touch of sun
made precious an oily puddle. 'I'll start tomorrow.'

II NIGHT WORKER

Jacko's been on straight nights twenty year.
He's got that pale look. No one envies him.
In winter, never sees the sun, except
weekends. You don't sleep right, the traffic, heat,
playground noises, doorbells, hammerings, light
fluttering the curtains. Then it's up at five,
supper for breakfast, pints and darts, till clocking-
on, and foreman's yell, 'Let's have yer, then.'

Twenty year! Why, even yet, at three,
when he's had his snap, head's down on messroom table.
The body never adjusts. Or when the shunt's
not up, nowt's doing, he'll stretch out beat on sacks.
Nights isn't natural.
                                        And yet he'll talk
of how the city looks at dead of night
as he smokes a crafty fag by the Humberstone wall
after the streetlamps go out, houses, shops
unearthly like, and it's all stars; or how
moths brush his cheeks out down the running roads;
how dawn comes up behind the Grain Shed, grey
or pearl, air stirring, cool light striking from
odd angles on wet slates; and going home
from barrer-running crates of fruit, the only
man in a bus against the rush, his pockets
stuffed with apples, straw stuck on his boots.

Weekends, he keeps indoors and watches telly,
Uses his holidays doing-up the house.

III TWO RAILWAY PORTRAITS

1

'We don't expect owt from Lennie.
He's puddled, penny-three-farthing.'
Rostered as 'miscellaneous',
he's given a barrow to trundle
out of harm's way. 'New foreman
once sent him over to help
unload bales of leather. Poor Lennie
tipped one load down cut, then ran
into a stanchion. Sat down,
took his cap off, great column of steam
shot up off his head, then he vanished
to shithouse for rest of the day.
Turn him off? No. You couldn't.
He'd not get any other job, 'sides,
he's a single man, no family,
nothing outside the yard.'

2

When Frank fell down the cut
and injured his back, they decided
his eyes were bad, gave him glasses:
'Bifocals. One half you're supposed
to look through for far-off, one for reading.
But ooh yer bugger, I'm blinded
with them on. I can't get right
what bit to look through when.
When I wear them I bump into things.
What's more they gives me headaches.
But I carry them round. I'm done
if they prove I'd not had them on.'
At least Frank saw that straight:
when he fell down the cut again,
by grabbing, before he passed out,
his specs and sticking them on,
he saved his disablement pension.

IV LIFTING DRILL

First size up the job.
Obstructions, greasy floors?
Sharp edges, nails?
If too heavy, get help.

Stand firmly, close to load
facing direction of move.
Bend from the knees, keeping
the back quite straight.

Get a firm grip, use
whole of fingers, not just
the tips. Keep load close
to body, lift

by straightening legs, moving
into required direction.
Put down with back straight, legs
bent, avoiding trapped fingers.

Carry this card until
safe, easy lifting drill
comes naturally to you.
Learn the rules.

'Sounds fine, but when it's coming
at you from all sides, no help,
and obstructions only found
by falling over them,

it's all sharp edges, and lurching
in unrequired directions,
time just for a grab that wrenches.
That's life. Sized up? Look at me.'

V TIME AND MOTION STUDY

'Hey-up, there's gaffers coming' – picking across
the running roads, grey macs and bowlers,
nervily holding back when the London express
whacks past, they make it at last, enquire

'What are you men doing?' 'Humping basic slag.
At it since dawn.' 'I see.' They see, notebooks
and pens out, suit-trouser-bottoms mired
a little, uneasy. Seymour, Worthington E.,

Simo, Knacker Orton, and I
slow right down so as the bastards can hardly
detect any motion, let alone time it: they've made
too many family men redundant this year.

'Is this hut your "place"?' 'Ah.' 'But there's no heating,
how do you keep warm in winter?' 'We freeze.' 'And where
do you brew-up your tea here?' 'We don't.' 'I see.
There's really supposed to be somewhere provided somewhere.'

'Thank Christ they've gone. Never lifted owt more than a pen.
Kid themselves their work's important. Think
they know it all. Let's over wall for a pint,
then round main messroom, rest, and mash.'

VI FOREMAN

Who'd be a foreman? Bimbo's never took
his coat off these ten year. Sits in his hut
doing the pools, just taking the odd turn
to sun his-self, or poke his nose in. And
he knows we've no respect. Show him a barrer,
or a crate to lift, he'd run off frit.
What's he got? – apart from his big head.
I've heard his new hats come in rain containers
unshipped by gantry-crane at Nedham Street –
two quid on his basic? We take home
far more than him each week, with bonuses,
and ours we've had to graft for, and that counts.
No, just a tongue gone black from licking boots.
Them gaffers up whose arse he crawls, they've no
more respect for him than us. You'll see.
He'll get no thanks from that lot. Why, my uncle,
twenty year a railway foreman, got
nowt but a plastic biscuit-barrel when
they'd done with him. That and his crippled leg.
Oh ah, and a handshake from the chief. He'd lost
the nerve to ask them how he'd live on that.

VII A BUTTERFLY

Even under the shed there's something outdoors
about the work. One side stands open

to stars and wind. You pause on your barrow to watch
dawn come up, or a shower across the city.

You're never bricked in. On slack shifts in summer
men wander off along overgrown sidings, embankments,

for a sun and a glance through the *Mirror*: a couple
have planted a vegetable garden back of Humberstone Coal Wharf.

Grass invades. Dustiest corners are settled
with unauthorised flowers. The Grain Shed sparrows

strut plundering leaking sacks, great rats
buck-jump away from right under your feet.

On a fine day wagons trundle in hung with glittering
waterdrops: somewhere rain is falling.

Even one bleak night, surrounded
by foggy blackness, and cartons, crates,

rolled netting stacked up on the shed platform,
hard graft, something broke in when old Gumble found

in the straw that wadded a cased-up carboy of acid
a sleepy butterfly. It crawled

onto his palm. 'Beautiful little bugger,
in't it?' It fluttered in his sour beer breath.

'Look at this, Jacko. Red admiral.' Wherever
he carried it, cupped precious in his hands,

men stopped, gathering under wan lights:
blue overalls, stubbled faces focused on

a butterfly, straw strewn upon the concrete,
and birds starting racketing for the new day in the girders.

VIII HARRY

Harry came on the Railways before the war,
stableboy. Small enough to duck under
the horse's belly for lifting up the hoofs.
His soft voice dwells like a gloss on the 'hosses':
'They were lovely. Human really. You'd talk to them.
They knew you. All had their own personalities.
Some were that vicious, kicking and bucking,
they couldn't be harnessed, or stealthy like, when you went
in to sweep shit and mush they'd close up and roll you over
on the stable floor. Couldn't take some of them near
a dray-load of carrots, they'd clean it out.
They weren't scrawny buggers, the railway hosses,

plenty of meat on them. They took prizes. We'd deck them
in red and blue ribbons for the May Day parades.
You could take a pride in the hosses,
not like them cabs they brought in in 'fifty-one.
More reliable, too, give a hoss a bag of hay,
he'd go all day. Them buggers always break down.'

On the night fire gutted the old Bell Lane stables, Harry
couldn't watch. He walked off, his limp worse than usual
from a foot a bay trod on, smashed twenty years back.

IX GETTING ON ON THE RAILWAYS

'There's few but me's just plain goods-porter here.
Soon as you've to read labels to know where
to hump the stuff they're tied to, grade goes up:
Special abilities. 'Sides, there's other things.

Take the motormen, allus arguing
with the men who load the trailers for their rounds,
how all's in the wrong order to pull off.
Both once were graded checkers. Motormen
got together, stuck out for how they must
get made-up senior checkers so they can
bollocks the loaders, call them every name
under the sun like they do anyway,
but by rights, for stacking trailers wrong.
Next the loaders found out that the forms
they list the goods on aren't straightforward forms,
oh no, they're multiple, carbons and all.
That entitled them to upgrading too.
So the motormen are back at square one. It'll
go on till they're all station managers,
They'd still waste half the morning arguing.

Another case: old Greg who checks out stock
in the Order Shed, he's not allowed to lift,
that's why they gave him that job. Can't hold owt,
poor old Gregory, not even his beer,
really shouldn't be working, no, the only
place for him is six foot under. Well,

he got so much wrong counting cartons out
they made him up a grade to give him an
increased sense of responsibility.
So now he draws more doing more things wrong.
Wrecking the bloody railways'd take him to
the big boss seat. He'd not be first, at that.

Me? I've no incentive. Oh, I graft.
But I can't stand the wife. I've no kids, don't sleep much:
the one sure way outside of opening hours
to stay clear of her whittling's being here.
I keep low grade to keep my basic down
so as I must stop overtime to earn
what buys her stuff for house and fancy stuff.
Not but what twelve pints a night don't help.'

X SIDELINE

'No satisfaction in this work –
load up a wagon or dray,
it goes off, and that's that,
never see it again.
And anyway someone's unloaded it somewhere.
My sideline, now, tables, chairs,
cupboards, suchlike – round my mates' houses
there's things I've made, solid – that's good.
Our spare room's full of the stuff.'

XI THE WATCHER

Bill's fair done, takes a breather
elbows on wall overlooking main road
mowed-out with traffic, shops thronged
with women and kids, all that coming and going,
beyond the workshop where girls wave back
and new carwash – pity you can't
nip out for a drench under that;
watched from the shadow inside the shed
by a spider trapped under a dusty
glass on a ledge, found last week
unloading bananas – 'Great hairy bugger' –
hunched motionless, patient to die.

XII THE INMATES

Some, one can't imagine outside the yard.
Dwarfed by the draughty Victorian sheds
they break down into their work.

The machinery, leaky hydraulic hoists,
splintered turntables embossed 1860,
frayed ropes, rusted tackle, bent crowbar,

unites with limps, maimed hands, greasy caps
grown to pulverised faces sporting
sellotaped Health Service specs, pink and white

wobbly false teeth, in a slow
organic deterioration. When not in use
they'll stand propped on wonky barrows till grass

comes up through their boots. A blowlamp would hardly
flake off soiled layers of clothing. Leisure
is sprawling on rotten casks

beneath weak lighting that yellows the skin,
sunning where a south wall holds the heat,
on a fine day pottering cuttings blackberrying;

in little huts scattered among the wilderness
of tracks they settle into a sludge
of used rosters, racing-sheets, calendars.

Red jelly one night in a washroom basin
meant Snowy'd gone after forty years: 'haemorrhage'.
The Railways had finished him off.

Bury his frame in Hoss Dock under
old sleepers, or let it rest in long grass
out of foreman's road back of the Grain Shed

till rank flowers sprout through his eyes, *Reveille*
folded over his knees, enamel
tea-mug gripped in skeleton hand.

At the Hermit's Chapel

Stone steps hewn
to the promontory's peak
where a chapel ledged
in wind overhangs
the Atlantic. The hermit
who carried stone to stone
to build this and lived here
knew the elements.

On fine days like today
people remote from him
come in cars that halt
at the cliff's edge, to climb
steps now dipped with wear,
and stand, in testimony
to the unimaginable.
The eye loses itself
drowning into light,
the ear receives only
the scream of wheeling gulls
in the wind, and wind.

Such height cannot be borne
too long. I descend,
crushing a snail I'd not
seen to a yellow smear.
It dries into the stone.

Solstice

Waking into
the landscape of my heart
it is snow.

Contours have
slipped. The loss of bearings
unfocuses me

and slopes I relied on
just being there firm
in every season

to pour
me back into myself
are blanked away.

Stumbling for paths
no earthly spring can find
I fall locked

into a backward
dream freezing a valley
once blossom and shade.

Turning Point

There is an evening moment when
the terminus cools. Oranges
glow from a kiosk, and light
lies unbroken in dust again.

Only a few dark suits straggle late
from offices towards
their train as it slides in from the sun.
And as the carriages shake down

fresh faces from the branches of childhoods
rooted in small parks in suburbs,
up for their first night in town,
coming to meet them across the barrier

the clerks see their young selves,
and all they once were surfaces again
through weighted, slackened features.
Unrecognised by new blank faces

passing on to the city that claims them;
knowing as broken these they push through;
not knowing that this turning-point
is their own, and it is gone.

Man Cycling Home in Donegal

A black coat flapping on a rusted bicycle
steadily pedalled beneath a vast sky,

he does not look over the spiky hedges,
intent on the day's end at the tarmac's end.

Intention contracts him out of the landscape,
a speck of absence; yet nags to alignment

all its passing through ignores,
the wilderness massing its greens and blues

under wide light ebbing where distant
peaks are null with snow. The contours

of centuries gathered behind pour through
this man, defining his substance, waste spaces.

His life is heavy with generations
of mist, of marriages silted with hailstones.

His slow deliberateness conforms
to outlines of ridge and glen, their scope

and lack of detail. He has no ideas,
being certain only of the earth and the stars

and – though tonight light flies from his hammer
about the cottage – snow dulling his pulses.

Hands

It is the hands
live on. I watch
wonderingly out of
the skull's shell

their slow underwater
tensionings wring
suds through a shirt,
their firm grasp

to puncture a can
of coffee releasing
the fresh aroma.
Peeling an orange

or in a mirror
knotting my tie
they flex intricately
like animate things.

How peacably now
they rest, lightweight
on knees, blue-veined,
dusted with hair,

before moving
unfalteringly on
to construct the spare
scaffolding of deed

assuring tomorrow.
They dress me to meet it;
record on this page
its intimations.

A Yorkshire Triptych

1 DEATH IN THE VALLEY

So it came to this:
the years of grit, of being
'beholden to no one'
contracted to a room,

her husband's farmer-hulk
dumped on a couch dying,
herself near-blind, arthritic,
still keeping the place tidy.

From the black mill-villages
clinging below the moorland
relatives call, take tea,
in the glow of hearth and polished

surfaces and shining
brass and copper things
watch the brawn hand twitching
at nothing, on the coverlet.

'Nurse says he'll not last weekend.'
They talk of their own ailments.
On the mantelpiece, beneath
three plaster flying ducks,

him in his striped demob-suit
that week they had in Blackpool,
and donkeys, and the children –
who now in distant cities

reading 'I can't write more.
I'm not myself since Father
passed on. But I manage,'
are steadied with a sense

of a lifetime's cramped persistence
dying in slow pieces,
leaving a world tidy
they'll not go back to live in.

2 THE RING

So she came back, it being
over, and walked through
from the kitchen door to find
her grandmother crouched scouring
the front step, where only
the doctor and undertaker
would ever call, as if
she'd not budged in four years
since the girl first came to tell
of the man she'd gone to live with.

The old woman, conforming
to the narrow ways
of the valley where mills point
dark fingers towards God,
had fetched out thirty pounds
from a teapot in the sideboard,
and the frail engagement-ring
her own swollen joints
could no longer wear:
'I'd like you to have it.'
But in church that Sunday
bending a submissive
neck to breathe in dust
like a sweetness sifted from
the generations of vows
given there, had cried,
that they'd not done things right.

Across silence now,
and sixty years, one sees
the posture of a life
stiffened undeceived
against sure attrition,

pitying the struggle
that has brought nothing;
the other pities freedom
from struggle that has left
nothing to betray;
except a ring the world,
whatever it's coming to,
no longer has a place for.

3 THE SONG

She sang the song the Belgian refugees
brought to the valley's mills in the Great War.
Straight in his narrow chair her husband sat,
blending a phrase. They were young then.

Their young have gone away. When her eyes went
he sold the weaver's-cottage, brought her down
to the terrace in the Bottom, fixed downstairs
for her wheelchair: bedroom, bath, no doors.

He does the women's work, and washes her.
When relatives call she talks of the old view
from home up on the Edge – moor, clough and sky.
But massive today in a darkening brown room

she sings the strange French words the Belgians taught her,
as if the mind's lens poured all summers since
back on one blot of light. She was young then,
the foreign music was the outside world.

Charged with its resonance the flowered teaset
on the Welsh dresser is set vibrating:
speckless teapot, milk-jug, rows of cups
she kept for best, and never filled or drank from.

Summer 1970

It is the season of death,
furred, feathered things crushed to the roads,
insects smacking themselves
to pulp on the windscreen, and
the bulldozer gouging back
ditch, hedgerow, root and branch:
gashed green bleeds red soil.
Community Relations Committee
campaigns to keep temperatures down;
but in town after little town
strident with union jacks
riding its fields afloat
on tidal flute and drum
the heat beats up. The road
dips from the hills into
the hazed pit of Belfast,
an army-truck gouts black smoke
over late-flowering thorn;
the sniper climbs to his roof,
wall blazoned ONE MAN ONE GUN.

Living with Dreams

When he dreamed it was he and Rosalind in the room
with orange curtains that overlooked seeping
redbrick backyards, dustbins and washing-lines,
discussing names they would one day give their children,
or her fears and failures in teaching, he caring so much,
and it was so real, the curve of her lip
so intimately known, and he woke and it was
Susan on whom morning sun streamed from the sea
through blue curtains, and on the pillow her wrist
with the pale band shadowing where the watchstrap went,
he felt pain, but was not bitter. This was real,
and the worries they shared walking the beach, and the comfort
each gave each, promising love. And later,

when dreaming of Rosalind or Susan he awoke
and it was Jane's black hair, her warm
leg thrown across his back in sleep, he was truly
grateful, having no choice, and learned
to live with dreams in which they lived with him
who were no longer his. And when it seemed
he had been here before, he also saw
that the view was changed again, the cups
they drank from different, pottery Jane liked,
and different noises troubled the evening quiet.
Things had been, and now were so, being Jane
with her own fears and hopes, who also dreamed
in this room with striped green curtains, and
must be in others' dreams. He could not say
there might not some day be two strangers linked
by Jane's and his dreams of each other from
their different beds. It seemed there was
this shimmering web of love and pain through dreams
at once uniting more than ever guessed
each other, and dividing each, among
those laid in daily pairs, where now
Jane needed him to listen, and they might
sit choosing names for unborn children.

Mother

I should be grateful. You
adopted me in a hard time,
the sound of guns from Dunkirk shaking
London, the bombs. You have told
how once you lay over my pram as a German
aeroplane swooped to machine-gun the street.
What made you, you never did say.

It was only 'You should be grateful' became
the theme you played on a subtle keyboard
(you'd not been an actress in vain):
grateful for supper, for half-days in Brighton,

for wellington boots in rainy weather,
'for all I have done for you'.
There was also your tone saying 'Don't.'

And when father left you said nothing,
except – remember? – when
I finally asked, that day in the park
at the rusted green cafeteria seats,
to distract me, 'Look at those sparrows,'
and did not notice rage boiling the dregs
of a nine-year-old's childhood away.

So I locked you from me in turn, as I locked
my schoolwork away in a case.
Where was I going? 'Out.'
And when leaving for good I came
to tell you, you carried on hanging up washing,
not taking the peg from your mouth just said
'Remember to leave your doorkey.'

At seventy now, arthritis
has withered the touch and range
from your piano-player's hands,
your first teeth are decayed (years after mine).
Hoarding a fossil faith
in Stalin, the god that failed,
you keep up the garden, read Dickens, see plays,

and we can be easier together,
and I am truly grateful.
If what you pinched and scraped once seemed
me, I know now it was for me,
understand things you still cannot say
as your talkative letters come, each signed
not 'with love', just 'as ever'.

Dingle

Here, where Europe ends
in great mountains weltering into the sea,
surgings of rock and cloud,

the past sticks bones through thin soil,
clochans, ringforts, earthworks, burial grounds,
casts up legendary arrowheads –

on Ventry strand
one might stumble on embedded skulls of the slain
scattered by Fionn Mac Cumhaill.

The sadness of the past whines through the people's music,
and the eyes of their barefoot children whipping
cattle down stony bohereens

under the summit where St Brendon the navigator
glimpsed between mists a clear view he followed
over the edge of the world.

Why should they stay: to scrape a living
from the tourist's pastoral myth?
They learn a sharp nose for his money,

and adult, given the chance, will trade
all his Celtic twilight and bee-loud glades
for a Hammersmith tenement, fridge, and forty-hour week.

Even in the village shop,
filled with students down to brush up on the language,
ancient gutturals are drowned

by the television dumped
among stacked Kelloggs, Surf, Flash, Alka-Seltzer:
on the counter a fading profile

of Padraic Pearse wilts by a gilt-edged colour photo
of John Fitzgerald Kennedy, the martyr who'd
first got away, made good.

Ghost

Remember? Wind and sea outside, and darkness
had seeped to fill the low horizons.
Together in the bed we lay apart,
pressed by the litter of her soft-whipped silver things,
brushes, boxes, mirrors face-down
on the dressing-table. At the bed's foot
her boots, in pairs, askew, suggesting torsion
in the body absent from them now,
crying for me elsewhere. I know. I knew –
but could not tell to whom was due
the single indivisible tear that came.

And our bodies, you and I,
lying taut the while in separate life.

In the end, of course, we came together
in the dark; warm flesh, cool-textured sheets. It seemed
natural to cling to what was there
ledged high in the purest element, pain.

Right too that her uncollected things
were cluttering the room, as she our love.

Her taking them has not tidied her away.
You whisper, 'I feel I am living among ghosts.'
I shiver, cannot reach you.
What lays this ghost between us in our bed?

The Dream

We'd hurt each other. Now I sat alone
drowsing on hot carriage-cushion where
along Lough Foyle the Derry train drifts wide
of anything like land: ribbed sand
ribboned and glazed with water mirrors sky
and the seagull's loop: which real, which mirage?

And it seemed you were with me: I said,
'A dream-blend of all elements – like peace.'
And outside the window a gull stilled
wings unmoving – or was it the train that stilled?

Beyond blue sea in which light steadied to
a million points, lay cloud-soft Donegal;
the other way, a sort of green fen spread,
trees, hedges, cattle in long grass, white stone –
the only movement bounding hares –
then suddenly Benevenagh's reared head,
sun picking out the topmost weave of grass.

'No,' you said. 'It is no dream, but life –
beautiful things, but you must glimpse them while
they're in your vision, you can't stop the train.'

'I am on the train too, we move together.'

The gull had fallen back, the glinting peak
receded. Then you screamed,
flung the compartment-door wide, jumped, were gone.

At least, I was on my own when the train pulled in
through wharves, warehouses, Derry's rank black walls.

Downhill All the Way

Ten-thirty. Bert from Sales Accounts looks in:
'Hatcha, Jess! your cheeks are pink –
did your old man give it you last night then?'

Mrs Wilkes pats her grey hair, grins
and bears it, goes on filing. Always does.
And Mike slides off down the corridor

to chat-up the Comps, and see where the tea-trolley's got –
rousing old Jack out of moaning about the blackies:
'Skiving bastard! – who you knocking off now, then?'

Eleven. 'If this bloody piss leaves your bloody gut crusted
like inside that urn, we'll be dead before our next increments.'
'Open the window, it's stifling.'

But when you do, black soot from the shop-floor vents
showers in, settling on cuffs, blotters, invoices –
and this time a butterfly – shrieks, a glissando

of flimsies and carbons as Joyce and Maureen the typists
flutter gaudily, batting it with today's *Mirror*.
Eric Hartree stamps a docket, frowns

intent on ten years time when he'll sit where
Mr Wells whom he stares at sits
in a costlier Burton suit in a swivel-chair

at a desk with drawers and a more massive ashtray heaped
with the cares of *Manager, Accounts Payable*.
Meanwhile the minute-hand limps past noon,

(the butterfly is limp between two panes) and young Doug
remarks, as this time every day,
'Downhill all the way now.' It always was.

Derry Images 1968–1971

1

Derry, Londoned Derry, jerrybuilt
and gerrymandered – yet turning
to sky and mountains a profile spiritual
as one of its dark appealing ghetto faces.

Close-up eruptions of disease,
on dank walls, broken gable-ends:
UP PAISLEY, BRITISH MURDERERS, FUCK THE POPE.
What flowers among this detritus?
slashing at nettles, a child runs barefoot begging.

2 NOVEMBER 1968

A volley of sticks, stones, bottles –
loyal Fountain Street rips up a Civil Rights march.
From Ferryquay Gate shut three hundred years ago
by apprentices, their heirs the police
gaze over shields unstirred from duty:
keeping inviolate the Maiden City.

3

One comes back to the walls. A bastion overlooks
Nailors Row, rotten stumps like broken teeth
since they stoned the Catholics out of the street.

Roaring Meg still pokes a swart muzzle
at Creggan Heights where James's army stood.
Now houses mass up that slope.
'Those people all came from the mountains, with their priests.'

What walls out, binds in.
Even bible-drunk Walker, defender of the Siege,
now petrified on his pillar turns
inward, cannot see on the road outside,
stolen in mockery, his slogan: NO SURRENDER.

4

From the battlements by the Apprentice Boys' Hall girls flaunt
union jacks at the sullen Bogside below;
mean streets, men standing about on corners,
on the burroo, forced to cadge from their working women.
They stare back up the embankment, waiting
to come into their manhood, their split-level city.

5

Precarious city, washed in a drift of rain
to almost a monochrome solution –
a shimmer of wet roofs, a mere
greyness wrinkling among the welter of mountains.

But stark on the wasteground dusk, vigilantes:
men bearing stones and staves;
and a toppled excavator sprawled
like a broken-backed dinosaur barring
the way down the Lecky Road where the RUC'd beat.

Back in the city centre
I walked into a lighted store, hovering
by a counter where electric lamps glowed –
that in the next affray were all smashed.

6

Flickering into focus on my screen,
electronically diffused through waves too thin
to body pain, it comes:
the latest riot: smoke plumes from a factory burning.
I go on peeling my orange.
But looking through my window to see the same
black cloud two blocks away,
put on my coat; drawn where what's felt is on the pulse,
by dint of a baton, stone.

7 AUGUST 1969, THE BATTLE OF BOGSIDE

So I was there, shooting
with a camera. Images for cold storage:

armoured cars bludgeoning through a barricade
into a storm of petrol-bombs, veering deranged,
to limp back beaten like scorched insects;

scaffold-poles, concrete blocks, steel reinforcing, built
into barricades – defence before housing;

teargas in the sun unrolling
like a voluptuous white carpet, beautiful –
its embrace scatters men like ashes;

night skies aflame, a hijacked
Mister Softee ice-cream van rolled blazing downhill
chiming silvery as the moon – till it hit the mob;

also a kind-faced man in a torn
sweater kissing his family goodbye after tea –
'No, you can't come with Daddy. Not till you're grown' –
as he set off, armed with dustbin-lid, stave.

And when, I wonder, on those frightened streets,
at what point of invasion, hurt, should I
have dropped my camera, to lift a stone, or run?
And which have done?

8 THE FENCE

Fountain Street's neat red white and blue. Wall-paintings,
freshened annually, show the Relief, King Billy
white-horsed, purified into primary colours.

'Our only trouble is we're too loyal here.
These lads would die for England. No one in England
cares, for us, or England, anymore.
The Fenian rioters get the sympathy,
and the army I served years with sent to help them.
Though now they stone the soldiers. So do our lads.

Things weren't so bad. I mind four years ago
I had a Catholic friend, lived up in Creggan.
Now, I do decorating round these streets,
some of these paintings. Well, I went up there
to set and paint the railings for my friend
round one of those wee saints they put in their gardens.
And his wife knew who I was, and didn't like it,
and got the neighbouring womenfolk who came
and threatened me, their weans all throwing stones.
And he jumped the fence, the fence was brave and high,
and hit her to the ground, and she stayed down,
and with a spade he warned the others off.

He was my friend. There was more tolerance then.
Though my Lodge didn't care for what I'd done, and warned me.
But nothing would get me up to Creggan now.'

9 JULY 1971

Black flags, plaster saints, fresh flowers,
compose at the spot of death a noontide pause.
The shadow might be that pool of blood again.
It lengthens, steeping oncoming evening.

These mourning candles will burn factories,
the tears wept fall as stones upon the soldiers.

A Summer Frame

Cogitate pipesmoke blue in a blue shade-dapple
beneath a garden tree, a water-sprinkler
rotating for ever, a bee bending white clover,
and I in a deckchair absorbed
in this greenness, its willing of something to come to pass.
A jamjar wasptrap full of sugared water
hung from a bough holds all the light of the world.

'It is summer,' we said, 'It is summer,'
thinking that accidental to the unique thing.
But the child squirming bare toes in the burning sandpit
grew out of himself; first love in the bracken,
with sunlight spinning in the wheel of a fallen cycle,
did not come true; I cannot even remember
that other girl's face (I could check, I have photographs),

only the great elm where we parted that
took root in an inner landscape with a stretch
of bridged canal, a field with burrs that clung,
certain walks, with others, or alone,
a white launch chugging past reeds, mown-grass scents, and
the garden sandpit, the creaking of these boughs
above me now, this bee, white clover.

A frame to hold all that through accident
survives merged into 'summer'; as if
a photograph, were one so sensitised
as to show, beyond the light-spectrum, the dark
seepage of everything thirty summers' greenness
has never brought to pass; and so composed
at a desk indoors by I who have no garden.

Room with a View, North Antrim

He was all too much motion.
She would embrace it.

He accepted. She hung up pictures, ordered
his living-space. Fixed things.

Her brooms drove through him. He eddied to corners,
under love's arc-lamp chafed to submerge

through mirrors – or, sometimes,
the window, beyond which sea ran crying

upon soft arms of coast:
such fluencies of outline, soarings, sweeping on,

still containing and calming,
reached peace through perfection of motion.

Dream-clear each cottage on far Donegal –
another country.

Gardens

'This is your garden. Dig it.'
Eight hummocky feet by three in a rancid corner.
Bored, I poked about, chopped at worms, bought seeds

at Woolworth's in vividly illustrated packets.
Such as came up looked shoddier, or were just weeds.
And besides, I preferred running off down the forest.

Since when I've had no gardens. 'And no regrets,'
I usually say, 'they enslave you.'
All those bank clerks pruning their privet each Sunday!

Not but what peering in on some shimmering lawn
with water-sprinkler rotating for ever, splodged
with immaculate flowerbeds there's not envy –

though the silver-haired bloke at the roller framed against
open french windows is not my style,
nor such casual-seeming perfectedness, not to mention

rustic bird-baths, phoney Tudor lanterns.
Still, as I move on, does the wrought-iron of his gate
bar his world or mine? I wonder.

And I quite like to haunt public gardens;
or those of stately homes, with statuary,
ornamental cascades and grottoes, hedges cut

into classically soluble mazes,
or some landscaped romantic vista along a lake,
trees shovelled up into the clouds.

And back looking out of whatever rooms I've got
at some rubbly yard with bins, or untended jungle
where you hear the tumbledown walls' stones grinding in frost,

I hanker after illusive gardens
from Adam and Eve to *Alice*; and that one
in the story everyone's read, through a magical gate

in a wall in a drab city street.
Some fertile green congruence: I can almost feel
its moss, catch its scent in the breeze, hear the sound of water.

'Concrete the bloody things over and leave yourself free.'
Yet now, if I found myself settling for one,
I'd set about digging.

Not That One Can Go Back

Not that one can go back and start again.
Perhaps, to a blue garden gate,
the momentary bloom of sunshine mute upon
pavement dust, dusty leaves, red pillarbox,
the pebbledashed house where my mother hoarded her worries.
'I'm going to quit school. And home,' I told a friend,
spinning my bicycle wheel till it kindled a blaze.

Or later, the river at Richmond, night:
against the dark flood a swan held its place and its poise,
neck arched, possibility questing.
'Marry me,' I said. She did. And that went wrong.

And elsewhere, to another, 'We'd best part.'

What is cast off, and what is taken on –
living, one acts from doubt, the contradictions
never resolve for waiting; and not to trust
those special moments when something blossoms or rides
a rising tide, is the greatest sin;
not less because sun is just sunny, and swan swan.

And yet, 'There is something inherently mean in action,'
Coleridge says; and I think of how each deed
destroys its alternatives; how most of pain
is burying them; and of this dream:
outside in a lightless street I am prising open
a drain. There issues a sulphurous underground smell.
And I lift out one by one translucent sopping

murdered embryos; heap them in the gutter.
A silent crowd has gathered. I cannot see
their faces. I know I am guilty.

Not that one can go back and start again.

The Two Roads

The fork in the path
came up before
I was ready to choose;
I found I had taken
the sky road. At first
I could glimpse through thicket
the other lane dipping,
escorted by water,
between flowering banks,
rollered lawns, white stone dwellings.
A turn lost the view.
And what with the rain
closing in, the unsheltered
climbing a stony
road riding blown grass,
it was only attaining
the ridge I could look
down through snatches of cloud
at the coast road whole:
past meadows where cows
stood in clusters it followed
the strand to the bay's
bluest haven, a house,
sunlit garden, child playing
as if who belonged there
might have been me;
who appearing now
did not look up,
would be deaf at such distance
to the nothing I knew
was all I could say now.

Lost

Rock, air, water,
a country resolved to brute elements,

raining down to grey sheets of itself,
tumultuously trickling and

splashing, mist-drifts
from which the mountains loom bunched and giant.

Up there, all tracks are lost,
in the great scoops between ridges where wind

hollows the skull like the strewn beasts' skulls,
almost distinction from that which is lost in;

for guidance only
in a momentary atmospheric

shift the granite's aimless
patterns of quartzveins brilliantly glittering;

also, those drystone walls,
meticulous, speaking of different weather,

kept purposes, reducing the mountain,
that might bring us down together.

Calling

I took it in when I first called to view,
through-traffic slushing beneath a railbridge,
peeling shopfronts, lustreless shut pubs,
a yard full of scrapped trolleybuses, dead
antennae aimless under a grey sky.
and the street I sought off-left, cracked pavement,
gardens all weeds, the odd house boarded up.

After knocking, I turned in the pause:.
across the road an open window framed
a headscarved woman moving, dusting, singing.
The massive pink door shuddered to let me in.
And I was led up past landing kitchenettes,
and round and up to a slope-roofed room, low bed,
bed-table, tilting wardrobe, cheap bowl fire.
'That's it, and there's the meter.' Then,
'You're young,' he added, 'where is your home?'
'Home?' I replied, 'Home's where I find myself.'

And so it was. Perhaps I have never left.
Coming round different corners since
I am caught surprised by a different door, red, blue,
wrong to my expectation of that blistering pink one,
and the strange accents of a different now.
My silences reassume the network
of those streets, whatever noise traffic makes
modulates to their noise; imagination
attunes to that cramped box. Which first
wrung notes of what it had for song from it;
where I settled for what calling found.

From the Other Country (1977)

Great Blasket

From land's extremity the island
entices, delectable with shadow.

The landing-place is clefted between rock,
and a green road loops up

around what have been dwellings, roofless,
foundering into blown grass set

with flower-constellations I have no name for.
Elemental enough: some sheep, the sea

they road in curraghs casting nets;
the long winters of inbred storytelling

in the Irish, the young drifting to mainland
jobs and marriages. Till all were taken off.

And if this twenty-year dereliction harboured
ghosts, there'd be nothing to be said

except agreement how across the water
always looks more alluring.

The boat collects us. From the stern
I see, before a shower cuts off, the broken

walls still marking each frail holding,
a longer stay than mine, and not romantic.

Epilogues

1 HOUSEHOLD

Names on the bellpush labels change
by the month; the house remains:
asymmetrical in rank garden
where nothing is tended but washing,
and a lurching pear-tree
still showers petals on grass,
worn wall, crazed path.
The iron gate hangs unhinged.

Tenants, not speaking
even goodmornings, edge past
on landings, behind partitions
listen to one another's private sounds;

share only the dustbins,
front steps kept by two pedestalled
stone lions, doggish and bird-dunged,
a thin pulse of tune from separate radios,
and a roof still crowning
all with a prodigal eccentricity:
green dome, castellations, turrets,
and a railed platform high for stargazing
Victorian paterfamilias, who kept
a home together.

2 CANAL

Climb through torn wire-mesh fencing
by the arterial road, and down
through nettles, rusting cans and flowering
grasses, to the canal.

It stagnates, loosening
the bricks of warehouses that have long
turned backs blank on it. It is quiet here,
where water detains passing clouds,
and out of bounds,
even the notices *By Authority*
weathered and fallen.

They are planning to do it up, a landscaped precinct,
flowerbeds, concrete wastebins.
A waterside lung for the community.

Meanwhile, unwatched,
step over fracturing flagstones set
with rusted iron mooring-rings.
Do not stumble. Come under
the mouth of this tunnel: deep grooves
scoured into stone where ropes have taken
the strain of a heavy bend;

a darkness that, stirred,
might almost disgorge, like slow prehistoric fish,
the corpses of drowned generations.

3 ANSWER

A single garden of roses, thickly wrought
red roses hoarding sun in the silence
of a low blind street end-on to a warehouse wall,
scheduled for clearance.
Blistering paint,
broken panes, the other small plots abandoned
to weeds, dropped tiles, gaped blank to what
had determined this immaculate aftermath.

Red blooms. Soft-burning still in vivid answer.

4 HYMNS

I

Dropped stucco, boarded
windows, aimlessly
spiralling dust,
one creaking shop-blind.
A lamp shattered by
the casual stone
arches an upstairs
window sashed high,
where a headscarved woman

moves dusting, singing:
'. . . through pastures green
He leadeth me
the quiet waters
by.' One street,
one minute, attuned
to impossible music.

II

Sudden access
of light, and green
sparking along
boughs lopped in winter
come painfully always;
a brilliant rush
that stuns itself now
into perfect stillness.
White blossom calms
the street, foot falls
steadily upon pavement,
a bird sings one note
over and over
on the sky's pure bowl.
We promise, we promise,
ingathered to a moment
helplessly credible,
already blurring.

III

An ice-cream van's chime
from parched suburb aspiring
trembles in blue air,
like seaweed in water.

5 LAST FRUIT

Planted behind today's houses
are fruit-trees spaced to a more lavish scale
ghosting the definitions of gardens
belonging to homes now gone.

Replaced by 'twenties villas,
mock-tudor semis, last season's box of flats:
high-density discord superimposing
tight limits out back.

And rooted where they always were, the trees'
disposition misses some lawns; while some
have apple-tree, pear or plum,
fruits for the picking.

With age, the yields are lessening:
branches fall, are lopped; and then the trunk,
to a stump good only for bowling at;
till hacked out and burnt.

Meanwhile, still lucky children
can play catching fluttering blossom in a cup;
and stray out on a frosty dawn
for the last windfall.

Coming Down

Our cylinder of hushed steel tilts, slides down;
and lives contracted to the beating of the engines

see startling, iridescent laciness
spread on the waters of the night, lit London:

whorls and radials of orange, blue,
turquoise, an insubstantial rainbow-froth

that might swirl away down its black holes.
Yet flashes stammering there the motivation

of an electric train, and smaller lights
moving, speak of human purposes.

Unreal, till grounded and bussed in, and stood
jostled on hard pavement, a quarrel breaks

behind me: 'I will.' 'You won't.' 'You'll see I will.'
Giving back local scale and weight.

I check my map. Above me, bowed lamps roof
intricacies shutting out the dark waste spaces.

He Woke

He woke, and it was true.
The light had wasted towards evening
and would stay that way for a while;
on either side of the tarmac a landscape

arrayed its ridges and dales
for his delectation, entertained
with discourse of water;
while tastefully arranged over fields

spread gently skirting the mountains
were men engaged in useful toil,
bent digging, restoring a wall,
a tractor rode its billowing acre;

and houses, decently spaced, of weathered
stone, sequestered in fruited gardens,
balanced spirals of hearth-smoke;
to each some lane would be leading.

It was all very pleasing.
Well-moulded trees alone or in clumps
on the dip-slope had unfurled
long shadows in the late sun

that yet did not sink. Though behind him
he was conscious of the road darkening backwards,
remembered the turnings-off attempted,
when the tramp sprang out of the ditch crying

'No!' and the lovers ran off
from the bushes giggling, the terror
as what enticed gave way underfoot:
black falls, pain, scufflings, cries.

Till back on the road. The scenery it seemed
was only disposed for his contemplation.
He had only the road, and in one direction.
Otherwise he was free.

And at least it held off night
for a time; though despite so many who had passed before
it was empty. As if in a dream.
He woke. It was true.

Suburban Eden

Booting a ball about, white shirtsleeves pumping
vivid on the summer dusk, until beyond
the trees red car-lights came flickering on
and the corner garage burned violet,

or in winter shouting for reassurance
in mist's stillness with black boughs dripping
it felt miles from any house,

or just to sit on the shelter bench staring out
at foliage darkening on darkening sky
till the pattern sparked live fire upon your brain,
or timeless hours up in those trees,

we grew. And there came girls, elusive as water,
awakening sharper pains. But still in a world
sealed by the sky's rim round the park's edges,

unaware to the last, to the day
the train shook us down in a gloomy rail terminus
fallen, clutching our season-tickets.

And one can never go back,
only to look: it is still going on,
on a stretch of grass boys are chasing a ball about,
girls call from the benches, the ball rolls loose, my foot
holds back; one kick might shatter glass,

as beyond the railings the Addiscombe train slides past,
dusty green, for the city; not yet for them.

The House

Yes, the house was there.
I noticed it young,
in a street round the corner:
built four-square
for every weather, windowframes
fresh-painted, never
a tile slipping,
grass mown, flowerbeds tended;
awaiting me.
I walked away, perplexed.

But later, when I made tentative approaches
from the bedsitter quarter: 'Well, one day . . .'
I ruminated over my gasring supper.

Then came, from time to time,
the invitations: to dinner,
perhaps overnight.
Beautiful getting up,
toes deep in carpet, a spacious
heated bathroom where I tried
scented soaps and shining
showertaps, paused for the sunlit

view over trees at the back.
My host at breakfast was gracious, but
perplexed, almost as if
I might steal the spoons.

It no longer looked like any house
that would ever be mine,
nor the pruning of hedges
and cleaning the watertank;
though, unconvinced,
I lodged in something like it
here and there. It did not
work out. When we parted
the wiring was faulting, the ceiling dripped.
I gave it up.

Now, when I venture back
to the street round the corner,
my contemporary
razoring his lawn,
a man of some standing in the borough,
would never recognise
it is his by default,
nor his well-fed children secure
in their stuffy inheritance.

Growing Pains

Green from Ireland,
and a childhood of pushing prams –
I can imagine your fireship innocence.

You danced all night,
telling them all the ways their lives were wrong;
kept up in London like treading water.

Grounded now, you laugh at yourself then –
until you gasp, as if
roots stirred with a sharp pain

of all that laughter is a loosening from:
home; a confirmation gown;
the candles of the faithful; on your cheeks

not these, but hallowed drops again.

Talking

Yes, he risked talking to others:
when light withered in long windows;
through evenings of wine; between laundered sheets.

It solved, to judge by the contortions
their lives entered into, none of their problems:
some gassing themselves, some marrying dolts. Nor his.

And whatever they thought him, he was not.
Nor they what he. At best, then, a palliative
rite, as the clasping of gloves extended on sticks.

Pressed closer, a clawed embrace rending.

An Ulster Garland

Close by my kitchen window juts
a wall, rich-textured, scarred
brickwork of ochre, grey and red
many times cemented, showing
faint whitewash from before
the house was last patched up.
And where the roof of split slates slopes
to its corner has somehow taken
root among fissures a sprig
of wallflowers, arching
luminous now in the late sunshine.

Delicate, the flowers
have survived nights, and many downpours,
found sustenance amid crumbling.
I have come to expect them.

No, they would not, should it come,
prevail against bulldozer or bomb;
nor admit their relevance.
And should these petals be torn by explosion,
buried deep under rubble, so
each unique thing must be lost, and is
irrevocable; yet always

others continue, reappear
contriving such root somewhere, so
configured on moving skies.

I drop my gaze on close
unfocused roofline ridges set
at jarring angles.
                                        This
is Ireland now, where mobs command
and kill, and terror grips.
The power system is at breakdown point.

Lightless, I look
again for the yellow flowers upon
their brink; also remark
among the streets' cross-hatching sprays
of answering greenery, deepening
as day ebbs in low
untended yards, how cranesbill, vetch,
sweetrocket, speedwell, flowers
run wild I have no name for,
sustain their points of colour; and grass
persists, unorganised; by kind
pervasive to outlast
what coming darkness.

26 May 1974, the Ulster Loyalists' Strike

Come In

'Can I tempt you?' she said.
I paused at the gate.
White wrought-iron tables and chairs
were set for tea on the lawn beneath
an appletree. Through
one window, a study, books settled in rows;
an upstairs sill showed toys.

Nothing moved while I looked.
The sun enriched the brickwork, shadow
did not inch over the rollered grass.

'Come in,' she said.
But the butterfly's wings were static above
the flowers, the sprinkler's drops did not drop.

'It is your home.'
                                        Could so
entranced my feet step forward not
bending one grassblade, not to find
her arms withering round me, glimpse
the hate-gnarled children's faces as
I fall in darkness deafened with clocks ticking.

Reading Habit

At the end of each chapter, the end of the novel,
some of the characters are always left talking;
they drift out on a blank leaf,
paired or alone, down indeterminate vistas.

I put down the book. Leaves cry out
on autumnal boughs, are scythed by the driving wind helplessly,
the sky ebbs violet over the rooftops.
It is the close of another day,

and the lights that spring on show some characters still left talking,
framed in their windows a dinner party, a girl
brushing her hair, grey screens flickering
news of death picking off others, elsewhere.

So with 'good-nights' at doorways and bus-stops,
assuring 'until tomorrow', 'take care',
we float wrapped in coloured dreams out on a pure
white sheet, its comforting blankness.

Those who are no longer with us, the tyrant
cut down in an early chapter, the drowned fiancé,
the aunt who fought cancer meanly, must have been different,
there not for themselves, but for us to react to.

Not in my book, one saying
'He, by what he did, and left undone,
and how, and why, helps us shape our perspectives' –
the untrodden page still realisable before him.

Lights While Travelling

Out from the close dark terminus roof our train
swayed into vaster darkness swimming with stars
and lights below and coloured lights tracing
the river's line of cranes, and separating
from other trains, lit windows carrying
heads reading, heads of lovers lolled in pairs
out to a scattering of rooms and homes
under roofs heaving vague as waves,
'and all the numberless goings-on of life'
I quoted. Cooling, we lay
in our compartment as we'd fallen, bitter
your opposite eyes, and you said, 'It is hard,
living as I do among these half-alive
is cruel for me.' The wheels beneath us ground
over some points, a factory cruised by
neon-lit, and blocks of flats

stacked up brilliance; while down among
grimed interstices of viaducts, sheets
of water fleetingly glittered the moon.
And up there was the moon, that stroked across
lit London spread out like a peacock's tail
its wirebrush rays soft-grazing our taut skin
as, opening fanlike, our gaze back
comprehended London, stars, moon, all.
'It is the balance I lack,' you said, 'to hold
the centres in equilibrium, different planes.'
Platform-signs paused, and went; doors slammed; and yet
it seemed our small lit oblong floated down
ceaselessly through a drift of lights
like fallen tree-blossom drifting on the water
past a punt. You said, 'The stars,
the most remote lights, stay with us as we fall.
And look!' – there was the sailing moon
that paced us deep in darkness. 'But we are on
the earth.' But not your eyes, on the far moon,
as now the train lurched, nearer lights
running blurred like raindrops streaked across the pane,
and we reached instinctive hands to hold
a fearful equipoise, all muscles tense,
hunching braced to meet the impact-shock . . .
My feet hit, and I found myself
alone: a platform, somewhere you swept on,
gone down in dark with a final wave.
I leant on a post for steadiness. Above
its single light stood still the moon,
your moon where separate now your lamp is lit;
inside my closed palm printed still your palm.

The Old, Cast Up on Lawns

The old, cast up on lawns in wicker chairs
sit waiting for the sun to drop,
humped shoulders towards a screen of trees,
hands fiddling with knitting or book.

What should we say to them?
That we have been far out, in passion, rain?
Patiently they turn
countenances rubbed, effaced

or scoured deep by more tides than they remember,
tokens of enough weather; not
distracted from branches charring
where gold dims at the garden's end.

Outgrowths of themselves, they hobble in,
from habit propped on shapes
long warped from what stood once
tall in hailstorms, distant lanes' white heat.

Removal

I was to pack;
the room persisted
in dead expectations,
chairs aligned so,
prints, record-rack there;
all comings and goings,
loss, breakage, accretion,
blurring but slightly
its fixed disposition.
Then the orange dropped
from its shelf, or was it
the fields outside
that after long bursts
of rain seemed to rise,

tilting, with greenness?
Foundations had shifted.
I sort, wrap, tear,
throw out, inhaling
dust that swirls gold
in a sunshaft, the filtering
windowgrime beautified.
The last cord is knotted,
makeshift I clear
the frame for time, dust,
other lives to settle;
leave only last year's
climbing boots, open
for stepping into.

The Mountains

I do not talk of daytime, when one can choose;
though whether, already exhausted, to follow what shrugs
beyond the horizon, knowing it always will,
or turn back, either feels like failure,
and the brooks raising noise like something wanting answer.
But it is the nights, when the mountains choose me,
bare, humped, unscalable, that prove possession.
The streets between are mapped with memories,
minutely familiar, some turnings now forbidden,
and houses to be called at or no more
allowed, such things deflected my purpose,
and the air filled with the voices of those I
had been in love with, or been young with.
Still hauntingly that clear brow beyond me.
The mountains are my sleep's wild hinterland,
they shift, usurp known territories. Once,
above roofs at the edge of a town a stile,
and path leading up the climbing eye; there were people
ascending, returning; some strayed to rest in the sunlight,
but down in the street they denied the stile,
and the slopes shut off, cloud spilling down ravines.

It was last night I hit the summit.
My glider had found a thermal current, and rising
rode it . . . After the smash I looked from a ledge
upon greenness strewn with white cottages by their turfstacks
and slate-dark lakes, all intricately rimmed
with yellow strand; far out to sea
stood Rathlin, Aran, the Blaskets; and I held
the whole world's curve, revolved it slowly . . .
Then came down; the man whose slant along
the upper slopes I crossed was real enough,
on Brandon once, he'd leant, told how all weathers
took him high as his sheep, and for no peak's sake.
Whin and heather tore my clothes, I filled
a shoe with peaty water, found the road,
at last crashed bleeding through swing doors. No head
glanced up. They said, 'There are no mountains.'

Hiatus

Departure comes as a relaxing; sheds
along the wharves leak light, and gemlike
lamps squander across black water,
orange and white flakes fretting lost to darkness.
Hulls and gantries ghost a formal stillness
passing, and the recessive land
is pricked as with minute abandoned faces.

The last buoy winks, the lough expands
to the steady rock and rock of open sea,
and companioned only by the wave-skipping moon
I, the woman profiled against a hatchway,
the crowd in the bar, are cradled weightless,
lives transfused by the throbbing of the engines.

Tomorrow the glittering rail
where screaming gulls pluck bread, the scattering
knock upon a different shore
luminous with the new day's compulsions.

Doubles

Dusk ghosts upon
this pane my spare
familiar, his single
room, with cases
above the wardrobe;
we smile, as in
complicity. Through
the reflection's skein
grass, evergreens,
brambles, thicken
untended, where
my rinsed shirt on
the line slowly
dancing waves
a vivid sleeve.

Tabula Rasa

Threads of milk risen in pools of spilt tea,
smoke rising above formica, and

'Going on needs more to go on. There's
too little basis.'
                                        Alternatively,
'We know each other through and through enough
to know we should have stopped before we knew.'

Opt out, find out, both come to such a place,
sea lapping outside, or traffic snarling;
close round, indifferent mangled faces.
And something massacred: conjured future rooms,
or a what-was whose makeshift furnishings,
hope's precipitates, now need dismantling
shelf by shelf, one taking sheets, one curtains.

Careless talk costs lives. At least, again
this moment in a public place
between might-have and has-been is, whichever
way the glass runs, that through which we know
the heaviness of how life goes;
whatever is, not necessary, not right.

Summer Truce

The weather holds. From Strangford Lough to Swilly
soft arms of coast cradle still water.
Sunning before our shore's edge cottage we
'enjoy it while it lasts', watch floated fronds
of seaweed among the rocks slightly
lifting with a glitter like broken glass.

And the radio talks into blue day –
to campions, sea-pinks, primroses run wild
over springy turf – of another sectarian killing,
a club blown up, several injured.
The tiny insistent voice is a black mote
in the mind, troubling the horizon

within which our concerns are local as
the cliff-path hesitating its few miles
to Portrush. We have our jokes, lovemaking,
morning-squabbles; John and Mary are at
each others' throats in phone-kiosks, kitchens;
another friend founders in private madness;

and 'Fuck off to Limavady' as the man said
last night to his girl, means over the edge
of the little world. But later ourselves beyond
Limavady, we find in Derry
the truce keeps up, with festive bunting and
the soldiers relaxed and eating ice-cream,

We drink campari in sweet evening air
where mountains pour down to the lough-side;
seething at Reggie, you shred a pound note with your teeth.
And this morning sit writing it up in your journal
here on the city wall, where ten days back
that policeman was shot from no personal anger.

All peace is imperfect. At last Belfast: the pub
where we talk poetry is pocked from old bombings –
nothing's worth fixing these days. In the gents'
a washbasin grimed and fractured, filled with glass,
taps issuing only a parched gush of air.
Outside, still sunshine. Everyone waits for the break.

1975

North Derry Nocturne

I

An unapologetic
Irish sky decays:
sunset, and Donegal's
ridge lies out on the water

crimson-rimmed, small clouds
like fluffs of ink above
on orange fading to blue.
I watch the embers burn

out. Now only far
Greencastle's twinkle, where
boats nose from the land's shadow
to harvest a salt darkness.

II

I load the Bendix – round
and round all goes in the wash –
and walk down Prospect Road
to raise my glass at the Anchor:

the old familiar faces,
the University matters.
These horses of instruction!
Where are the wiser tigers

of wrath? Outside and headed
this way last evening, a car
blew up: they found an arm
tattooed *For God and Ulster*.

III

We talk our last pints through;
your man here, blond, flush-faced,
degree in Greek and Latin,
grew up inside all this:

'But those were quieter days.
The big house was still owned
by mad aristocrats –
the goings-on up there,

locking each other in cupboards,
disowning heirs! I'd go
for chestnuts to the estate.
They chased me waving shotguns.'

IV

Now the gun's outside
the plantation wall, and trigger
pulled. The headlights catch
only a moving swathe

of scrubby verge, with bracken
smashed, and one dead hedgehog.
We pass the Bush round, sip
its thread of warmth. Unseen

the billowing hills pegged down
by stony farms attuned
to ancient disciplines,
bringing to growth, to market.

V

'My uncle's a country man,'
says one, 'he's not been known
to construct an entire sentence.
But he could keep a farm.

He knew of just one way
with vermin: take the gun.
And so he'd keep the country.
But he couldn't hold his son.

Des married a go-go dancer
from Strabane, a Teague.
They've two weans now, in England.'
All's black outside the car.

VI

As last month in the Tube
before I came back from England,
I watched straphanging faces
assuming some next station

and thought, What if we stopped
for ever in this tunnel,
or, not rising out
at Finchley Road, the train

dipped, and whooshed straight through?
So – we read the papers,
plan lectures, double-glazing;
now, coffee-time again.

VII

Dropped back from which, indoors
I leave the curtains open:
desk, paper, anglepoise's
glow, ringed mug, and dimmed

bookshelves – thus to cruise
night, the town's few roofs
heaving vague, subsumed
to the Atlantic groundswell;

precise in focused light
ink's strict notation charts
the spinning nebulae,
the labyrinthine self.

VIII

Where the Minotaur of soul
bellows darkly, ramps
mazed in intricacies,
gorges on pale ideals.

All, killer in the night,
the poets, demagogues,
take as they find for world,
apotheosise these

confines. But mine those walls
with imagination's fuse –
poor souls in a rough field
adrift in stars and sea.

IX

And I, returned, who hang
these blanched sheets to the moon,
feet tangling in wet grass?
I think three weeks back to

that girl in the Penge Chinese:
'They send you anywhere,
I see it all, meet friends.
But you know how it is.

It's like you're in the dark,
and strike match after match.
I could chuck the agency
I know . . . But it's not that . . .'

X

And so, I wait for dawn's
pure green and silver, sea
calmed by soft arms of coast,
Portstewart clarifying

around me, white and frail
as shells these houses clasped
to rock, so rootless might
be gone with the next tide;

as when, in skins, men first
leant upon spears to see
dream-clear Donegal
sunlit across the water.

From the Other Country

But you do not consider how long I have lived in this country.
Its skies move through my skull, and the changing light
over the water; like whales the humped mountains
surface in my dreams, and never were trees
thwart like these in flight from the salt harsh gales.

The customs of the people, it is true,
are not mine; in farms and one-street towns
they enact strict rituals of thrift, worship, pleasure.
Lights burn late where slow accounts are reckoned,
the drunk crashes prone in dying embers,

and beneath tribal tokens, ancient recitations.
Often indeed through main-street and glen
drums throb savage annunciation, the door
opens to a rain of bullets, car-lights pick out
the corpse in a ditch. 'It's a madness going on,'

they say. Did you think madness so dull?
Look: how finite among the weltering green
these settlements, no margins to nourish the odd.
Knowing their place, they grow, pray, wed, kill, die.
Even their knowing smiles have a terrible innocence

which you do not understand. Nor, though you hear,
how their soft gutturals and singing intonation
infect my accent. I am welcomed
in bars and corner-shops, with 'It's a soft night.'
And yes, I have loved their girls.

See, where fine white clouds drift high above the meadow
the small farm daydreams all doors open:
they are all gone round the bend of the field, out of change.
Behind the clock on the mantel dust thickens on letters
strangely deciphered, from children 'across the water'.

From where, too, on my screen come shimmering
images of the old labyrinthine cities,
sanities. Which I can revisit, resume
undetected; noticing how they find
bestial or glamorous our banalities,

and do not see the detail beneath stark outlines.
I am no longer sure that I wish to return,
even though it is winter here now, the sky and land
seeping greyly together. Unsettled, defined
by difference, I find I can live with this,

am strangely involved in, call it, a climate.
Yes, as the mad wind rises, sets the sea
resonating, whips waves white, and plucks
tiles from thin roofs, above which gulls
weave lamentation's dissonant vocables.

Intimation

'Aunt Ginnie's dead.' Aunt Ginnie's dead. The words
stilled a garden, butterfly in mid-loop,
each leaf and bird, the cherry petals fluttering
down, the child with cup held waiting.

Until his father came down from the loft,
reading the telegram walked out with his mother.
And the world rolled on. The sparrows ate the crumbs,
flew off, were eaten; leaves browned, trembled, fell,

and were replaced by leaves. And I am here,
my mother there, my father elsewhere. Something
holds, like a photograph; rather, a landscape
I find myself re-entering unprepared.

The child, focused on some far point, is blank
to me, the ground he'll cross to where I see him from:
him, a butterfly slipped from time's arc,
and the dropped cup no more petals will be saved in.

Over the Wall
(1980)

In Highgate Wood

A flicker of sun through leaves in Highgate Wood,
this moment of recognition: I who know
no kin find myself open intently
in a willed, almost religious relinquishing,

as if to diffuse among this ceaseless play
some latent thing so near in me it asks
to be named all that I now forgo
as what it might have been: I say, 'My son.'

Whispering translucencies take up the merely
personal into their green going-on
ageing within each season's restlessness.
Another spring. I lean against

a hornbeam's fluted trunk to follow up
the frail slant of a silver birch bole hung
with tatters of bark like peeling paint.
Slow bramble smothers cut lengths of felled tree,

and the bones of a dumped pram are patiently
digested. Always the forest, underfoot
its dead green softening to renew; and nothing
I can bestow: this is, as from a child,

a receiving. See how delicately wrought
that cherry-tree declares its blossoming,
drifts of flowers like conjurings from snow
almost, so pure and candid:

luminous thing, it tricks the eye
to seem itself condensation of mere air
floating it, yet is earthed in darkness.
Brief one of many, time unique as flesh.

Stepping Westward, Donegal

And stepping westward seemed to be
A kind of heavenly *destiny.*
Wordsworth

At times I could believe I'd even reached . . .
But the land shrugged on and west, and west again,
through Creeslough and the hedged pasture giving way
to drystone walls, a frail net cast

over what heaved savage now, huge boulders standing
intact like eggs, and the sentinel long hump
of Muckish rising. Then the other side
where the gap road wound close under the mountain.

In slow processional cloud-shadows ascended
a calm flank filigreed with scree, and water
somewhere ravelling hoarsely; the climb
unfolded vistas bluing to far ranges.

And from Calabber through the afternoon
lines of turfcutters bent to a brackish landscape
as like a further planet Errigal
reared its serene cone. A turn looked down

on a lough spread in the rift: intensely green
those deeper fields; some dwellings, planted beechwood
smudging the shadow of an old estate
beneath the frozen surge of the Poisoned Glen.

So to descend, and find the church roofless, lapped
with thick grass starry with milkwort, speedwell, vetch,
and pedestalled on the little stone bridge
old stumps of statues long since knocked away,

but bees weighting wild rhododendron and
the bank tumbling primroses down to a stream
that sustained between alders a flickering dance of sunlight,
seemed to reach some meant core of the day.

But was not all. One last extremity:
green, violet, glittering white, that strand's heaped stones,
and no more to do with man than the unnameable
light on sea ringing to the horizon.

That carried along the whole return, with travelling
lines of mountains, past the turfcutters crouched
still over antique spades, red weathered faces
lifting incuriously after the car,

till Muckish sank behind like a slow whale,
telling nothing. Brought back, just this one
crystalline pure ellipsoid, paperweight
here heavy with all it holds unbroken.

Playing Through Old Games of Chess

A crane-fly trembles in the windowpane
as it has since before there were windows . . .
I play through old games of chess: their rich diapason
a blossoming in the room, as of huge heavy-headed roses.

Outside, the hottest summer since records began,
and the traffic-lights signalling insane morse,
a jabber of red green amber, somewhere a computer
has overheated, fouling the traffic and tempers

are overheated, and all along the Thames
the bridges shove themselves over from metal expansion.
Ah, the ecologists say, it is carbon dioxide
irreversibly building up in the upper atmosphere

due to industrial waste, and all kinds of waste
accumulate irreversibly, and we record it,
even the mineral ores of language processed through
to a standing slag beyond recycling;

and economists say it is the economy overheated.
The plane trees shimmer through rising petrol fumes,
and children's voices ascend to tinkle against the bowl
of a blue sky hazed with entropy, our last heat-death.

I reset the pieces and start again:
Steinitz versus Tchigorin, Ruy Lopez, Morphy Defence,
Havana, 1892, and decorously
the opposite knights step forth, the kings are castled to safety

for a while. And still for a while
beyond the cities in meadows (but a hum of traffic hanging)
the cows, as then, stand four-square over their shadows,
while one by one white petals slip into sun-dappled water

to float, for a while, and the woods are dark with summer,
greenness sloping to greenness to a far
horizon marked with the faint stroke of a steeple
as it has been since before there were

– steeples, I almost said. At least as when
all history seemed a sort of sunlit incline upwards,
with problems like the Balkans, abolishing cholera, crime,
certainly soluble, and change meant improvement,

hygiene, gas cooking, fast travel, the bioscope.
Beneath *Truman, Hanbury, Buxton and Comps Entire*
the old photograph shows clay pipes and boaters around an ale-bench,
and Spoonbeam is not out at lunch for Lancs for ever,

while at dusk, his cycle-lamp catching gold motes
along deep lanes where roots twist and convolvulus clings,
comes Cholmondeley to talk, over whisky by leaded windows,
of *The Origin of Species* or *The Idylls of the King*.

The pawn-structure looks sound, across the board *andante*
the full orchestration unfolds, with recurring motifs and grace-notes,
rounding Good Hope the *Ariel* bringing home tea from China,
cablegrams under the sea, while in Afghan hill-posts

or where a delta's archipelagos of bamboo huts
coalesce to a port of old palaces, crumbling pagodas,
men with iron moustaches bat out their time
outstaring all sundowns from the verandah.

Of course, through the looking-glass all was different,
and moving forward got you nowhere, the miners
stonily piling their barrows after the latest eviction
cannot see their great-grandsons' Cortinas, package-tour fritterings,

and the husband who tended with flowers the most honourable intentions
is hanging his stovepipe hat on the bedposts of whores;
and every life dark-edged, the hushed death-rooms, the infant graves,
and perhaps it is all the tinman's dream

who stationed at the street corner pedals his grinding-wheel
for ever. And as for the countless hordes
of Indians and Chinese, it is not their game
at all, they have nothing to learn but patience.

Exchange of queens: the general liquidation
which follows seems to favour White, a sacrificial
manoeuvre clinches things, for a while. If today
in Flanders the farmer again wades through barley where all nature

was murdered, still the old dynasties have toppled like chess kings,
and however we go through the motions again
(the squares are being done up, houses wormy with their past
are scoured, the cellars blocked off as if there were bones down in them,

layers of cheap flowered paper torn from each wall),
or trace the lines not followed, unrealised combinations
in notes as much as the moves played part of the game,
the quality of that long, lost summer cannot be restored

– when June rang like a gong for Pax Britannica,
and Europe's chordage held the world enthralled;
and in London, St Petersburg, Vienna or Baden Baden
the old chess-masters' arias thrilled. Until Lasker, who

would research Relativity, talk with Einstein, flee
the Nazis, shifted a piece irrevocably changing
the chemistry of the game, its lovely architectonics;
while a crane-fly trembled in the windowpane.

That Pass in the Night

A hush of fine rain,
upon deepening lawns
each house drifts back, settling
round TV's wan glow.

Then clear over all
the streets' loose ends and aimless
wires, lights, I see
a ship in the bay.

Or where should be the bay:
the headlands have vanished,
no sea, nor horizon,
just an indigo-grey

solution, that black
lozenge suspended,
red port light and rich
gold suffusing the stern.

Enviable far world!
close under dim steam-pipes
hot soup, jokes, card-playing
– now perhaps looking back

through a finger-rubbed port-hole
on this shore's lit filament
afloat upon fathomless
space, as to home.

Tomorrow will bring back
bold street-fronts, curved headlands,
sea clear: the ship gone,
or our world rolled on.

The Winter Talent

Fifth-Floor Pulchritude's down for a quick thrash
on the duplicator, her Antrim and my London speech
are mutually impenetrable, she doesn't drink,
thinks God's a hard-line 'anti' on sex, but gave me
a sweet . . . Should I trust that Lawrencean *otherness* stuff?

And Bridget has stirrings for that stripling who
is spoken for; while playing the field Des finds
Miss Riding Hood's holds only horses. The Phantom Fencer
prinks her bum through the corridor unaware
Paul spent last night on her porch in romantic stupor.

Our circus animals are all on show.
Who are these people? What will happen next?
Have we all taken leave of our senses? Is then perhaps
self-irony the stuff that dreams are made on?
Maybe what we all need is someone we can't talk to:

for under their duvets, or over the Bordello Rosso soul-mates
kamikaze each other, spelling out death;
female poets are punching their lovers; ignoring the telly
(*International It's a Knockout*) they're at it,
'I've told you before . . .' 'Why we married . . .' 'My values . . .' All that.

While ours may be that true Shakespearian comedy world
of cross-purposes, shaping fantasies, and mistook
identities, that unfold purifyingly right.
Well then, *Time, thou must untangle this, not I.*
So I'll buy myself a digital watch for Christmas

and live in the present. Where, through the window, bird-throngs
wheel and settle kaleidoscopically beneath neutral
sky, slaking what's left of their lusts on such worms
as the sodden ground yields, or whatever they're up to. Survival,
the winter talent. Some somehow contrive to reach summer.

The Scent

Left to wash-up, I touched the lacy glass
collecting sunlight on our dinner-table,
gingerly sniffed the gold dregs it still held
of cider, that our visitor had sipped
in our non-drinking house and laughed and set
my mother laughing, me intent
at the intimation of a fearful change.

This, then, made somehow different. I put
aside its cloying taint, to keep it from
our dishes; these cleansed, dried, reached for the glass:
a wasp simmered drowning in that sweetness
– the same perfuming summer evenings when
pub-doors are bolted open, and I'd pause,
catch music, laughter, dark interior cries.

Ludicrous, looking back. School-cap in pocket
I was soon worming in. And now near every night
mere background and I'm covering the whole range,
wines, spirits, creamy Guinness. Yet, again
turning my key flush from a good evening, a girl
met, talk of eternal things, the room
is terrifying with apples' fermented sick sweetness.

Jersey, Channel Islands, 1959

It almost seemed there was
no night, each day such light,
and working all summer through
a hundred hours a week
I walked to my room as dawn
reclarified the streets'
pink and blue washes, air
wine-sharp, high glints of gulls.
Three hours, then up again,
sweat stinging my shaving-cuts,
the hotel kitchen a furnace
of hurry, heat and anger:
'Quick with that toast!' 'The lift!'
'A porter he calls himself!'

With that job, no cash, nothing
but what one suitcase held
and that half books, past severed
and vagrant from my future,
I didn't know enough
to know how lost I was.
All shadows were sharp-edged,
I leant into the sun
sloshing water on
high windows; every Sunday
afternoon ledged high
in flowering cliffs read on,
Orwell, Conrad, Forster;
bees simmering, glitter of sea.

One evening, free at nine,
at an outdoor red iron table,
girls jabbering French, I stared
beyond the prom into
liquid light-fluencies.
And yes, I'd got it wrong,
the tide had turned: slowly
black rocks emerged, the waves
cringed broken now. Day drained,
and strings of coloured bulbs
came on, and cigarettes;
and the whole sea went vague.
Tide-scarred through centuries,
the rocks grew dark and hard.

Greenhead Ghyll

Therefore, although it be a history
Homely and rude, I will relate the same
For the delight of a few natural hearts;
And, with yet fonder feeling, for the sake
Of youthful Poets, who among these hills
Will be my second self when I am gone.
Wordsworth, 'Michael'

So, from the public way we turned our steps
up *the tumultuous brook af Greenhead Ghyll*
– this August just at first parched boulders, cobwebbed
and dusty, there a grey feather resting,
and thornily overgrown. We parted branches,
bent and sweating; underneath the bridge
where houses crossed, barbed wire, corroded pipes
taking off any higher water from
the brook. I knocked a shin, stood one foot slipped
in a stagnant pool combing greenfly from my hair,
through closed eyelids sunlight flickering.

And remembered the cottage: his skates in a glass case,
'His cuckoo-clock. It has its off-days,' said
the guide to blank women in woollies, rucksacked men,
the blonde in a *Southern Comfort* tee-shirt, ourselves;
then ushered us through to let the Italians in.
'Their cold-store for perishables': scrubbed, bare except
for a Minimax extinguisher bracketed to the wall;
behind now, 'Ecco' this, and 'Ecco' that.
Outside, under rowan-berries,
I imagined Coleridge calling, having walked over
Helvellyn to urge on 'the philosophical poem';
moon-faced, fretting for Asra, his marriage, health, talent,
all now going wrong; three cherishing decades before
her madness Dorothy bringing in tea.

Earlier, above Rydal Water,
I had noticed your tears in hot sunshine. 'What is it?'
'It's that poem,' you answered. Where you had read
His bodily frame had been from youth to age
of an unusual strength, his mind had been
intense and frugal, apt for all affairs;
of the son so cared for leaving, foundered in
the dissolute city, ignominy and shame,
Michael dead, and the plough gone through the ground
on which his home had stood. 'It's wrong, it's wrong,'
you cried, voice thin in blue indifferent air
and the gorse all round bursting with summer, our summer
that the lake mirrored back as if without depth to its water.

Now, climbing out beneath blank sky,
fresh tricklings hoarse through the pebbles of the ghyll,
we walk lovingly up blanched slippery grass.
That dead sheep half-devoured by scavengers
we pause beside, belongs on every fell,
the living nibble before us. Until the hills
opening yield to a high dell, and there
a straggling heap of stones touching the place
with a faint usage that is part of it,
Michael's unfinished fold. On a sharp edge
I sit, eat chocolate, and look round:
so many different swathes and shades of greenness,
dark where ferns come down, the nearer grass

flowing, and distant Easedale's fields and farms
lit with a delicate gleam, and water-noise
enough to take me now into a dream
in which the day completes itself, where Michael
in the story, desolated, brooded
by the fold he'd started with his son,
and never lifted up a single stone.

Nine months ago. I hold the photograph, stare
back at myself seated there. And this, of you.
Each in turn outside the other's frame
of things. Or so it proved when we returned
to the city, through to our agreement to part,
blaming the different geography of our lives.
And nothing admitted of ignominy and shame.
Today is my thirty-seventh birthday, outside
my Irish window this water is open sea,
its million quirks of light, cloud-shadows passing eastward.
'It's wrong.' But we erased our shared ground;
those mountains have folded back in a changed perspective:
still burnished by our passing through.

At the Sea's Edge

This sea like shot-silk, every day such light
gilding my window-frames. I drowse, afloat
in summer; and some sound I have always known,
say that lawnmower's gritty whirring, makes believe
there are continuities woven through the years.
Even that mad-looking spiky hasp of a thing
that palpitates on my pane, I have known before,

fastening to me one childhood evening when
I sifted through my coin collection, francs,
marks, annas, coins with squiggles, blackening
silver threepennies, and the massy copper
George III penny, perhaps then the last time
dropping back in the soft bag, me not realising.
So many things put by for the last time!

Or lost. All that was meant. As when, sun gilding
our handlebars I cycled out with Pam
whose back to touch was velvet. Who is she now,
with daughters maybe older than us then?
Well, but we got beyond Coulsdon anyhow,
stood mazed in hot fields tasting ears of wheat
under blue vacancy empty as today's.

Some purposes are approximated, reached
provisionally, as day floats into day
each where we point ourselves from, promising,
no place to linger, but for drinks and chat,
brief sexual crestings. 'But what next?' we say,
and then distracted perhaps only because
of chance conjunction: girl, sun, bluebell-wood.

The expense of spirit for so much betrayed!
I founder into it; until again
the lawnmower chirring, insect on the pane
steady me, beachcombing what swims up,
flotsam, precipitates not all beautiful,
but hard; this ring kept which the world whatever
it's coming to no longer has a use for.

One wants things should mean something overall,
at least be shaped from one act somewhere back
– as picking a single flower can ramify
past sight to huge loves or unblossomings.
But that dog trotting by now with wrapped meat
as such dogs always have, connects with no
last pattern, is familiar to deceive,

and the sea refulgent with a creamy light
where tiny crestings randomly repeat,
pure freedom merely; plunge in off the strand
and feel its coldness. I have heard it cry
all night upon those outflung arms of coast
– soaring fluencies of line perfecting
motion to far paradigms of peace.

Pictures from Donegal

for Vic Willi

Through Rathmelton, then
six miles of turns and lanes,
'Ask for Greer's cottage'

– in the heart of silence
and greenery dripping fuchsia.
We'd sit outside all day

sunburning, the chessboard
aligned so you could manage
all moves but knight-leaps,

and talked, of everything –
your transatlantic voice
a buzz-saw in the pure air –

but most, of what you'd come
here to, sick Ireland
and its maddest flourishes:

'Some Provos dressed as nuns
robbed a Coleraine bank,
were lifted drinking at Garvagh . . .'

'I used to have,' you said,
'a laugh like yours before
my chest-muscles went.'

Vic, I envy your
clear sight: from your wheelchair
gazing across the Swilly

to pick out where light gleamed
on Inishowen, far
fields cut since yesterday.

I had learned to empty
your drainage-bag, hook
the cup to your withering hand,

had come, having the time,
to be 'of use', and surely
wasn't much. We loafed

till the girls drove back from Derry.
– Which you'd seen also, bombed
to bits, the soldiers,

and an old dear yammering
'When yous go back, just tell them
we're not all monsters.'

Then every evening out
around mountains and valleys
firing your camera at

glittering heather, turfstacks,
sunset over more bays
than you'd ever remember

– remember the seals off Fanad,
with Donegal flinging
wild arms to the Atlantic?

It needs a place far gone
as this for me to realise
our science-fiction age:

'Yes, probably the bomb
will drop,' I think
for the first time in years,

while you are staring at
intricate drystone walls
netting tiny holdings

on an empty headland. Yes,
people have starved here,
been driven away;

this cottage, where returning
to fumble with tilley-lamps
and well-water is for us

a week going primitive,
for two hundred years
cocooned remote lives

that never saw towns,
our electric civilisation
a car-ride away

– yet were near as first light
woke me. You too perhaps
(as well as the tang of Guinness

and 'Is it an Anglo-Canadian
consortium yous are,
these your secretaries from Derry?')

have taken back what camera
and eyesight are blank to:
beneath the flowered wallpaper

old scuffmarks, burns, an odour
outlasting us and all
on our chirruping radio.

Over the Wall

So I came over
the wall, over
a wall from which
long grass-tufts blew.
All was composed:
about the lake
what else to say
banks, willows, and wild
rhododendron told,
sweet nameless scents;
and fields of flowering
grasses, yes it is

near mowing-time;
and one great tree
locking earth to sky,
sky so dazzlingly
pointilliste, such
greenness, surely
utterance pured
to last legibilities.

This is the strange
land I have always
known, always known.
And listen, the birdsong.
Insistently though,
sustaining it, somewhere
a waterfall crashing
to nothingness over
and over; nor
when I cross the terrace
to opened french windows
is anyone there;
only dust on mahogany.
Dialled, the phone
gives back an eerie
whine, disconnected.
Maybe a call
will come, says the voice
in my head, *if you put*
the receiver down.

To affirm means to share:
even for mad
John Clare it was
his *Mary in truth*
and nature my own
made all nature cohere;
she a phantom by then,
dead many a year.
And I would invoke . . .
But I glimpse only
moments scattered
with different faces:

a mountain chapel;
deer nuzzling at
another hand; also
the arrowing wake
of a water-vole after
which two lovers stared;
usually somewhere
a waterfall crashing.

It wants some sleight
of light eliciting
figures in focus,
some trick I have missed,
for this world to be born
footsure, the hole
in my map earthed-in.
Now, as I turn,
its green invitation
curdles, lake shrills,
bitter to be
betrayed once more;
flickers, blows out
as I fall through thin air . . .
Awake, in my ears
Edward Thomas's words:
And I rose up
and knew that I
was tired, and
continued my journey.

On the Mend

So now you are on the mend. Upon the lawn
outside the Female Ward we lounge, eat squares
of chocolate, and drink apple-juice; like stars
the weave of speedwells blue in springy grass.

It was not thus when we first visited,
the ambulance that had brought you from your last
bitching, sleepless, frantic, then mad week
outside, you called 'the Celestial Insomnibus',

your mind raced manic, spinning wheels with no
purchase on the real; unsteadily
you craved to see life whole: 'Bring me a globe
I'll reconcile Marx and Christianity' –

in tantrums at a world that would not see –
'I'd turn it upside-down and find my twin
in the Antipodes.' So David said,
'Take that lawn as the globe's top bit, start there.'

The door between was locked then. 'But I'll shrink
until I go through the keyhole,' you explained.
Meanwhile, confined to nightwear, scribbled reams . . .
The doctors said: 'Her judgement's very poor.'

We soft-shoe-shuffled down a corridor,
noting your institutional drugged pace.
And, on the wall, a fire-alarm beside
which the standard printed notice read

IN CASE OF FIRE, then every usual clause,
1. Break glass etc . . . Some loony had
crossed these through, in staggering capitals
substituted just, I'D PUT IT OUT.

– Regardless of ferocity, extent?
Infantile omnipotence! the new
problem-solving technique for all! IN CASE
OF BEING SICK – GET WELL. IN CASE OF LOVE . . .

'Wouldn't it be nice if we could fall in love,
marry, have children,' confided your friend Anne
childishly. But, 'David frightens me,
like telly's Space-Doctor Who.' Your polar twin,

schizoid, depressive, Anne talked of her 'fears',
when she talked. But mostly hunched in trance
gazed into no-space; roamed in odd forays
as we tippled the hospital-canteen Lucozade.

Then once, while fingersnapping patients lurched
failing to dance (others impassive stared)
to TV's *Top of the Pops*, Anne deadpan told
how, this time, it had happened she came here:

'I was going to hit my mother with a saw.
She was sawing. So I took the saw
to hit her. So my sister got me here.
My sister's right. They make me well in here.'

Anne's fears, your hypomanic ferment of
ideas, aggressions, such are impulses
we all know. 'Health' is pragmatic, it appears:
can the world cope with one, or one with it?

'It's chemical,' they say. When you snapped back
at my mild 'no' to your 'All growing-up
is coming to terms with one's father,' since my tone
'recalled' him, *She needs help*, I thought, self-curbed.

Well: you 'got your clothes' (the idiom here
and emblem of recovering); and then
your room's french-window was unlocked, so we
and others visiting walked you on the lawn.

And Anne, as if a switch had dropped, clicked back
to 'normal', talkative, interested, live;
and has her clothes. So now for the last time
before your coming-out the four of us

sit on the grass, your sunlit room behind
decked with flowers, cards, its pastel shades
a cool interior; all here you know best
are on the mend. It's garden-partyish.

Except, of course, more are brought in each day.
'That beautiful girl', you tell, found pregnant, fouled,
in a Derry street; the youth who blew up an ice-cream
van, 'for the ultimate onanistic thrill'.

And also in the Male Ward, there's our friend
the alcoholic poet. Who yanks a door
to wrench off Lucozade-tops, and blood gouts
annoying the cleaners, and by turns he fawns,

insults, then turkey-faced waddles away
huffing down the corridor. Insufferable
the suffering can be, outside they'd smash
his face for less . . . But, 'He needs help,' we say.

So the bell rings, calling you for lunch,
quietly to accept your 'medication' where
three weeks ago they'd hold you down, inject,
as you curled screaming distant in lost time.

Outside will care for you. But may not care
to be always pleasanter to you than you
to it which falls back on no such 'needs help'
exoneration. Judgement that is poor

will be called bad, not 'illness': morally
health entails responsibility where
infantilism never puts fires out.
Meanwhile, for outside, you've fresh-waved your hair.

Accounts Payable

'That's Mr Sims's office. He's in charge.
But off this week having all his teeth out.
So meanwhile we've got Eric. He's all right.
When he's all right. Here's what we do in here,
we match these delivery-notes with invoices,
checking the quantities, we mustn't pay
for more than what we get. So query all
discrepancies. Mr Anderson will start you,
he's been here in Accounts Payable forty years.'

Someone has felt-penned SILENCE: WORK IN REGRESS;
but of course there's chat to help the whole lot down.
'My friend Doris said, she said when she
was a nurse she'd fed a patient custard who'd
died. Well he could only take slops and
just lying there you'd hardly tell, she said,
I mean she'd spooned it in for ages,
but he'd passed on in the night. Gave her a turn.
I'd rather be a filing-clerk than that.'

But Maureen is wondering whether Eric
really is fucking June the Comptometer Operator,
and can you tell from the look of them now standing there?
No flies on Eric: 'Fancies himself. Still, rather
him than that old Anderson stuck here
a century and all he knows or cares for
is writing copperplate. Them times have gone,
"You've been dead you old fool for years," I said to him,
only I didn't. His legs, all blotched with bloodclots.'

So, lunchtimes stroll about past flyblown shops,
hotels, that kiosk where oranges glow;
note the chiropodist's window cluttered with plaster casts
of feet deformed or maimed; at junctions meet
beneath plucked brows the distilled gaze
risen from multitudinous spoiled beds
(and how much pain can one head hold?);
or in the museum stare at the mummified princess,
lids shrivelled, which four thousand years ago . . .

While, between the sweet and the bill,
'It's easier anyway to say yes than no,
they're mostly married of course, but that means nothing
these days. Friends? Oh, friends are all right. I've friends,
I'm not the type to be much on my own.
But you, you're deep, so you know what I mean,
it's someone to really talk to. And there's more to sex
than just sex. The Agency send you anywhere,
I could chuck the Agency, but it's not that . . .'

And the aeroplanes are catapulted over and over
all afternoon and gently in stained hands
Mr Anderson lifts his tea-mug, half
hearing Mrs Wilkes ('I told my Jan
when baby's sick you don't wanna give it milk,
milk lies on its chest, milk's thickening . . .')
and thinking how all is different now. 'Take care',
they part, 'Don't do what I'd not.' And indeed
one might as well say yes as no. 'Until tomorrow.'

Escalators drag them Underground . . .
But this is another tunnel, and longer and darker,
still tilting down, the carriage-lights wan,
and many who used to be in the compartment are gone,
and anyway everyone really journeys alone
to discrepant destinations; and what lies thickening
on the chest is not milk . . . 'I saw his false-teeth drop.
By the time they took him out his face was blue.
Old. Anderson. Well, his account is settled.'

The Interviews

Ledged high in glass and steel the Committee Room:
'So why do you want to be . . . ?' That is, to join us.
From ten stock replies, you select for your mood,
almost say, 'Choose a number, try for the jackpot,'
while your gaze slides out to that dying orange cloud-rent.

Or they are 'unsure of the lines of your career',
'Of course, it's a battlefield here', or 'The crucial art
is delegation' – and can you think of one reason
why anyone's right for this except (which you are)
the sort of woman who on principle would refuse it?

Often, they like you, you seem 'creative',
though 'here we've developed a team philosophy'.
You are interviewed longer than anyone else, and given
a second tea; but the post is given
to that dud in a deep-pile suit, or the mouse from Garstang.

Long after the cleaners have crunched up the debris, leaving
these rooms in a mist of purifying aerosol,
in the icy misshapen hours when you cannot sleep,
or delegate not sleeping, and facing the final
questions finds no reason for anything ever,

you take all night to the high lines of the moors;
there are forests with silence folded under their leaves;
and every motorway-mile phones on posts skid past
your hurtling box, each *Why do you want to be?*
foundering in your wake's black wastes unfurling.

Out for the Elements (1981)

Way Back

Clearing after a party or
another lover come and gone,
before the Tube and the next cup,
there swims into her levelled head's

conjugated retrospects,
as her eyes admit fresh snow
giving urban sunrise back,
that winter twenty years ago:

'In twenty years we will come back'
they kissed. She could go now alone,
see emptied husks upon such white:
mill, village, church, and youth. Composed,

unsuccouring. Suffering no loss.
Each spring rinsed millstone moors blank green,
fresh water fills the valley's throat,
black chimneys faintly suppurate.

War Memoir

'Jim went down with the *Hood*' brings back
my war: carried beneath cold stars
to earthy shelter. Those bangs? 'Just
night-time noises buses make dear.'

Before-the-war, all sweets and fruit,
an Eden missed by being born
in its refugee-camp. Which transferred
me in '44 to a farm:

one windmill locking sky on land,
'Eyetie' prisoners, Nellie the horse;
the barn where I touched tongues with June.
And as I grasped the universe was

War, again the city's skein
of trolleybus wires spread overhead,
strange 'Peace' declared, leaving for years
my playgrounds, bomb-sites, pillbox, tank-traps.

Those Moments

That atmosphere like powdered gold
say, when figures down the street
are blurred to seeming innocence
of motivation, or perhaps

a sunlit snatch of some old song,
or greenness deepening in the parks,
and not minding missing the wine
and roses wherever they're going on,

recur so accidentally
and, though finite, what of calm
they give so shares their homelessness,
wherever one is, one checks, to find

here, for instance, inland, wheeling
over the high-street parapets
gulls, to tell that five miles off
some huge percussion storms the strand.

Bunhill Fields

Crammed, blackening, subsiding, warped,
some weathered past deciphering,
Dissenters' gravestones; railed off from
what's smoothed to lawn and flowerbeds,

where pensioners put out to grass
and girls with limpid eyes and prams
sun through the weekday afternoon,
as Milton, blind nearby, once did.

The risen City overlooks
here Cromwells, Wesleys, and the bones
of Bunyan, Blake, Defoe. Above
and underneath the grass now, stillness.

Broken by what taps my cheek
flaked from the opulence of trees
repeating autumn's fall of life
to headstone, greensward, marking time.

A History of Ideas

When I was eighteen I took up a blank white sheet
and heading it CREDO wrote out the lot,
needing to know what I thought, and especially why
no God exists: nobler so, if a pity.

At thirty, notes jotted while travelling, on margins
and envelope-backs, some shimmered to poems
nagging fragmentarily at why so much seemed
a pity, not noble, no God now in question.

Near forty, dark with my words, I helplessly dream
heaven where all that's been broken moves healed
as in dance: blue jug on its shelf; summer walks we intended.
Wake knowing ignobly such hunger self-pity.

The Ould Boy

Cold as ice. He'd never notice you
when you four were all weans. left all of that
up to your ma. Just came in and went out.
Friends? He'd boozing mates, no real friends
you'd say. Asked 'What's he really like?' say 'Hands.
They're his gift. He could do anything.'
In wood. Or stone. 'That picture in the hall,
no educated taste, but details perfect.'
And never trained. Did nothing with it. 'Just
a housepainter, when what he should have been's
a craftsman as few can be, say restoring
roodscreens for old churches wrecked with dry rot.'
What reared him offered swagger, drums, King Billy.
'The Ould Boy's maybe kicked his life away
not knowing his way out from under it.
Modelled himself instead on Cary Grant,
even curling his lip like his when talking.'
'He'd come home stocious late on Christmas Eve,
no food or heat in the house, and never caring.'
Yet made that garden shed, slats firm, all wired
for electricity; those amazing toys:
'The jack-in-the-box, it's in the attic now,
pops up like *this*. He made the spring, the box,
from scratch, and it'll last two hundred years.
You felt he'd done it for himself, not you.
Yet really he's done nothing for himself.'

Twelve years back, when your mother hurled one more
burnt supper out, he'd packed and gone. And showed
no interest since. You'll see him now, round bars,
hair still that black there's a blue sheen off it.
'He'll reach you ten pounds now, it's sad as if
he's lonely, but who'd know what's in his head?
He used to read. Read poetry. Aloud.
Fitzgerald's *Rubaiyat*. The only times
I mind that I felt close. His voice so, slowing:
"What! . . . did the Hond, then . . . of the Potther . . . *she-ak?*"

When Rain Sweeps Over

Say I am in a train when rain sweeps over
killing all glow from the landscape, masking hills
and pounding amorphousness of grasses blown
till the eye founders and the blind heart leaping
out there in icy whorls of it lashed by the fall
of an absolute element threshes unbeaten knowing
this teeming borne as of love's desolations must
be conjured to what bears survival, and it can swim in,
and my empty body rocking from there to here
in some day's compartment, what matter that the train
will carry me out of the storm, or the fury pass over,
the story continue, when that is only a story,
whose bluest skies are engulfed by such scourgings of rain?

Death in the Family

i.m. Leonard Waterman, 1900–1979

'I have to tell you that your father died,
suddenly, a heart-attack, last week.'

Who am I weeping for? Mother,
is it the first time of your own accord
you've mentioned him in thirty years?
You write: 'It was a comfort knowing him
there somewhere. It's my young life cut away.'

'Father. My father,' has the distant flavour
of childhood's liquorice, convolvulus
along the lane to Highams Park where he,
bespectacled, in brown, rowed us on water.

And you 'could never talk of it' until
five years ago: it seems he'd kept away
reluctantly; sent money; was in the Shropshire phone-book.
My sister dialled, heard far burring, then
put down the phone. Nor fearfully
did I track to that door. Now never can.

Paths closed, for you, me, that vestigial man.

Yet all once cherishing stays somewhere true:
you both aged my age now adopting me;
and, dapple of light or time disfiguring
his face, those careworn clerk's hands still upon
the oars, on summer's trembling lake.

Retirement

At ease with a glass of wine,
sunset pearling the sky above
Shropshire hills, blackberries
ripening in the hedges.

Gaius Mannius Secundus
of the tribe Pollia, 31 years
in the Tungrian regiments, after
the fighting in North Britain

having discharge, citizenship,
settling for this:
Viroconium's paved thoroughfares,
forum, and public baths;

secure from the murderous rites
in the uncivil mountains westward,
not to speak of the wheeling
hordes of the German forests.

As for fabulous Rome,
its poisonings, coups, executions,
(other veterans have seen it)
– better this peaceable periphery

where the writ of the Emperor
Caesar Trajanus Hadrianus
Augustus, son of the deified
Trajanus, and such mumbo-jumbo,

is pared of insanities
to a network orderly as these roads,
bureaucratic routines
enjoyed by the Romanised Celts.

*

Fluorescent lights reflect
from glass over unearthed denarii,
a holed kettle, Samian ware;
a model-reconstruction of

that place then not knowing
England due to go over it
like a tidal wave, a succession:
the blood-edged Saxon darkness

slowly civilising to churches;
more fighting, fortifications;
blackberries ever ripening
through a land's long cultivation.

Beyond the museum's windows
Shrewsbury's traffic snarls;
and *Timberland*, the *Home Improvers,*
Credit facilities.

On Mannius's tombstone
still crisp Latin; lions and pinecone
are sculpted symbols of afterlife:
reclining, wherever, beneath us.

Out for the Elements

PART ONE

1

Starry tonight, and repetitious
sea harassing the empty strand,
as when it first cast adventitious
staggering life upon the land;
through sleights of wondrous generation
since to attain a consummation
in filaments of light I see
stacked on the Prom: humanity
with all its complex apparatus,
deep-freezers, televisions, cars,
banks, supermarkets, churches, bars,
shows what once kindled to create us
subtilised now to a weird grace-
note shimmering on time and space.

2

The sand beneath my feet caressing
negligently each emptied shell,
dropped cans and condoms, spreads expressing
only conclusive flatness. Well
clear of its first-and-last mnemonic
and breakers issuing their sonic
premonitions, mankind who feigns
whole worlds dreamed to exalted planes,
within those intricate wired boxes
saying things like 'computer sales',
'topspin forehand', 'don't tell tales',
'I'm not contracepting' foxes
comprehension with monkey-tricks:
arts, avocations, politics.

3

Marvellous are the anthills, skuas,
acacias, zebras, whales, yet none
gone so tortuously askew as
man so inventively has done
from first imperatives. How did it
come about? How could nature bid it
we should attain such livings as
insurance, market research, and jazz,
mining for coal, or crawling under
purring metal contraptions, or
inspecting wickets, or the law?
It all bends the mind, and no wonder
that some are put away, convinced
they're parrots or the Queen, brains minced.

4

Small babies born to suck, laugh, cry on
their mothers' breasts, pure animal,
grow to learn how to tie a tie on,
and say 'Don't get emotional,'
budgeting life away, its flicker
never possessed streams ever quicker:
first toy, first fuck, child, grandchild, stroke,
then that's your lot. I could invoke
anthologies of the grisly ending,
mad, murdered, maimed, mocked, crucified
by surgical art. Most just subside
slowly though into what's past mending,
shopping around until they're gone,
unmissed where fleets of prams roll on.

5

Take that teashop in South Norwood
where I grew up, named *The Horst*
Café: every year more and more would
alter it with paint to read *Worst*
Café, and the man and his wife who
owned the place change it back, a life you

could hardly envy, soldiered through
repainting *H* on *W*.
Such can't be meant. Other dimensions
to their existences? No doubt.
But none improved what they slopped out
as tea. They've gone now, on their pensions
somewhere, paintbrush at last hung up,
crouched to the dregs of their last cup.

6

Which brings me to myself, revolving
such matters on a starlit beach
on Ireland's northern rim, and solving
none of my problems as I reach
perhaps my own half-way, at forty.
Pure romanticism, each sortie
risking its leap before the look
jells, has run into Life's left-hook
absurdly often. Once more home is
dwindled to little more than these
shoes I stand here in, where the sea's
belling as wind gets up, and foam is
whitening now to topple sheer.
There's plenty of the void round here.

7

But what I've journeyed to it out of
can't reclaim me. Visiting where
I 'left home' from triggers no bout of
nostalgic oh-if-only: there
today, now stuck in mortgaged houses
staring across the rug at spouses
they married at nineteen because
a year of 'going steady' was
sufficient for a blind society
subtly to put the screws on, kids
that I once played with flip their lids
or bear it, swallowing a variety
of tranquillising pills; sustain
hope with annual trips to Spain.

8

A half-mile stretch of Epping Forest
surrounded our first house: vaulting boughs
of oak, beech, hornbeam, where bird chorist-
ers thronged, sometimes a dozen cows
turned loose, and silver birches peeling
bark like paint. All conferred a feeling
prelapsarian, pure and free.
Nine was the perfect age to be
I knew, just old enough for straying
without one's parents, not yet hit
by homework, exams. But then the writ
of adults intervened, conveying
me across London, stripped away
that world, friends, woods, flash of blue jay.

9

Now in South Norwood, sent for shopping,
I'd take a ball between my feet
and book in hand, and saunter, stopping
to trap a rebound. Along our street
people considered thus combining
the two things odd; my mind was mining
the black depths of galactic space:
our island-earth, I read, a place
speck-like, lost, infinitesimal,
due to be swallowed by the sun;
life randomly from gas begun,
a sort of freak recurring decimal.
Perspective there on hacks who'd bore
at school of 'what you're cut out for'.

10

Also, the library held the ocean:
fascinated by frigate, barque,
galleon, longship, my emotion
hovered most round the *Cutty Sark*;
I travelled in imagination
great voyages of exploration,

Frobisher, Cook, Magellan, Drake,
and fought with Grenville, Nelson, Blake;
and in Marryat's books through pouring
suburban indoor afternoons
adventured tropic blue lagoons;
I clung to wind-tossed park trees roaring
Eternal father, strong to save,
Whose arm doth bind the mighty wave.

11

No clues or reason then for guessing
vagaries bringing me here to stand
where waves are mightily depressing
this winter on Portstewart strand.
Our setting-forth's exhilaration
can never tell its destination;
nor can what's reached call back and warn
the younger self of not-yet-born
defeats and pains. That ghost still living,
a phosphorescence of the tide,
in me here as I walk beside
the North Atlantic is not forgiving
my failure to resolve distress.
Nor I him his ingenuousness.

12

And no, I never joined the navy;
but knew it through the school cadets:
hammock-slung mess-deck, awful gravy,
foul 'heads', illicit cigarettes
on *HMS Dido, HMS Bermuda.*
Sailors' conversation was cruder
than in books; and it seemed to be
the case they hardly got to sea
at all, that 'fifties Home Fleet rotting
greyly in Portsmouth, Devonport;
till mothballed, scrapped, or sometimes bought
by Turks and such. I liked the yachting.
But not the whole thing's purpose: war.
Also, my eyesight was too poor.

13

At sixteen I ran out training
each night, past the lit shops, rows
of residential windows staining
the dark with brilliant cameos;
then up the last built road ascending
the tilt of downs, to halt, breath rending
my chest. The artificial light
from London blotted out the night
behind me; but ahead stars studding
deep black wastes. I leaned to rest
against a humming lamp-post, vest
sweat-soaked and my heart still thudding;
then dropped into a homeward track.
Knowing one day I'd not turn back.

14

And so, I walked out on my schooling
in mid-term. Some thought this was mad.
Then left home. And I wasn't fooling –
intent, excited, frightened, had
outgrown the adolescent years of
make-believe in the park, the tears of
first love; talk about God, sex, cars,
and sunlight on the handlebars
cycling to Keston. I'd the notion
I must test out what Conrad meant,
In the destructive element
immerse, and cast upon life's ocean
discover whether I'd sink or swim.
I found myself out on a limb.

15

SINGEL ROOM GENT NR SHOPS. BUS, STACION
1 MIN US BATH on boards outside
newsagents led to education
different from anything school had tried:
rickety chair, bowl-fire, asthmatic
washbasin in a slant-roofed attic

room, where if I sat up in bed
forgetfully, I'd bang my head;
others' intimate sounds through meagre
partitions; furtive landing-smiles;
cracked front-steps spilling bottles; miles
of strange streets all round I was eager
to roam, where boughs in lamplight cast
black beams of shadow as I passed.

16

Cramped boxes, from imagination
wringing what it might have of song,
where I read, dreamed, yearned: my conflation
of life's wonders congealed to long
novel-drafts; but I found I'd outgrown all
as fast as written; have long since thrown all
that away; but never what went
into its making. One could rent
in 1958 for two pounds weekly
a window with a piercing view
beneath Parnassian eaves. And who,
looking from drab street at that bleakly
glinting pane, would ever have guessed
who lived there, rapturous, distressed?

17

Those were the days! All I owned going
into one suitcase, everything
possible, unbounded, flowing,
everything serving my turn. I'd fling
myself nightly on the bed, mind reeling
with all it had taken in (the ceiling
with its Africa-shaped damp-
stain emblematic), and Art's lamp
glowing, pad on my knees I'd hone a
couple of thousand words – for what
else, to harvest life, have we got?
So, for a period, being a loner
flukily squared with what, time's shown,
is less put up with – being alone.

18

Meanwhile, I earned my bread and butter
in offices, kitchens, bookshops, through
my bloodstream London's twilight mutter
insinuated: Waterloo
Station's cavernous rush-hour; whisper
of escalators; cash-tills' crisper
echoings; news cried; scraps of jazz
from gratings; starlings twittering as
each dusk in millions they settled
on ashen roofs along the Strand.
I changed jobs often, which made bland
Personnel Managers somewhat nettled:
'You've been a drifter, it would seem.'
They'd tell me of their pension scheme.

19

Those singular London years conceivably
shaped me more than any. I found
myself, fallen now irretrievably
from childhood's boughs, cast on harsh ground
whose maps deceived; so, solipsistic,
created my place, direction. Mystic
apprehensions persuaded my soul
it saw life steadily and whole.
And then – I fell in love; and walking
along the Thames at Richmond past
swans' arched necks questioning a vast
ebb-tide at dusk, we realised, talking,
we would transcend the flux, abide
each cherishing each. So, 'Be my bride.'

20

I could go now, and find uncaring
swans glimmering beneath that white
bridge, green fields and willows sharing
us then unmoved; a scatter of bright
new picnics down the gardens dropping
to water, on and never stopping

the rites and play of innocence,
the couples, rowing-boats, and tents.
And a promiscuous view. Whatever
might, for us, have all come true,
have become our case – home, children, *you* –
now gleams as a figment of never-never-
land. The four years it did last took me
to Leicester University.

21

And five years later, through the mixture
of choice and chance deciding these things,
to Ulster, where the past's a fixture
stark in the moral landscape, clings
like mist to human vision. Trying
my luck, I found myself applying
in 'sixty-eight to teach at their
New University, somewhere
over the world's edge built in very
empty farmland through which the train
through blazing gorse wound to Coleraine.
Posted my first year to the Derry
campus I saw the helpless slide
through to the Battle of Bogside.

22

From marches, watercannon, patrolling
vigilantes, stones, things bloomed
through a year to teargas rolling
down Rossville Street, the city doomed
to – all the water that's passed under
Craigavon Bridge since. But the wonder
of those bemused Welsh soldiers brought
out on the streets first! – and I sought
to picture London thus, and couldn't.
An old man jerked his thumb: 'I've seen
them off back in 1919,
and now we welcome them. I wouldn't
bank on that lasting. Politics
will turn them on us Catholics.'

23

A lovely setting Derry City
has on the Foyle, against the hills
of Donegal; and a great pity
for the beating it's taken fills
my heart. By 'seventy-two each day was
rocked by bombs, and children's play was
stoning the military; each night
around the centre a gunfight
punctual as a ballet, soldiers prone in
Waterloo Place directing fire
up William Street; the funeral pyre
of factories; all shop-fronts blown in;
impassioned anti-Brit parades
behind 'free Derry' barricades.

24

A siren, then a rocket flaring
brilliantly over dark sea mean
somewhere far out a vessel's faring
direly, tossing about between
wild wind and water; like this battered
country. Recalling me from scattered
recollections to where I stand,
head among stars, feet in the sand,
out for the elements, where spacious
wastes most nearly touch this our earth.
It's late, I walk back. Banshee mirth
flutters Portstewart as tenacious
drinkers are voided from bars, some girls
whoop among blown cans, litter-whirls.

PART TWO

25

And now, beneath me, huge fluffed ranges,
promontories, lagooned with sky,
otherworldly, passing strange is
the cloudscape over which we fly
in aeroplanes. Obscured, receding,
Ireland subsides beneath me. Reading
a book up here, one's freed from care
temporarily. Empty air
cradles this frail shell in suspension
from earthbound gravities, the hum
of engines densens to become
almost my heartbeat through declension
to gentle touchdown. Which restores
the scale of streets, roofs, corridors.

26

On 'sabbatical' twenty years later
than in my London days, I stand
makeshift again, my usual fate, a
suitcase dangling from either hand;
different place, the old sensations,
in Manchester. The railway station's
bustling with focused purpose. I,
among not of all this, a shy
étranger randomly alighted,
hoping to find myself some stay
against the tides, and seek what way
my will can conjure, uninvited
pass through the *son et lumière*
of city centres everywhere.

27

Amid lit plate-glass, on tall buses
swaying down wet streets that unwind
into expanding suburbs, thus is
an anonymity I find
more enlivening than depressive.
And walking pavements past recessive

gardens where lit panes show assured
gestures adrift on dark, not moored
in human contexts, this precarious
homelessness feels more like home to me
than any scoop of space to be
captured by four roofed walls, my various
rooms and flats. I dodge the cars,
in puddles tread among the stars.

28

Uncertainty's winds have a cutting
edge that keenly intensifies
identity, prevents the shutting-
off of imagination, lies
and self-deception. Yet, it's later,
bleaker, now than then; and greater
by far the luggage weighting me,
too much these days to handle: three
trunksfull and furniture arriving
by van; books left behind; and in
my heart, more than enough. Within
the drab flat I take here reviving
old memories, I sweep the floor,
start to unpack myself once more.

29

Cold grips this city, it is snowing
as I begin to get about,
see my few friends here, write. And knowing
I've time to saunter, just hang out
listening, is nice. Being a poet
cannot make life's blessings flow, it
does not assist one to one's needs
among life's store of comforts, creeds,
the dailiness of what needs solving.
A slow thaw. Motionless grey air,
on twigs and railings everywhere
pure distillations of dissolving
snow bead, drops that do not fall.
In pubs I chat to one and all.

30

'I was once in them flats, then get a
small council house. I've moved up, see
– except that it's no bleeding better.
Fed up with fucking ferocity
I am. You get a corporation
tree at the front. It's just temptation
to kids like there's round here. They bashed
it flat. I saw them, out I dashed,
"Fuck off and slug your own trees!" Round the
Protestant school they've put up thick
wire. Good luck to them! Catholic
I am, until I die, but found the
Church's schools out years back – a hoax.
Those Prod kids learn from cultured blokes.'

31

'Get her, right bloody trollop, standing
across the bar' – split-skirt, perox-
ided – 'You'd have a cushy landing
on those boobs mate, except she'd pox
you, like as not. Last Monday she was
sat in here with some pick-up. We was
creased when she turns to him and coos
while she was knocking back the booze
he'd bought, "I don't want sex" – he winces
at this of course – "it's friends I need."
So Bill shouts, "Quid an hour, agreed?
That's all I'm asking." Out she minces,
spitting foul language. Bill just leers.
Another pint? No? Off then? Cheers!'

32

'Listen, I'll tell you truly, Andy,
the fooking Micks is twice as bad
as curry-swilling Hindustandi
coloureds. I think you're bloody mad
living in Ulster, I won't mince words,' said
the red-haired girl, 'I'd bomb the turds dead,

let those ones as wants out of it
get out, I'd blow the rest to shit
I would, like fooking Hishoreyema,
it's the only method at all
to solve it I see, why should all
our English soldiers die there?' I'm a
little put out. 'I've lived there years,
know friends. The troops are volunteers.'

33

And where the army's roll of honour
includes thirteen unarmed men shot
on Bloody Sunday, people on a
Strand Road bus, a deaf-mute, I've not
much inclination to be pally
at check-points when they try some sally
of wit; I keep eyes hard, lips shut.
And what's a soldier really but
a thing without a conscience others
point? – but behind khaki and guns,
from homes that could be anyone's,
grown up with mates, girls, hobbies, mothers'
love, scared lads in the Ulster dark
fall as the sniper finds his mark.

34

Once, at a car-check on the Border,
I had my legs bashed with a gun
by one man, after I'd deplored a
few things the soldiers here had done,
annoyed by their naïvely greeting
my English accent. Next day, meeting
coincidentally in town
the soldier who had knocked me down,
he looked quite sheepish, recognising
me, and said, 'Sorry about last night.'
We stood and chatted. 'That's all right.
Safe home yourself, mate.' Scrutinising
passers' eyes were accusing me:
See him – talks to the military.

35

And how tell England? So, I've seen Derry
pointlessly wrecked, and soldiers shot.
Yet three months back, in Portaferry
down at the tip of Ards – I'd not
been there before, seemed off the planet
travelling, savage foreshore granite,
a wintry sea tinged amethyst,
delirium of trees through mist –
I went for a stroll and pint, and after
five hours it felt I'd been there years,
welcomed, bought drinks, buying them, cheers
for Ireland and England, friendship, laughter.
'Slainte! Come to the ceilidh can
you tomorrow?' said the lighthouseman.

36

And – 'Wait till I tell you' – her recalling
Christmas seasons in Belfast:
'Inebriates, as bars shut, falling
into the churches with a last
carry-out under their oxters, quaffing,
smoking, blethering, puking, coughing
prayerfully through midnight Mass.
Then after seven days drunk and crass,
swearing they'd all go on the wagon.
And as the midnight chimes struck, half
the city, stocious, Christ you'd laugh,
firing full bottles in the Lagan,
embracing New Year rectitude.
We're chaos. But the crack is good!'

37

Yet some of those I teach have grown up
throughout the 'troubles' in the Falls
or Andersonstown, and yes, they'll own up
to working for the Provisionals
at twelve or so, performing various
tasks, not usually too nefarious,

hijacking cars, hiding a gun,
sometimes a hit-man on the run
from soldiers whose pre-dawn house-searches
have torn their rooms apart, who'd shot
some of their relatives, put a lot
behind the wires, despoiled their churches:
'Sure, we had buried arms there. So
the priests aren't keen? They daren't say no.'

38

By fifteen they were mostly mitching
school, maybe hooked on drugs or booze,
through courts, or variously ditching
sanity; and yet somehow cruise
their way through 'A'-levels, to reach us
blitzed in ways beyond their teachers'
experience. But: 'Now, I've got
sick sore tired of it, there's not
much future being a rear-gunner
on a Belfast milk-float. Nor them as pour
at shift-ends out of Gallaghers or
the dinghy factory, taking a scunner
to their whole lives while clicking bags
arm-in-arm to hoke for fags.'

39

From Belfast now, where like a flame on
ruins a wild vitality
dances – whoever you'd lay blame on
for all destroyed, deformity
of spirit, craven adorations –
west and south by slow gradations
modulating, Ireland yields
itself: white stone farms pegging fields
that fire with whin each May, cool rivers
winding through alder, green townlands
tricked out each Twelfth with flags and bands
and Orange arches; country-livers,
marketing in slow one-street towns:
byres where the searching soldier frowns.

40

Jaguars parked on mud outside the
disco-lounges of shore hotels
(each weekend's hangover must ride the
sabbatical tumult of bells);
fishermen out on Lough Neagh steering
frail boats; tenebrous packed bars hearing
Carrickfergus, Mna na hEirann,
on uilleann pipes, flute and bodhran.
Night over all, a full moon bowling
through cloud-slipstream glitters from
pooled water and that milk-churn bomb
triggered for Ferret-cars patrolling
the border lanes, lads homesick for
city-lights far from this mad war.

41

Each morning, Radio Ulster's prattle
about it all, as bread-vans drive
past hedge and sheugh and mist-wreathed cattle
('Three dead, one serious but alive')
delivering nourishment to rural
estates and lonely farms. A plural
half-listening regret's expressed,
'Surely, it's dreadful. Sean, get dressed
or it's the school bus you'll be losing,'
lost among purpled peaks and slopes
where high springs generate like hopes
gushing what filters downhill, oozing
to loughs where Ireland in chaste dress
kneels to its mirrored loveliness.

42

Two tinker kids with switches bowling
a tyre down a remote bohereen,
the background mountains, and sheep strolling
among dead sheep's bones: I have seen
wildernesses of greenness barely
netted by drystone walls, one squarely

imperturbable Norman tower
perhaps by water; with each shower
bounty of rainbows arched on passes
where windswept wayside shrines gleam or
some tumbled cabin, roof and door
jaggedly gaping. Over grasses
in derelict graveyards by the sea
light blows in waves, swarms each bent tree.

43

Crying on cliffs, the western ocean
utters itself to fishermen
intimate with its ficklest motion,
trusting in what they have to when
the tide allows: in Cleggan, Downings,
Cahirciveen, families with drownings
throughout their ancestries like knots
in sea-wrack. That horizon's what's
lured since the early hermits shivered
in stone chapels clinging to bare fangs
of rock where the Atlantic bangs,
their skulls blown clean till vision quivered
alive on solitude, stars, night,
conjuring ecstasies of light.

44

But life has ways of interrupting
poetry: I had better say,
however it may be disrupting
sequence, what I have learned today,
March, 1980, an ironic
circumstance of my being, yet tonic
also. Born 1940, when
war raged, and adopted then,
I've never known my real kin. Mother
has said that the agency would not
at the time give her one jot
of information. Sometimes other
people have urged me on to find
out 'who you are; and don't you mind?'

45

Of course it's something that I've pondered.
Once, chancing past the building where
all births are registered, I wandered
inside, but my enquiries there
drew a blank. My adoptive father,
not seen since I was nine for rather
intricately sad reasons, died
late last year. I was notified.
'From his papers' proof of my actual
parentage comes, astounds my day:
*Nolan, Dermot and Moyra (née
Enright)*. Both Irish. A strange factual
fluke for me to assimilate.
I sit, and let it resonate.

PART THREE

46

Spring comes round again, and what is
pushing up through the verges, parks,
is fresh, is daisies; a waste lot is
rioting vegetation; sparks
of bud on trees, exotic clumps of
blossom on roundabouts; garden dumps of
compost heap up, lawnmowers whirr,
cut grass perfumes South Manchester.
On pavements, shoals of cotton dresses,
cruising pushchairs; earliest white
cherry blossom: still nature's trite
annual flummery impresses.
My underwater hands wring clean
bright shirts to meet this rush of green.

47

Out and about's the way to scatter
disjecta membra of the mind.
Where I'm living doesn't flatter
anyway: once again I find
furnished rooms, rickety bed, sagged chairs, are
where I'm at. The chipped mirror's stares are
uncondoling. It's later than
when first like this. I wonder can
this now be irreversible exile
from everything I've always known
I really belong to; sought, it's grown
more distant, shivering to flecks. I'll
do as they say, no doubt: *He's strong,*
he can cope. But now something vital's wrong.

48

'The boys from Killybegs come rolling
home' resounds in this Moss Side pub;
though where the Irish here are bowling
off to is some Manchester club,
the Top Cat, Ardri, Ritz, or Kelly's,
or a Chinese to fill their bellies.
Or just back home: scarred Lingbeck flats,
Whalley Range, Chorlton Road. Well, that's
my lot again; I drain the whiskey
bought to help make my last pint last,
talking to Pat Quinn of his past
in Derry. Philomena's frisky,
whooping and boasting how she'd been
a 'forties Sligo beauty queen.

49

Among the hubbub, a girl weeping
near me. 'So what's up, love?' I say.
'Nothing.' But then her tale comes seeping
out: 'My sister. It's my big day,
my twenty-first, that she's decided
to get engaged on. Dad here's sided

with her. I'll let them organise
it. Won't go near it.' And she dries
her eyes with nicotine-stained fingers.
'One of my kids is five next day.' 'You've
children?' 'I've four.' 'Time up, friends, move,'
the landlord interrupts. She lingers:
'My husband's off serving the Queen
two years.' 'The nick?' 'That's what I mean.'

50

'We're five, my kids and me. There's Maire
who I was talking of, she's great.
Sean died at three months, he'll be four, a
beautiful son. Martine and Kate
I lost at fifteen days. September
they're two, the twins. Oh, I remember
all their birthdays, to me they stay
alive and growing every day.'
Cellophane in the ashtray crackles
as she stubs her cigarette, flares
brilliant as magnesium. There's
life answering academic jackals
who, reading Wordsworth, have demurred
at 'We Are Seven' as absurd.

51

'The afterbirth come out in sections,
hitting the ceiling and the wall,
the midwife giving me directions.
And then they hand me him, and all
bloody. I've always loved that baby,
'cause of the pain I'd been through maybe . . .'
'In Failsworth at the Cloggers Fred
first downs his pint, then drops down dead . . .'
'Them black clubs, friend, don't take your wallet.
They roll you as you leave the door.
The prozzies there are rough, and sure
a jump would cost you . . .' 'Grabbed her doll, it
broke my Lyn's heart . . .' 'When dark arrives
keep off the Precinct, they use knives.'

52

Interpersonal situations
of conflict most arise, we find,
among those whose accreditations
if societally defined
extrapolate as, well, inferior.
The buggers would be so much cheerier,
display aversive stimuli
measurably reduced, if we
contrived, despite their results status,
some alternative paradigm
for them . . . Meanwhile, at closing-time
round Moss Side jobless blacks may hate us:
within our field's parameters
mortality-response occurs.

53

Still, in the sun in Alexandra
Park, buds freshening sooty trees,
all's harmony. I've taken Sandra,
thirteen and 'handicapped', her knees
bumping, head lolling, hands tight-clinging
upon the pram, her brothers flinging
about the grass (one's Peter, he
is 'hyperactive'). Anthony
the baby peers from my arms enjoying
the slide. The black kids want to play
with Sandra. 'She's not well,' we say.
Gently the roundabout. 'Annoying
her is it?' for she almost-screams.
'No, that's just how she laughs,' it seems.

54

'So have some tea then. I feel rested
with that break from the kids. With Len
away, I've no time, not digested
a meal before I'm up again,
and Sandra takes some looking after.
But she went backwards like, got dafter

when in that institution, so
I'd rather have her home. Although
Len's always been good, and in work, he
can't earn so we have luxuries.
We cope. I make sure the deep-freeze
is kept stocked. Have another turkey
drumstick? When we was kids we got
"Here's a jam butty, that's your lot."

55

'Our mother sent me and my sisters
out for to knock off coal and scrap,
you finished up all dirt and blisters,
climbing those fences, through the gap
underneath gates. If we got back and
had nowt, then we got fetched a whack, and
with anything to hand, a pan,
the iron. Me, Louise and Anne
got hammered rotten. "Get along the
chippie for me," our mam would yell,
"and don't forget me minerals!" Well,
she didn't know her ways was wrong. The
schoolteachers griped, she kept us home
to send us out to fetch and comb.

56

'Louise got into trouble, sent to
Borstal. But always lively, till
that day ten years back when she went to
cross to get cigs in Cheetham Hill.
A Strangeways screw in a Cortina
hit her. His fault. Well, if you'd seen her
in hospital . . . It hurt her brain.
Mam settled out of court, she's plain
stupid, for just two hundred nicker.
Our Anne's grown houseproud, tight, her three
kids daren't be kids, you never see
toys on her carpet. Makes me sick, a
belting they get. She banks Steve's pay,
then draws the Social, that's her way.

57

'How would Anne cope with mine, I wonder?
She'd murder Peter or Sandra, then
there's Nell, my eldest, got took under
the Authority three years back when
she was just twelve and lifting money
out of the house, it wasn't funny,
she'd hitch to London. She's in Care.
They done a termination there
on her last year, then told me after.
I went in mad. "It's a police
matter," they said. They got a piece
of my mind. "Fuck, I'll wipe the laughter
off your jaw with a clout, and tell
the police myself. She's my girl, Nell."

58

'The first time Nell was in, I brought her
along, was one where once I'd been
myself, but never thought my daughter
would know the like. In seventeen
years nothing changed. Bare, dark, and stinking
of disinfectant. And I'm thinking
my little Nell was me back then,
and me my mam. Could taste again
that mouldy bread. Imagination
plays you strange tricks. But there's the same
grey warden woman. "What's your game,
handing things on a generation?"
The cow. Food's better now, it seems . . .
The life I'd like . . . But that's all dreams.'

59

Pleasant in the late sun to ramble
circuitously back: the locked
and disused church, choked round with bramble
and nettles, in blue air its pocked
steeple still gracefully aspiring;
down Chorlton Road I pause admiring

a proud Victorian ornate
corner-frontage, chopped like some great
wrecked prow; scarred cliffs of overlooking
flats, a low sea of yellow brick
estate. But gutter-drifts of thick
may-blossom temper smells of cooking
in Whalley Range, where whores on low
walls watch the dandelions grow.

60

Above worn tarmac gnarled old branches
interlock forming dense arcades
of foliage, where sunlight dances,
slithers in glittering cascades
as air stirs. Even in this depleted
so-often built-upon, concreted,
weighted and riddled stretch, there is
still inexhaustibly the fizz
of earth's most basic growth, forever
grass pushes splitting pavements, knots
of living colour splash waste lots,
crumble walls, smother rubbish, never
mind which are flowers, which called weeds,
so long as greenness blooms and seeds.

61

Yet utterly England's still two nations:
twelve miles away in prettified
Prestbury, different expectations
and accents resonate inside
half-timbered pubs hung with expensive
shining brasses as loud offensive
business-types in immaculate
and costly 'casuals' talk of VAT,
and stocks, shares, deals, consumer markets,
riding, antiques, priorities
unknown in the brick congeries
of drab square miles where after dark it's
the blue HARP LAGER factory sign
reigns, not the constellations' shine.

62

And round our earth more generally, a
poisonous human blight; obscene
new photographs from Kampuchea
adorn the colour magazine
beside my breakfast coffee: dumps of
skulls on pink soil, with brownish clumps of
grass thrusting up through sockets where
eyes once were: victims of the Khmer
Rouge. Small mechanised wars. Pollution.
And now a racket on TV
distracts me to look up and see
'live coverage' of the armed solution
to London's embassy siege: gout-
ing flame, shots, hostages fetched out.

63

Only two weeks ago though, during
a trip to London, rocking down
familiar rails at six, enduring
merely the homebound rush-hour, brown
brick arches fanning Southern Region's
tracks out above the usual legions
of scrapped cars, metal drums, the sprawl
of rigid log-jammed roof-lines, tall
boxes of flats, high windows flaming
with sun, the whole place felt once more
the same as ever, so that for
a moment, twenty years back claiming
me utterly, my life since seemed
like something woken from, just dreamed.

64

Next day outside East Croydon station
confirmed the otherwise I know:
hugely concrete obliteration
of – almost me, it feels, although
environmental demolition's
impersonal. Part of our condition's

experiencing this orphanage
by the accustomed as we age,
even things once disliked, lamented:
my school, its cloisters, fields, brick clock-
tower long expunged for a high block
of offices, shops; among Boots' scented
toiletry counters, thoughts that sear
are, *I did maths, carved desk-lids here.*

65

Then, on a 12A bus, through shoppers'
chatter, I heard: 'It's marvellous
the life that walked this earth once, whoppers
them dinosaurs were, ponderous
as whales, but up on legs, a hundred
tons, and others had wings that thundered
bigger than planes about the sky
beaks snapping tree-tops off.' And I
looked at our planet's tie-and-shirted
and trousered heir, some aeons on,
to brontosaur, pteronadon,
as he continued, 'It's asserted
all this here, Croydon, yonks BC,
was miles beneath the bloody sea.'

66

Still, my love for green trains grinding
over Hungerford Bridge towards
Charing Cross, powered barges winding
leisurely past the House of Lords,
green populous Embankment gardens,
Big Ben, the river's glitter, pardons
even the blocks that screen St Paul's.
That day, inside the County Hall's
slabbed edifice, I watched them playing
chess, a world abstractly profound
conjuring harmonies around
carved wood in silence. Smiling, greying,
Korchnoi moves a piece, creates
imbalance, tension; complicates.

67

Chess, so unfathomably various
more different games might be played than
are atoms in our multifarious
universe, is itself but an
infinitesimal detail only
of life's brief flicker on our lonely
planet mislaid in emptiness.
A spasm in some maybe purposeless
vast game's dynamic, we conjecture
fragmentarily, our unique
signatures – microchips, bezique,
Joyce, teasmades, popes, string, architecture –
doomed squiggles. Still we weep, and think,
notice that girl, or clean the sink.

68

Quantum theory has thrown up notions
positing that the universe
which we experience, its oceans,
cities, stars, all we love, or curse,
may only be one chance projection
out of a limitless confection
of transient cosmic images,
alternative worlds that ghost *what is*
(that sunlit afternoon; the frost in
a spider's web); some postulate
reality multifoliate
occurs, is not just latent. Lost in
such infinite chess, we find *what might*
be haunts our days, and dreams at night.

69

Illimitable reflections . . . Scattered
by the hurtling of a stone
through my flat window. I pick shattered
glass from my carpet, slightly thrown
myself. Some passing drunk? Teenagers?
A clairvoyant Moss Side umbrageous

Samuel Johnson refuting me
after the manner in which he
disposed of Berkeley's speculations?
The lamplit street outside yields no
clues to what dropped the actual so
concretely in. Well, an ovation's
due to some neat slip-fielding: there
the missile rests, caught by a chair.

PART FOUR

70

Diffracted fire across the water
in the bright morning sun, as past
gantried and dry-docked hulls, at quarter
speed, the ferry glides up Belfast
Lough; and beyond the city's ravel
the clear brow of Cave Hill. I travel
through County Antrim once again,
hedge-blossom foaming past my train . . .
Portstewart's thronged, milling confusion
of dogs armed to the teeth with teeth,
cars, pushchairs; but outspread beneath
blue sky Donegal gives illusion
of paradisal zones beyond
Atlantic calm now as a pond.

71

Behind the convent's castellations
the cliff-path clings above sheer fall
to igneous black rocks; constellations
of wildflowers, blue, pink, yellow, all
nameless to my town mind, grow scattered
precariously on this long-battered
northern shore, vivid proofs of blown
seed flowering where it can, cleft stone,

cascading grass, wherever landing.
Against odds. For miles inland trees,
such as there are, the trickeries
of June's cosmetics notwithstanding,
protrude misshapen, in this place
where hard survival cripples grace.

72

I press my palm on long bleached grasses
over the sea. Today, this view
innate now to my life surpasses
most of the world's; so different too
from all I grew up with. A tension,
this geographical dimension
of my cross-channel life: we find
our frameworks shape our frames of mind.
Much in my verse, notes one reviewer,
of 'comings and goings between
Ulster and England', which is seen
as about 'freedom'. Scarcely. Through a
long aggregation by degrees
my lot, it yields strange plangencies.

73

Places, like people, grow intensely
part of one: here Portstewart Strand,
Derry, the Causeway Coast, immensely
the ranges of glens and mountains; and
so also, haunting through recurring
dreams, verdant Leicestershire, unblurring
images of its small red brick
arched canal-bridges; and trees thick
in Whalley Range, such huge profusion
must have stood first when all was
open country. These things, because
dispersed in space, in me crave fusion.
And wood-less Norwood underneath
them all, with heath-less Thornton Heath.

74

Through all, the personal life is woven.
I look on this refulgent sea
caressing levelly cliff and cove, an
azure and fragrant sky, with three
white yacht-triangles, and remember
listening all night last November
to Atlantic roar and shingle-scrape,
gale screaming through a fire-escape,
and in the lull after each wave, a
hissing of rain on water. I
lay in your arms in your room, my
old flame; and warm, let my mind savour
thoughts of far fishing-boats that spark
the ocean harvesting salt dark.

75

And you? 'See her,' they'd say, 'she's way out,
drinks like a fish, and doesn't care
a damn.' A bottle saw each day out,
and from a bottle your red hair.
'She's brains to burn,' 'She's hell-for-leather,'
hands always waving, one green feather
ear-ring, clothed 'like a fucking heap'
you'd wryly put it, so short of sleep
and long on talk, 'a myth', 'a riddle', a
perpetual-motion cross between
a Malcolm Lowry hell-raiser, Jean
Rhys tragic heroine and Bette Midler
in *The Rose* – when I was sad
to sickness, we met, you made me glad.

76

You burned, the purest of flames, owning
no shape's dead encrustations, scorned
all ashen cautions, nothing toning
you down, and no one (plenty warned);
cindering days most build to boxes
walled into refuge from life's shocks. Is

our shared suspicion of their plush
living-rooms, gleaming doorknockers, lusc-
ious flowerbeds, stasis, what united
us? – our complicity an innocence
not of lived experience
but form: quick brilliance is blighted
when outlines worn that it might face
harsh world congeal to carapace.

77

Attuned to a dance beyond the dancers,
among a bar's wallpapered fake
stars and comets you kindled answer,
would slip the net of all they'd make
us. Yet what moved me was a dark shimmer
beyond your flame's tip. Something grimmer
than even what you've had awaits;
and that, knowing perhaps your fate's
self-destruction, you rush toward it
– 'I get on best with drop-outs, dope
fiends, drunks . . . I tried but couldn't cope
with lesbians . . . Eat? I can't afford it
if I'm to have my breakfast beer
and fags, and books' – is youth, I fear.

78

Well, *compañera*, I suppose you
reading all this – where are you now?
New York? Or Amsterdam? Who knows, you
orbit beyond me, anyhow:
one of your attic pads with ash and
empties and novels, dropped rings, cash and
matches and clothes strewn on the floor,
holed blankets covering you, the roar
of sea or traffic through frayed curtain? –
you'll laugh that I should elevate
you as a true exemplar: 'Wait,
I'm catastrophic, and for certain
I don't know what I'm all about –
look at this room! I'm clearing out.'

79

For you, impromptu flitting started
back in beleaguered East Belfast,
where each day your school bus departed
stoned by Prods; to escort it past
them, British soldiers, whom you hated;
an Ulster education; fated
in your case to be cut short when
the UDA sent ten armed men
who scourged the house around you, wrecking,
yet when your father lunged, fled quick
– 'Just one Fenian waving a stick!
I thought they'd shoot him' – you all trekking
out to a squat in rural Down:
oil-lamps, and miles from any town.

80

'The Ards gentility talk money
in plastic lounges. Where we went
to school they thought our accents funny,
"Belfast common" – so I'd absent
myself, read, drink, crash out wherever
I landed up, and with whoever
sometimes. When I was just sixteen
and into pencil-skirts, hygiene
and vodka – Christ, I'd even dab a
perfume on – I'd light out to bars
and pick up vapid guys with cars
– "I own a factory" and such slabber,
"I've watched you in here, you're all go" –
to reach a disco or a show.

81

'"Take a big stick to her," our hateful
obese priest said to my da, who's
simple and stay-at-home, a grateful
by the turf fire's his nightly booze,
then cries for Ireland when he's stocious.
They love me, but think I'm atrocious,

him and our ma. She slaves, the poor
dear, heating water day-long for
washing and cleaning. They both hope a
better life for their children, but
I can't become what they want, shut
in some drab office. The Europa
floor-shows where I once stripped and danced
were my scene. From which I've advanced.'

82

Into the radiantly gregarious
loneliness drawing me to you.
And so, forgive me this vicarious
leisurely versified trip through
what for its liver has got bleaker;
kind, touching, talented truth-seeker,
just 'get your head showered' as you'd say;
I wish you focus. If one day
you find yourself, still travelling light and
further, crashed out beneath the cold
stars finally, may there unfold
for you a heaven in that goodnight, and
you'll angel-sweet-talk past the gate,
and keep the music loud and late.

83

Meanwhile, the fishing boats go trawling
winter or summer, for what catch
they can; and still my right hand crawling
on paper waits, then moves, to scratch
ink nets upon unfathomed oceans
of experience, complex emotions
more subtle and vast than words can say.
The poem knows its only way
is trust in craft, collaboration
with elements; some lucky tide
remote from dock-lights, that may guide
and buoy its venture, saturation
in inchoate stuff; that just might
net lustres shoaled beyond its sight.

84

Intricacies of patient labour
attuned to whispering darkness past
the vessel (not to friend or neighbour
advising, warning) may at last
fetch home some glints of those elusive
harmonies; hinted unobtrusive
musically perfected notes
which life aspires to as it floats
afraid on the imagination's
undercurrent that comprehends
the chaos wrecking human ends,
our purest hopes and expectations;
yet through which only we compose
life towards verities each knows.

85

Today's bright sheen on the Atlantic
flatly denies all depths, reflects
diffusely sky and sun. Romantic
to a casual eye, effects
dazzling as if of shot-silk shaken
are superficial, could be mistaken
for membrane rather to thin air
than that opaque interior where
slowly unlighted vegetation
coagulates on sunken wrecks,
and blind existences perplex
our surface-minds, such propagation
and ravening still where life begins,
dark sea-floor of our origins.

86

O, but anyone might find them
within me, silted, crumbling
sad hulks of what, when I designed them
set out to be . . . Past salvaging
they rot and shimmer in deep water,
haunting my nights. And I have caught a

visionary glimpse of full proud sail
while washing-up, or opening mail,
clairvoyantly from such diurnal
routine cried out to see come home
unbroken upon gentling foam
that ship, its children, love eternal . . .
The apparition fades away,
goes sailing by, leaves empty day.

87

Turning from which, I speed my visit
with talk, drink; at a party sport
a silly hat ('It's borrowed, is it?'
'No.'), as usual wince when caught
among the campus's endemic
sheep-head blether, stale academic
trivia; post cards of the view
of sunset from Portstewart to
Manchester friends. Until I'm back in
good time to see it on their wall.
'A pleasant trip?' And is that all?
– I cruise the nights insomniac in
what welters in me, take unseen
soundings, subversive, submarine.

PART FIVE

88

I am invited to a christening:
First, at the house, we drink a toast
(the baby girl sleeps on, unlistening,
shawled, bonneted); then set forth, most
on foot, for church. Hot sunshine blesses
beribboned toddlers in bright dresses,
flowers on Moss Side lawns ('Looks nice –
who'd think it muggers' paradise?').

Duly, the infant's soul is grafted
onto the body of Christ's church
('And just as well, because you'd search
in vain for a father, so many've shafted
my sister'), as in wooden pews
tired feet are eased from high-heel shoes.

89

This baby's grown life will be in a
different century from mine . . .
Tiring among the party's din, (a
great deal of food and beer and wine
has been put down, loud music's playing,
the children gone, most adults staying;
around the room some quarrels start,
it's growing dark outside), I part
the curtains, pause a while reflecting,
a little muzzily, about
mankind's perpetual reaching-out
to unknown future; recollecting
also how I stood yesterday
looking at mummies on display.

90

O! Osiris live for ever!
emblazoned the museum where
the long-dead were laid out. Whatever
convictions motivated their
arcane embalming many thousand
years ago with religious vows and
rites, it was what's left human stirred
my feelings: amputees interred
with spare mud feet; an infant wizened
in its reed coffin, scarcely born
before its future was withdrawn;
the royal Perenbast's bedizened
carrion. X-rays show beneath
the wraps, disease, worn joints, bad teeth.

91

The simple ills that flesh is heir to
connect us with the distant past;
moving from frailties we share to
the tricks man's learned since Perenbast
was laid to rest though, raises thoughts of
her astonishment at all sorts of
phenomena could she come back:
astroturf, cars, the cling-film pack,
print, nuclear power, supersonic
travel, credit-cards, disco-noise,
non-biodegradable soft toys,
skyscrapers, phone-taps, electronic
space invader games, fruit-machines,
acrylic clothes, sex magazines.

92

We've bent our minds to sociology,
radar, the Sydney Opera House,
psychiatry, hijacks, clones, ecology,
extruded chipboard, Mickey Mouse,
Ceefax, the seaside pier, the quango,
hermeneutics, the Pill, the tango,
multinationals, the football mob,
and *Danish Dentist on the Job*,
and holding mummy exhibitions;
reached for the moon they held in awe
along the Nile, with no time for
such antiquated inhibitions
sauntered upon its ancient face
to check if we can use the place.

93

Moon rises now, above these local
roofs and inchoate streets, as though
offering us a lucid focal
point for desires confused below,
a platform enabling perspective
on what is piecemeal and subjective

seen from where we must live, inside
our heads. I watch its brilliance glide
free of all geocentric weathers:
the poets', lovers' moon; and now
uncertain why but knowing how,
the scientists', who stepped light as feathers
out of their fragile craft, to stare
for something elemental there.

94

Touching empiricists, collecting
data with scoops to put in jars,
prodding, measuring, stooped, inspecting;
who turned to see among cold stars
harmoniously our blue-green planet
spin steadily and whole. Nor can it
for mystic, lover, astronaut,
endure so; for no life-support
systems sustain unearthly visions
long – and all must re-enter through
spoiled atmosphere and touch down to
a world that peers and makes incisions
in what's ineffable and mocks
us with its grey shards, moondust, rocks.

95

Like those long-buried, this new baby
ignorantly through its brief span
will quicken to whatever may be
our true desiderata. Man
cannot construe his teleologies,
always played false by the mythologies
and forms of his own time and place
settles for shapes that seem his case,
half-hearing larger orchestrations.
I leave the christening-party, stroll
under the dateless star-pricked bowl
on which all human civilisations,
today's, or Egypt's long ago,
melt as a single flake of snow.

96

And given time for adaptation
('You can't eat them, they're cigarettes,
breathe in the smoke for the sensation' –
'Don't you know how to play cassettes?' –
'We've got no slaves' – 'No, use the toilet' –
'Your dress smells queer, you ought to boil it')
and so forth, Perenbast might find
that what ticks in the human mind
in Manchester in 1980
is not much changed through all those years
since she once knew them: hopes and fears,
wanting love, and to love, such weighty
matters; a sense of wonder links
this christening with what built the Sphinx.

97

Times change, but the deep aspirations
centred within mankind abide;
with few, if any, correlations
between how far they're satisfied
and our material wellbeing.
Any Victorian mill-hand seeing
what's owned by his great-great-grandson
might think Utopia's begun;
and yet the ratio of pleasure
to misery's much as it was;
and only fools suppose because
we've central heating, planes, more leisure,
anaesthetics and extra years,
our lives are richer than Shakespeare's.

98

And when I was a kitchen porter,
or penniless in slum bed-sits,
I had no less of what I sought, a
great deal of it since shot to bits,
some grown with time, and some that wouldn't.
Dean Swift, rich in his own day, couldn't

stand it; while peasant John Clare found
his Eden-fields and green lanes wound
towards the mad-house – elementary
surely, to see what was too much
for them was not their lot as such,
but being them. Staid Yorkshire gentry
doubtless found what intensely stirred
their neighbour Brontës quite absurd.

99

Nor do the Bomb and concentration
camps make us really worse than when,
horse-back with no administration,
Attila ravaged Europe. Then
we weren't so dangerously efficient
at evil, that's all. And sufficient
use is still made of primitive
methods – babies whose parents give
them burns, for instance. Hatreds harden
people to enact what yesterday
occurred in Northern Ireland: they
impaled a woman with a garden
fork upon her own carpeted
lounge floor, and beat her father dead.

100

Few grounds for hope, yet much to honour
in people as they are. I heard
two girls all rings and ear-rings on a
bus pouring forth each trashy word
of some 'hit' song; and thought of Emma
Bovary, offered just like them a
meretricious and second-rate
range of expression for her great
hunger of spirit for life's beauty.
Our public world supposes what
we need is more of what we've got,
consumer-goods topped with tutti-frutti.
Yet listening around finds out
most know that's not what they're about.

101

Intellectuals fear 'the masses',
or idealise; won't let be
people much apter (when the Bass is
flowing) than they whose tendency
in talk's impersonal or woolly,
to utter their deep being fully;
whose prejudice and platitude
are free of cant; from whom obtrude
germinal yearnings, satisfactions
charging them, yet so marginal
to what the ads, political
parties, ideologues and factions
are on about; and some will boast,
some shyly tell, what matters most.

102

It might be woodwork, keeping whippets,
gardening, wild-life, music, their
children or friends, a lakeland trip. It's
true people breathe what's in the air,
are superficially excited
at wins by Manchester United,
soap-opera, murder mysteries,
or 'My Val's passed six GCEs.'
Beneath induced false-consciousness is
a truer knowledge though, its flames
famished for life; its feelings, aims,
knit to what poetry expresses.
And rare, but not élitist, art
keeps faith with the bruised common heart.

103

True poetry, articulating
what's smothered in our slipshod lives,
restoring us, through its creating,
to truths by which mankind survives,
even when most abstruse or vatic
thus is profoundly democratic,

against the casual tide that tugs
us from ourselves, our daily drugs.
And the poetic imagination
is moral too in making us
feel other lives, transmuted thus
'by sympathy to an incarnation
of the spirit it breathes' – so said
Shelley. Intolerance is ill-read.

104

The people I like, or find least galling,
are loners, writers, plain folk, brats.
May I continue my appalling
relationships with bureaucrats:
collectively on a committee
mild-mannered dons would without pity
concur in genocide to keep
the boat from rocking. The least deep
chatter of sales-girls, clerks, yobs, dockers
('This pub's where shop tarts drink, we're made' –
'Great car' – 'Blue Bols and lemonade' –
'My friend's got freckles on her knockers')
still helps us through to closing-time,
while Caesar's staff hatch global crime.

105

Locally now, Moss Side's late summer
expires in rain and seediness.
The park looks tired, September's come, a
new school year's started (more or less:
the absentee-rate here is greater
than flogging's in my *alma mater*).
And you, friend, struggling on as best
you can with Sandra and the rest
through poverty, work, family, crisis,
admit 'life's heartbreak', with a wry
grin however. Yours has been, I
know all offered as advice is
useless. But I would honour what
irradiates its cruel plot.

106

You're brave, perceptive, complex, humorous.
Much of your life's been swallowed tears.
One of eleven all-too-numerous
children yourself, your early years
not gifted with much indication
of true human signification
or potential, and left without
any true schooling, knocked about
(I've quoted you before), you married
and started your own family
before you knew how to be free.
As for the problems you've since carried,
they make a painful catalogue,
a pitilessly uphill slog.

107

Untutored to high aspirations
craving in you for happiness
grows lambent in approximations:
a binge in town, that new red dress,
a joke, that day with all the nippers
in Southport, riding the big dipper's
huge undulations, showing sea
for the first time to Anthony
your powerful toddler, still called 'baby'.
I wish that I could conjure true
your dream: a café run by you.
The books you've missed would show you maybe
your notions of good times lack exact
basis – I'm just glad of their fact.

108

Begun by ocean, in the tavern
often to catch life's utterance, here
the poem at last comes to Poole's Cavern
deep among peaks of Derbyshire:
many-chambered, echoing, wondrous
tinctured rock above and under us,

pink, green, orange, black and blue;
and water percolating through,
so every drip's minute deposit
lengthens the spear-like stalactites,
stubbily phallic stalagmites
erecting at, the guide said, was it
an inch each thousand years? While I'm
in here I've entered slowed-down time.

109

To these caves once arrived the clever
and predatory ape, cast out
from Eden by his knowledge. Never
since our forefathers lurched about
here have we healed our alienation
from nature, or found true relation
with each other; though what once gnawed
its supper here has since on flawed
premises built such huge dominion,
its been no moral leap to sub-
stitute the H-bomb for the club,
for tribal prejudice opinion
polls. Still like frozen waterfalls
the flowstone creeps down limestone walls.

110

No outside vagaries of climate
perturb the cavern's temperature:
9° Centigrade. No time at
all, it seems, since clad in rough fur,
with bows and spears, they took its shelter.
Concurrently with the Nile Delta
this too was civilisation's womb:
all-purpose, part a living-room,
and part a tomb, for human bones are
found here; and that recess a sort
of prehistoric fridge where caught
animals were stacked on dank stones. Are
our modern towns and countryside,
I'm wondering, still there outside?

111

Time tricks one here. I feel a million
hours or miles from when strolling round
Buxton's grey Georgian Pavilion
and Crescent. After which I found
myself in Grin Low woods unsure of
my path, the forest dark, the roar of
treetops in strong wind blowing clear
from Axe Edge; scents close round. And near
also, glimpsed among trees, elusive
as momentary sunshafts, seemed
that figment I've pursued or dreamed,
our brief encounters inconclusive:
My *doppelganger*, with home, child, all
I might have been. Deaf to my call.

112

As if he feared me. Yet somehow directed
me down here, where things in my past
and origins gather unexpected
nimbus around them, then at last
illuminate me with a vision
pre-empting all bleak life-revision,
admitting only gratitude
for what has been. And in this mood
belonging to a peace occurring
unreasonably, anywhere,
I saunter round myself to stare
at moments flickering and recurring
like sunlight when small breezes shake
it out like petals on a lake.

113

As that last flash of greenness lighting
landscape before the sun sets may
assure tomorrow in igniting
detail of the completed day,
or as the unrecorded golden
long-lost cornet of Buddy Bolden

inventing jazz blows sweet and clear
to the imagination's ear,
authenticating recollection
blazes within me, so that I glean
by guiding-lights from what has been
a future focus and direction;
axial truths that harmonise,
answering the undone self's cries.

114

People of course. Friends, shared laughter.
All love's unique epiphanies
still sharp, despite what happened after,
in memory's lens. Wheat in a breeze,
the windmill turning. Voices, glances,
places, evenings. Poole's Cavern dances
as if the seas off Donegal
boomed through its chambers, as I recall
finally, numinous, no moral
beyond the peace it knew, when I
on childhood's lawn – its butterfly
still loops my mind unbroken, laurel
leaves glittering, 1951 –
sat shelling green peas in the sun.

In the Planetarium
(1990)

1981

Green drumlins swept delectably with light,
pegged by kempt farms, an old truncated tower;
sheep belly-deep, rose gardens, dappled lanes,
flowering hedgerow and July's quenched whin.

'Only two snows this century round here . . .'
Such rich confection seems life's natural ground,
no transient conjuring. Stone eagles gaze
at the Mournes' far serrations, wilderness

reduced to décor. Just one pool reflects
some troubling essence dark beyond thin air . . .
Till sign-stuck petrol stations, country shops
coagulate past our windscreen to Belfast.

Funnelled down the Ormeau Road we hit the blitz,
or what's left outcropped: gable-ends, gapped streets
leprous with scrawled SMASH H-BLOCKS, FTQ,
RUC MURDERERS; black lamp-post flags

for the hunger-strikers. Then, abruptly, THIS
IS UVF TERRITORY, red white and blue . . .
The steel-engirded city-centre stores
are tricked with royal wedding souvenirs.

Clear above all Cave Hill, where in high grass
bloom coloured galaxies perennial
since ice inched sculpting this terrain. Brief foam
on the blank welter out of which all comes.

Birth Day

1

The waters have broken. Now your body's slow
convulsions irreversibly begin.
Packing, I finger-lift a slat of blind:
low roofs sleeping, tree-traceries
rising like dreams, faint watermarks on night.

2

Admission seems a languid dream
of birth inverted: sunken entry lipped
with flexing doors, a lift ascending through
dormant entrails to the labour ward . . .
My overshoes squeak on aseptic floor
around the candid trolley-bed where you
are laid; dawn greying past your pane.

3

You are subdued to process,
an intravenous drip tamped to your wrist;
divested of your clothes, belongings, watch,
almost of me beside you. Shifts
of nurses, midwives, come and go, abstracting
to ink on paper your identity;
while, irrevocable hourglass,
above you the translucent glucose-drip-bag
decanting sheds its luminosity.
You cry 'I can't bear this' as yet again
the shark's-tooth jag of a contraction shows
ticking through the monitoring-machine.
Like metering needles your gold earrings shaking.

4

'Bear down . . .' Your palm grips mine,
your body opening like petals and
ah! the bloodied head emerging,
a wriggled slither and, suspended there

as if a tiny astronaut connected
by the umbilical's rich purple coil
to life-support, 'You have a son,'
the doctor says. Steel cuts the link. Adrift,
lost to the close dark amniotic warmth,
his spasm gulps wide world's thin air.
Brute fact miraculously born.

5

The fallen world rolls over into night.
Two army vehicles splash through lamplit rain,
miniskirts throng a disco. Things
ongoing register again.
My 'Goodnight' left you hazed on a ward bed;
and you, our Rory, ankle name-tagged, parked
one in a row of wheeled transparent cots:
beautiful accident, success
in lieu of whose unique incipience
like failed intentions cells in millions died.
You are fallen on history's brink. Unthinkable,
'one bomb no bigger than a cricket-ball'
could shrivel Belfast, gunmen, parents, all
who have been babies. Meanwhile
my mind with doubled vision now pursues
my own childhood paths among
green forest, and I sense
my first-loved books re-opening their wings.
Half-conscious at a crossing I come to,
I carry myself with novel care,
like a cup trembling to overbrim.
Frail lighted streets diverge into wet dark.
The world rolls hurtling you beyond my sight.

Beauty and Truth

Wide shimmer of mountains
and sky. From Horn Head we
threw stones at bright ocean.
How tiny our leisure!

Turning back as the lane wound,
a craving for detail:
harebells in crevices
stacked turves, sunken trickling.

A bend found the cottage,
ledged sunning and roofless
enclosing a culture
of thistles and nettles,

arched by a sycamore
scroll-like, a formalised
wave, its grey branches
encrusted with lichen.

Our brief footfall troubles
a whisper in grasses
still meshed by a stagger
of drystone long after

huge sparseness uprooted
from native ground all but
this tree: emblematic,
wind-tortured to beauty.

Outside

Outside for a minute fetching coal, I look
back through the window: a luminous vignette,
the laden dinner-table, bravura fork
conducting discussion, lustre of poured wine,
composure of faces, dress, for it. Chill night
revives perspectives from when such wasn't mine.

Twenty years back, frozen pavements where great elms
erupting in lamplight splayed black beams across
opulent gardens, animated films
of the good life behind glass that shut me off:
wit-spangled comeliness arguing the toss
on Art, Truth, uttering 'fifthly', 'fugue', and stuff.

Not that I'd not thought then they might be jerks.
Nor that these are, on cars, schools, roles, pay, laws,
things not what life's about, just how it works.
I sense, re-entering with a full scuttle,
all ideality is sheen we know because
of the cold outer dark. 'Another bottle?'

Romance

When I toiled at a library issue-desk
old dears who had long since lost their looks
came battering up with thrust tickets to ask
me to pick out their next armful of books:
'Romances, love. Any. Don't matter at all
if I've had them, it's stuff you don't recall.'
Where typists jet off to chateaux or sheikhs,
loves are kiss-consummated in spotless dusk,
the girls are all peach-blossom, men rich and tall.

It took them out of themselves, fair enough.
So, better than romance remembered too much?
The staff Christmas party, nerved up about if
you'd get off with Di, till the beer made you retch.
Their make-up-smeared spots. Being too skint for taxis.
Years on and balder, their hangups, kids, exes.
Searing blossoms of 'always' buried in such
aftermath snows. Not my ticket-of-leave;
what I'm stuck with. Spinning me whole on its axis.

In Time

From birth, we counted you in days,
each one sufficient to amaze.

Then it was weeks were marked off while
you inched your way to that first smile.

Baby, it's months I notice now
you play, crawl, clutch a spoon. Learn how

to become what's birthday-ticked by years,
vessel of memories, hopes, fears.

Who through the decades' windows will
gaze at stars, constellated still

as when Rome's great empire fell.
In peace of heart? Ah, time will tell.

Cushendun

I stare at the whole contraption:
stone bridge, hotels on the quay,
crescent of strand, boats, sea.
That place one has always sought, a
miraculous refraction
above its shimmering water.

As if just off the map.
Sweeps of glen when I turn;
trees escort the burn.
In the cottaged street, a shop.
Tentatively I post
a card, feel like a ghost.

Of course, all's real enough,
rock-firm as its sandstone caves.
Talk I join in the bar
is travel, jobs, A-levels stuff;
as also no doubt on that far
Scottish coast across gilded waves

like yet another dimension
tranquilly outlined. The era
of Gaelic and turf and flax
is over, however its aura
persists, or we pay no attention
to TV news at our backs.

The hotel Family Night's
packed tourists and locals in.
The area's Irish class
presents disco-dancing: mites
gyrate to anywhere-noise;
new steps, old discipline.

Last whiskeys. Kathy, Sinéad,
three farmers. 'I want more
than the life here.' 'Protestants
won't come these years, they're afraid.'
'That murder . . .' Dark elements
outside. Staff sweep the floor.

At breakfast, feeling rough,
I gaze out at the ocean
through glass, its assuaging motion
cradles the headland. Enough
stir in its time to knock
that arch clean through black rock.

I read in the morning papers
of bombings, disasters, crisis,
states' and their foes' mad capers.
Nowhere a paradise is
untainted. That blue Moyle screens
our nuclear submarines.

Then, history's chill seep:
although by trick of the light
belying all connection,
slopes ravelling streams and sheep
have borne famine and eviction,
pogroms, the '98.

That ruin along the shore,
ivied and picturesque,
is Castle Carra where
the MacDonnells, beaten by
him at Red Bay and Glenshesk
lured Shane O'Neill to die,

cut down after the feast;
then gave his head to the Queen.
Only a clansmen's putsch, a
few years and the Sasanach seized
all Ulster. Today between
kempt hedges dripping fuchsia

the Mobile Library lurches;
doorstep milk's fetched in.
Though no one was astounded
when a British frigate landed
a party conducting searches
last week. Old discipline.

Fragile in time and place
on the planet our heuristic
aggrandisements may blow
life off or waste through slow
entropy, a grace-
note, anachronistic,

these Arcadian fragments stake
irrefutably green claim
to a world that keeps some room
for images we make:
waters for heart's retroflexion,
contours shaping direction.

Coming Back

'Home': low streets so intimately mapping
childhood: junction, crescent, alleyways,
bridge, railway station; fly-blown plate-glass trapping
shop-soiled sunlight; litter, petrol-haze,

frail lawns; that bough's configurations steady
above the kerb just as recalled; and there's
the door – but different-coloured now, unready
to admit me. Upstairs sills show dolls and bears.

It continues: hedges trimmed, excited voices
skirling in the park, the kids maybe
of girls that I was young with, Annes, Pams, Joyces,
before I knew this lot was not for me.

They now, whatever their green years chased after,
shrug half-disclaiming what instead they got,
and shop and cook for, deck with care and laughter;
doing what came naturally – why not?

I am not their affair. Among the nettles
past palsied fencing where all falls away
untended to the glinting branch-line, settles
a ball some distant June bounced out of play.

This morning, drawn around a nearby corner
I paused at a grey terrace-row, a door
and two-step front path here among my former
life, as if by sleight of mind I saw

a young man moustached and nondescript emerging,
his bag full of marked schoolwork, but his head
of pit-blotched farmland, gaslit childhood's surging
chiaroscuro; Jessie; mother dead;

'the roofs of the village, pitiful, beseeching'.
Stuff blossoming to poems, stories, when
calm pooled amid aridities of teaching.
Ghost, exile here, who wasn't 'Lawrence' then,

not as the world would make him – an abstraction,
a mental football all can have a go
at, size up, boot – he glances for direction
at the crossroads, and is gone. Decades ago.

So all who somehow bound beyond retrieval
by our first place, weathering its neglect,
spirit ourselves away, toward a level
of being more diffuse, its dialect

self-conscious measure of the gap between us
and those who fill life up with what we left;
are translated to ideational arenas
arguing our toss, missing our drift,

or bending it to goals not ours. Returning
unasked we stand, as here by the park fence,
tuned to the clamour of fresh starts; discerning
how bleak our freedom from such innocence.

Whirligig

Headline-hopping through racial wars,
strikes, drug-scares, fashions, cricket scores,
I've missed this morning build its high
never-to-be-repeated sky.
I let the Sunday papers drop,
and watch my child pump at his top,
regenerating spin; it hums,
successively each colour comes
to perfect circle, blurs, then dies;
usurped by what next clarifies.

An accelerated paradigm
of history's images: each time
form coheres, illusory stasis,
some gathering shade within displaces
it. New definitions break.
Sunk fragments gleam, as in a lake.
No refinement of infrared
photography conjures back the dead;
yet lingering perturbation floats
from buried centuries spectral notes.

A goblet, say, struck by a spoon
one leisurely late afternoon
by the Garonne. Immaculate
around spreads the matured estate,
tended by slaves: woods, ponds, herds, plough;
once more ripe apples weight the bough;
grape-clusters mirrored in the stream,
reeds, banks, are sealed there, as in dream.
What if Germans have crossed the Rhine?
He raps again, commands more wine.

Bangled barbarians can't stampede
law, legions, libraries. All's greed
and glitter back in Rome; but here
carts trundle straight roads purged of fear.
Later than common sense can know.
Too near the day his son will go
to Bordeaux, and just not return,

Goths seize these lands, his villa burn.
So much gone. So much yet to come.
Give it a whirl, and let it hum.

Pining towards a harmony
that earth-bent eyes can never see,
the medieval field of folk
scatter their seed, past beech and oak,
backing towards us, looking back
on infants laid down in their track;
in time, all falling into place.
Shrovings, tabors, maypoles, lace;
beyond night's huddled eaves, wild beasts,
the Fiend with reap-hook, witching feasts.

They labour, revel, stink, recoil
craving abstraction, ritual,
in frozen surge of stone entomb
space incensed as God's ante-room.
Life is a scrabbling at greased rungs
between the Pit and choiring tongues
of angels. Earthly state's ordained,
those who mince in silk have gained
nothing of Heaven. From Traitor's Gate
void sockets quiz a fled soul's fate.

Dissolve again, quicken the pace,
hazard frail caravels to trace
the planet round, chart silences
blanched by combers. Metasteses
of trade and power, the suffrage, shares,
din of machines, dispel dark fears:
ancestral spires' quaint maquillage
embellishes a railway age.
Safe as houses. Shires repeat
a trance of cumulus and wheat.

The earth's a project, a resource.
Uncloistered, the starched sahib tours
his district on an elephant;
iron ideals, box-files, and plant
reduce bow-culture, fever zones

to cushion laurelled English lawns
where daguerreotypes they posed for frame
pride braced in fashions new to them;
remote from basements where the soul
gestates revenge, cast out, unwhole.

Twelve chimes. A radiant cab; the driver
dozing above, homeward . . . and over
the brink of 1900, new
century opening, landslide. Two
by two those twined in Lover's Lane
are severed. Bluebells pool again,
but shellholes pool in the morass
where he disintegrates. A pause,
jazz, joy-rides, screen-dreams. It renews,
sifts gold from ashes of gassed Jews.

Ramps dizzying on, all now replaced
only by aggregating waste:
bombed villages, dustbowl, dumped foodstocks,
poisoned estuaries, tower blocks.
Dialled wires click, the wilderness
expands. Wrong number. Wrong address.
Deathwish aerosolled on the wall.
Aircraft show homecomers sprawl
they never chose; space-probes beam back
a coloured bubble lost on black.

Sad retrospect! Horizon gone
for ever . . . Oh, but once upon
a time, a track, half knowing why,
his universe what met his eye,
something in us reared to walk stark
upright, a staggering landmark!
Galactic spindrift fertilised
miracle we've destabilised
to cities where the human heart
is sick, and people lie a part.

While guardian angel submarines
patrol pre-Cambrian capes. Machines
twinkle in bunkers, warning lights

monitor girdling satellites.
'200 50-megaton
nukes on the Russians, and we've won.
They're more exposed, except for mere
biological continuance. Here
the industrial fabric will survive,
control, the President alive . . .'

A top lies toppled on the floor.
Bored with it, calling from the door,
my son, you'll play another day.
The spokesman from the USA
fades on the screen, unreal beside
our here and now, noon sun outside
immune to slipstream, hung there staid
and homely as this room's lampshade.
I walk you out, we pass a brown
horse, grassed lane lifts us beyond town.

Through your delight I relive grace-
notes squandering in this casual place:
petal, hedge-dapple, shade unfurled
on gleaming slope; world within world.
Pouring me back to what might be
our ancestor at gate or tree
inwrought to such inheritance,
trusting its dynasties of chance.
May they enfold you. Some day too,
somewhere, your children after you.

Over the hills and far away
flickers reiteration of May;
essential green here immanent
restores intact all we once meant.
Let none loose counterwise the power
at the universe's core,
the nuclear blossom's candid white,
all history vanishing in light.
In quasar spectra a redshift
measures lights out. We catch the drift.

No strength in me, your fragile shield,
can salvage Eden in a field.
Gossamer flutters what had wings,
a beak stabs; yet another wrings
pure arias from this underplot
to large design. Leaves whisper what,
like metaphor, to truth refracts
meanings plain speech makes inexact.
Ours for the asking, as years take
us, circles widen, bubbles break.

A Derry Farm

A five-mile reach of pasture elevated
into June and larksong, strewn with reeds,
purple orchid and gold-smouldering whin.
The clipping-shed's oil-fuelled generator
rackets on the skyline, till we dip
losing it for the trickle of brook water
through boulders, with a trodden path that leads
to the escarpment's fenced top. Congregated
against the foot below, woods ripple green,
as if a garment that the farm's let slip.

Ewes break down there when they take a notion.
You drive right round by road to fetch them back,
that land's no use. But yours to the stone wall
faint as a thread. Beyond the railway track
reticulated fen bordered by yellow
strand curves to the Point and squat Martello
Tower, where the Foyle turns into ocean
glittering like a harp, about it curled
cloud-soft a lambent arm of Donegal.
You might suppose you'd risen above the world;

At least, compared with what you left for it,
that this world's nearer something we all dream
of as if exiled from. Not heaven, exactly –
a whirr along the cliffs and sudden scream
as gulls mob a marauder pull us round;
and as we saunter back, matter-of-factly
you show an empty buzzard's nest the crows
got at last week; and skewed upon the ground
a dead sheep rots, its groin a bloodied pit,
flies crawling from void eye-holes down black nose.

You heave it off the precipice, stench whooshes
up and wool-shreds flutter to the grass.
In fallen drystone that walled tiny fields
and rubbled cottages, a hungrier past
obtrudes its lineaments. Eased now by cars
and subsidies, life at this height, where bushes
grow flinching from what the Atlantic wields
in winter, when snow drifts and torrents roar,
still takes the brunt. But closer to that core
our days would bite to; fitted to a vast

sky's indifferent shifts of grey or blue
subduing all to unity we guess
or part recall as ours back somewhere when
we did not know time moved, that growing older
lost the vision, left us settling wryly
to sort its fragments – down here, where again,
in my mind's lens, stray lamb across your shoulder,
you trudge broad undulations for its ewe;
outlined on the far horizon Islay
rising lucidly from changelessness.

On Farthing Downs

Through seas of grass you run
ecstatic at what's given;
light-soused blue above
what you might think the glens
last week at Cushendun,
but is, an airflight thence,
Coulsdon downland's curve
fitting a Surrey heaven.
I compose you in a frame
of background still the same

as I grew up with: Sunday
walks, then from the school
I got translated to
friends living hereabouts.
I asked, invited one day
to tea and scones, 'So that's
your mum?' A pause, then, 'No,
our servant.' Like a fool
I flushed, plucked at my trousers.
Still those copious houses

are anchored along valleys
where car-wheels scrunch on gravel
meandering past mature
cypress and flowerbeds.
A world of golf and rallies
whose fathers lolled in tweeds
at wide french windows sure
of providence as civil
as their doucely shrugging day;
and saw no close of play.

As each man's out, replace
the bails, call the next.
In panelled calm heirs ripened
to an honours roll
remote from wilderness
of polity or soul.
Suez, Strikes, Sex, happened,

foxing a set text
that knew what England's for,
sandcastles found her shore.

Nearly three decades' lapse
since I last trod this chalk
convexity, took in
vistas hard to call
home now my inner map's
clouded by the pall
of Ireland in between:
changed county-shapes, the bulk
of mountain ranges where
all glitters in salt air.

I press down with my thumb
and snap! your photograph
is taken where, my son,
you've never been before.
Where still the insects thrum,
minute ephemera
of eternal summer one
parches after, half
believing it the place
where its state of grace

descended long ago:
cork-tips and cherryade,
a bicycle wheel ticking;
to lie balancing the sun
on raised knee under slow
sky-passages; or run
for running's sake or kicking
a ball about. I shade
my eyes at that red kite
so motionless it might

be 1956's
still high in homeless blue.
For which I cut adrift.
As you may, from your place,
in time, that meanwhile fixes

contours we can't efface,
histories we've left,
heart-deep: for me, this view,
and luxury flotillas
of dozing greenbelt villas.

That taught me to call dinner
lunch, and knew the score.
Not even my own streets –
what ambiguities
made me as a beginner
find charms of paradise
dressing people I thought twits!
A lacquered enclave for
composure entertained
to hear itself arraigned.

Playing Armstrong's *Tin Roof Blues*
I imagined negro faces
under a full moon,
battered instruments
letting the night suffuse
subtopian lineaments,
like lava thrilling down,
shooting-star-burn traces
along this ridge, pure jet
of trumpet, clarinet.

Child's play. Put aside.
Revisitant, I laugh:
all looks so as-it-was
yet can't be, a time-warp
denying that it's died;
to your play blank, a drop
of backcloth weightless as
in squares of photograph
one day you'll inherit.
Fated not to share it.

On the March

After the plastic cups dispensed in fields,
two nights on packed school floors inhaling chalkdust,
rain-darkened banners winding past the airport
on the road from Aldermaston, 1960,
suburb enclosed us: small cherished gardens,
segments of lit shopfront. 'Ban the Bomb!'
fell on indifferent children, strolling couples.
A junction halted us, the band stopped playing.

Then, in the pause, a woman's high voice singing
Barbara Allen – and the evening shook its
last gleams across a park where trees etched chance
configurations on my mind for ever;
rinsed in such light sheer blocks stood beautified.
An odour too of wool where droplets clung.
Then, *Didn't He Ramble* rasped, we shuffled on
towards Trafalgar Square's speeches tomorrow.

Did we think we were changing the world? Not really.
Though we cared all right, the madness of nuclear warfare,
the dangers of fall-out; we'd posters of Hiroshima.
Those children are parents now, small gardens are tended still,
things scaled to our dailiness. It's not our ideals
that are not good enough for us, but rather we
who don't measure up. And whatever we think we are doing
the fall-out will differ – may, with luck, be a song,

transfiguring a time, a place and some weather.

A Father's Tale

LULLABY

Child, so beautiful
in repose,
tousled silk hair,
pale snub of nose

gently exhaling,
nails pearl-clear
on small fingers curled
round your teddy bear;

outside your cot,
and moonlit room,
spread fens of exile
from what meant 'home'.

Where I stare at the moon,
as if love might
a pulley-rope drawn
by your feather-fate

over it, toss
me to you. Sleep
my darling, nor ever
dream that I weep.

But when from mists
wreathing you forms,
bent to your slumber,
a ghost in your dreams,

assuaging your core –
hearth's flickering fire,
a hug when you fall,
guiding hand on the stair,

first friends, places, ball
beneath trees, river, town,
Pates Lane ponies;
all whirled back and gone

as if but a dream –
O, should you stir,
reach up to kiss
and meet thin air,

those purest blue
eyes would know
the intruder not
my vanished shadow

but the upstart world
shrilling your soul,
and cry to dream
of all made whole

again as before
its madness threw
the terrible switch
abducting you.

I dangle shoes scuffed
with your toddler-fun:
one day, retreading
their steps, my son

you'll discover clear
of what spells it dead,
like Donegal
or Benbane Head

truth endures
patient to bless
trust in its slopes,
its fabulous

peaks restoring
all lost ground,
reknit the whole
horizon round.

Christmas 1983

'DADDY MEND IT'

Summer sealed the garden as you played,
gentle with petals, smiled at the black cat
lapping milk you poured. Green habitat
intact against whatever edge of shade.

One fallen leaf on the lawn's grass. You ran
and tried to put it back on its low bough;
then said 'Daddy mend it', knowing how
I've fixed a light, your broken top, toy van,

and gave me it trusting that yet again
I'd make all right. And found that wasn't true,
there is no trick of screwdriver or glue
for growing things; but how could I explain?

Or now. Since mad October's massive fall
whirling you over salt estranging sea.
Hail-scourged in dark yearns the stripped weeping tree
precarious greenness hints, and can't forestall.

ACCESS

The Welfare Officer says, 'Sit down, please.
How was your journey?' Teacups stand between us.
Casework for Beginners
Chapter One: set client at his ease.
'I met your wife last week.
You know, bad spouses need not therefore be
bad parents.' Yes, I know that stuff, can we
take it as read and get to what's unique?

Like what that shrink said. 'Look, I know you're busy,
but . . .' One more file to you, it's my son's life.
Meanwhile, 'I've told your wife
it's reasonable he should see you.' 'Is he
coming?' 'She's extremely
averse. But yes, at three.' Put on a spot,
she's calculated that she'd better not,
while you're assessing her, seem too unseemly.

So, four months ten days after 'the event'
I'm ushered down an office corridor,
enter – and on the floor
he stands. A little taller. Wonderment
transfixes him. 'It's Daddy
darling.' Eyes lock, and a world's restored.
A snooker table, stacked grey chairs, dartboard,
scuffed toys, a plastic scooter, car, soiled teddy.

Like reference-library books you can't take out,
promiscuously used by one and all.
A ball is still a ball:
he chuckles as we chuck the thing about.
And she's there in the corner.
'Don't speak to her, she's said.' That guilt-born horror
of discussion! Two score letters wasted, or a
handset slammed down when at first I'd phone her.

I hear her tense voice curdle vacuous
small-talk, as we grand-prix round the table.
She must be miserable
somewhere, quelling all she lived as 'us'.
'Daddy's the winner! Kiss?'
Once more his soft mouth puckers to my lips.
One hour, so much, so little, to eclipse
waste aftermath of two years' dailiness.

His small talk's added words, connectives; yet
'window' for the frames upon my nose –
'No, Rory, "glasses"' – shows
time hazing detail. But he'll not forget –
here are the photos – where
only last summer he so loved these beaches,
caves, dunes, and huge, 'The castle, look!' He reaches,
points, 'Daddy!' – tiny in the two-inch square.

As if receding. Feigning not to see,
she packs his bag. The book I've bought goes in,
to be thrown in the bin
I guess. O love, remember, naked we
pitched him into being,
unlike our mingled sweat, 'eternal bond'

indeed . . . Back in the office, 'Yes, he's fond
of you: it worked.' I nod, blurred eyes unseeing.

Daddies lose, in the textbook. My hopes plummet.
'You won't gain custody, for she's the mother;
the status quo's the other
factor.' He'd that before she ripped him from it . . .
'Just look at *this* case . . .' Then,
three hours of clapped-out diesel train to Crewe;
the platform buffet; sleeper, dozing to
wheel-beat night-track's *when again? when again?* When?

Deep in the darkness, keeping pace, a star;
near, ever-present as my heartbeat, you
my son. I start these few
stanzas as the train slows to Stranraer,
sea-welter, pitching boat.
Frail structures offering your spirit room;
love's poor substitute for a lost home.
Where emptiness coils, flickers at my throat.

TYROLEAN RETROSPECT

Will he remember this? we wondered. In
your pushchair from the Hahnenkamm you stare:
distant peaks like blossom spike clear air
that tinkles cowbells, burnishes your skin.

I turn the page: dirndl and *lederhosen*,
wrought iron shop-signs, flowering balconies,
falls of green pasture draped with Alpine trees,
the Golden Roof, small figures on the frozen

tongue of the Grossglockner glacier; ledged
chunks of *schloss* from the Imperial cake;
a Salzburg palace mirrored in blue lake.
All sifted to this album. Double-edged,

the foreignness – north meaning Germany;
bitte and *danke* – was entrancing fable
owed no living duty, so destabil-
ising us because it set us free

of all except ourselves, home truths beyond
what the camera framed. For you, not knowing
where you were, or where we might be going,
abroad just added on to native ground.

Innocent of history, you crawl
the Hofburg ballroom's marble floor as if
at playgroup, past idealised Habsburgs stiff
in antique finery upon the wall.

'One day we will come back to stand again
here on the *Panoramaweg*,' we said.
What she's done since has knocked that on the head.
All family perspectives down the drain,

may one, which as our cablecar dipped, fed
your gaze, persist; against life's ugliness
immunise your soul. Who could not guess
such exaltation hung by a mere thread.

ACCESS AGAIN

The Welfare Officer's 'come a long way'
since I last came by sea a month ago
from Ireland. 'Your wife's so . . .
Well, everything you've said seems true.' I say,
'What she needs isn't lawyers.'
Then you, my son, arrive. With her. Asked whether
this time I might take you out, your mother,
glacial with power, 'won't allow' us.

Since she abducted you, her ploy's inversion:
pretence it's me who'd whisk you off . . . I shrug,
and give you a big hug.
A length of corridor, improvisation
of games . . . You point through glass, say 'church', 'dog', 'cars'
– which speed into the world expanding out
of sight I long to share, tell you about
again: its byways, creatures, wildflowers, stars.

My child, I know a shore beyond a shore,
where whin and harebells fringe the bluest bay,
and in its cave, they say
the wellwater has magic powers to cure,
and on that Rathlin beach
past and future, sun and sky and sea
merge glittering into all life yearns to be,
unspoiled and peaceful at its farthest reach.

FOR MY SON

Again May's blossom foaming past,
indifferent to what since last
time round has exiled me from all
attunement to its seasonal
bag of tricks. A pavement tree
lopped back last winter helplessly
conjures from black stumps a dance
of fresh leaves; daisies take their chance
in galaxies; red blooms adorn
municipally tended lawn.
Each form unique, and rooted here.
Replaced by much the same next year.
New pushchairs trundle past the sea
here in your place, my son. Since she
revoked your birthright, all I'd share
with you squanders against my stare,
falling to ashes. You are gone.
Uselessly spring's show goes on.
Drawn by its weather to this coast
families sprawl or stroll. A ghost
infiltrating, I retrace
old steps, as if once more your face
might bob past on the carousel.
One blink, all magically well
again. An empty horse glides round.
And round. And over there the sound
of laughter from the Slippery Dip.
Far out, incurious, a ship
pointing away from Ireland, buoyed
on a blue flux beneath blue void.

I walk again this curve of strand,
a shine of wet on firm gold sand
blanked by 500 tides since you
knelt watching Daddy as I drew
a little boy, inscribed your name:
RORY WAS HERE. Here looks the same:
dunes, headlands, ocean charged with light
as then, rippling to its long white
ribbon of foam, where bubbles break
in millions for each breath I take.
Standing on its edge I stare
at the expanse of water where
ceaselessly varying one theme
waves crest and lapse; a cosmic dream
wherein what shaped our selves first stirred,
progenitive subsentient curd;
then instinct tipped with jaws, routine
rendings and matings, submarine
aeons never asking why;
crawling at last beneath the sky
beyond which constellations spin,
their chemistry life's origin.

Innumerable stars and sperm . . .
Interrogation can't confirm
my almost-faith that you were meant,
no sport of chance, but heaven-sent;
and yet, as sandgrains on a plate
stimulated to vibrate
by sweet notes from a violin
gather to a pattern in
the nodal lines, so when I hold
you in my arms next will the cold
welter of space-time reshape
to lucid focus, stellarscape
vindicated in the rays
of love that interlock our gaze.

As fourteen days ago: again
a boat across to Scotland, then
the night-train dreaming southward to
ticking wheels, a shave at Crewe,
and halting curve through the spoiled heart

of England, as commuters start
their workday. Scented typists cram
the carriage into Nottingham,
spill dispersing; Lincolnshire
expands monotonously. Dear
child, lost to the sea-surge, light
on soaring headlands, wheeling flight
of gulls, Glenariff's waterfalls.
I greet you within office walls
among the Welfare Service staff.
She sits and glowers, while you laugh
conjuring from a swivel-chair
'a roundabout – Daddy sit there'.
        All now depends upon the Court.
The Welfare Officer's report
assesses *your best interests*
are served best if the Law invests
custody in me; although
she'll argue as the 'status quo'
what she's brought you to; presume
the 'mother's right' must overcome.
        Rory, all your future ought
to be pleads fate may not abort
its sunrise on mutual hopes,
cloth spread for three on picnic slopes
where insects thrum, your basic right
to childhood's freedom and delight
beneath the overarching love
of parents intertwined above.
That world, like a baby seal
lifting its eyes in mute appeal
against the club, knows no redress;
and is crushed into wilderness.
        I lift you to a windowsill
to watch the world go by, and thrill
as round my shoulder your small arm
curls gently. What's done cannot harm
our bond, bright gold that will not rust
hooping our two souls in trust.
        With me on that 'access' day
was Dermot, joining in our play.

Strange ravellings of bittersweet
chance and change and choice complete
inscrutable design in our
conjunction in that Lincoln hour,
three generations grouped to look
at pictures in a storybook.

South-east Leinster is still thick
with Nolans. As when, famine-sick
they crawled the bohereens scrabbling for
raw turnips, died of scurvy or
the bloody-flux – grandchildren to
the famous Boys of Wexford who
rose in the '98 until
massacred at Vinegar Hill.
I can't know whether Patrick wept
for the once-proud O Nuailláin sept
deGaelicised, dispossessed, denied
subsistence. The green countryside
of 1847 stank
of corpses. Slowly Ireland sank
astern. By exile he survived;
enlisted in Liverpool, arrived
in Bengal as a gunner, rose
to Quartermaster Sergeant, chose
an Irishwoman for his wife;
and died of cholera. A life
residual in fading ink
on scattered documents; a link
with a lost provenance. Nolans won
place in the Imperial sun
climbing rungs of the Raj, but still
ancestral Catholics. Until
you were born to Burmese days
in 1913, Dermot: blaze
of flowers, ricefields, the caress
of heat, whirls of stirred-rainbow dress,
lashed teak logs piloted downstream
past gilt pagodas. A charmed dream
of childhood, its still lotus pool
cancelled by England, boarding school,
Cambridge, and your regiment.

Thames holidays with punt and tent,
halcyon motoring Junes before
Europe's storm-clouds broke to war –
the week a child was conceived.
You married Moyra, and believed
'it would work out'. Her maiden name
Enright tells her forebears came
from Clare and Limerick. The frail
private tie, dwarfed by the scale
of the times' impersonal
coercions broke. Before the fall
of France you were agreed the best
course, in the infant's interest,
would be at-birth adoption . . . Cared
for under skies where searchlights flared,
those London air-raid-shelter nights
my earliest memory, droning flights
of bombers, bangs – yet innocent
of what that huge commotion meant,
unhorrified, intact, I grew
alternatively. And never knew,
through asphalt years inlaid with parks,
brash, dreamy, bookish, teenage sparks
of wondering what it's all about,
bedsitter drifting, finding out,
pain suffered, and pain caused, the real
eroding poster-paint ideal
to lay bare given world – that if
we open to it from the stiff
coiled self is patient to requite
us, use us as we sense it might.
Until, uprooted, grafted for
twelve years to this northern shore
where green glens trickle water, I
learned, following the death of my
adoptive father whom through sad
unmeant imbroglio I had
not seen since childhood, who had kept
the papers, details I thought swept
beyond retrieval, of my true
parentage. So I found you

in the London phonebook, kin
met for the first time: freckled skin,
bald, bespectacled . . . Among
your pot-plants, bric-a-brac, walls hung
with horsey Stubbs and Munnings prints
we've come to know each other since
that meeting, Dermot; and I have
lost, youthful Moyra's photograph.
And here in Ireland, as if some
hidden wheel at last had come
full circle since his ancestor
Patrick fled so long before,
native beside the River Bann:
Rory John Nolan Waterman.
    Till casually as one might swing
a stick she lopped that blossoming.
    My son, six footprints interwound
along this sand last year: you found
small shells I've kept, along the beach
burnished by wind and water, each
the candid husk of some minute
brief living impulse. At the root
of all creation, stars and cells
proliferating, parallels
and mutations, cryptic hints
of pattern, random process, since
the original Big Bang
kick-starting the entire shebang,
we crave some purpose, to confer
meaning upon our petty stir,
latecomers to a blue-green speck
of spinning planet we may wreck –
one madman's itchy fingertip,
or 40-cent computer chip
malfunctioning, to activate
our holocaust. And yet innate
gratuitous imperatives
by which our human nature lives –
so that as small seeds buried in
the earth respond to an unseen
light and striving upward may

flower at last to unguessed day
the soul aspires – compel us. Laws
of physics cannot be the cause
of prisoner Kolbe's 'Take me instead'
when one picked out for dying shed
tears for his family; to refute
the Nazis with an absolute
their ideology denies,
yet Auschwitz could not brutalise.
External circumstance can break
us; the response is ours to make.

Art seeks to forge atoning sense
and shapeliness from violence
and hurt we may be powerless
in life to help. These lines confess
sheer impotence, as they complete
their formal pattern, to defeat
or solace discord which has ripped
you from your home and father, stripped
away known places, play and friends;
yet while it cannot make amends
for wrong endured, the poem sustains
truths life would void; by taking pains
composes our essential form,
inviolable through the storm.

Unfathomable, transmitted through
quantum leaps we can't construe,
and multimillion flukes of chance
encounter, whim, and circumstance,
the force that moves the galaxies
shines now incarnate in your eyes,
specific in a soul's unique
flowering from birth to seek
fulfilment. Rory, far today
from where you've watched this ocean sway,
successive heaves and crestings each
toppling to froth washed from the beach
by the next breaker, trust the flow
of life's wave through you as you go
intensifying onward, bright
parabola beyond my sight

into the microchip and space-
culture future of our race.
May love, which science cannot spell,
by grace alone of which we quell
devouring impulses, attend
your great adventure to its end,
your gift according as it can
with the brief music which is man.
　　And, in spite of everything,
mend, next time round, our broken spring.

Thoughts of Blaise Pascal in East Anglia

for Christopher and Joan Speake

Suave Wroxham lawns mown to the water's edge.
In this flat country even rivers stand
still, or as good as. Reeds and sedge,
sun-dappled foliage, liquid sounds, expand

through winding miles of Broadland peace. We chug
past other launches, triangles of sail
for two hours, circle shallows dug
for peat in ancient times. A pint of ale,

then back to leafy Norwich cul-de-sacs
where television prattles: Mozambique
babies are boiled alive; Iraq's
bombed Gulf shipping; new Cruise Missile leak.

Lost in this corner of the universe . . .
'We play squash several evenings; jog.' Me too,
guest of courtesies fearing no worse
than showers to spoil a garden barbecue;

sure of this man-made part of England where
no natural features, mountain, waterfall
rearing untamed and always there
measure our human lives as brief and small;

and on far, farmed horizon trees stand clear
at sunset, neutralising Pascal's sense
of nature as *an infinite sphere*
the centre everywhere, no circumference.

Who knew as *useless, dubious*, Descartes
assembling life's traffic in appearances
from 'cogito', setting mind apart
from world. For *man is bound to all he sees.*

All this visible universe only a drop
on the ample breast of nature, infinite
beyond where even imaginings stop.
No idea of ours approaches it.

Yet also: *Take a mite, its legs, veins, blood,*
drops in that blood. And see a new abyss
immense within the atom . . . A flood
sways us . . . The earth yields, voids craved certainties.

Full of itself, his vain and gaudy age
attended salons, cock-fights, or the shout
of Frondeurs. Blood flowed. Centre-stage,
an armoured Church cast bat-winged Jansen out.

Themes change. Now pickets and police replace
forgotten social turmoils. We debate
no longer God's 'efficient grace',
but embryo-culture, votes, the Welfare State.

Or wearying of such matter, idle at
video-games; my joystick guide a 'frog'
through the screen's hurtling 'traffic' . . . Splat! . . .
The next one makes it, hops from log to log

across the river, dodging crocodiles;
and so on, till five lives are lost, and then
GAME OVER: YOUR SCORE . . . Well, it whiles
an hour away. I press, and start again.

Diversion soothes our miseries, yet it
is our worst misery, functioning to stop
us thinking of ourselves. We hit
a ball for points; chase hares. Until we drop.

Like one in prison, ignorant of what
his sentence is, who to secure repeal
has one hour, killing the time he's got
playing piquet! It is unnatural!

Discoverer of the syringe, calculus
and, asked by gamblers, of the laws of chance,
your clear mind discomposes us
into stark elements, as we advance

stupefied by our technology toward
perhaps the day its fires burst in blue air
above Thorpe Road or Hickling Broad;
and then the nuclear winter, everywhere . . .

Game over. And we never knew the score . . .
Meanwhile, the weather holds, six weeks of drought
have finished the roses off before
this year's GCE results are out

for parents sprawled on patios, conifer
secluding this from that house, who turn pages
of the *Sunday Times*. Bees stir
among Virginia Creeper that assuages

this residential redbrick which somehow
displaced what greener impulses pursued,
never defined. Their children's now?
Uncertainty. Ennui. Inquietude . . .

Alone on Halvergate Marshes in a bleak
November twilight you can stand attuned
to bitterns booming, and the creak
of derelict windpumps, opening like a wound;

apparitions, cows and cattlegate
among the wetland's random clumps and spikes
of grass; a world still inchoate;
moonlight shuddering in drainage dykes.

Man is only a reed, the weakest thing
in nature; but a thinking reed, thereby
nobler than forces that may wring
the life from us; because we know we die.

In nature. Knowing it unfalsified
to a Cartesian mechanism we
might infer, but verified
upon our pulse experientially.

Pascal, the creaturely empiricist,
when Descartes claimed by reason vacuums
in nature could nowhere exist,
devised fit tests, observed, and did the sums.

But analysed this apple has no taste.
Heat is mere movement of small particles.
And you are, my good friends, replaced
by unconsenting stacks of molecules.

As lines, squares, cubes – or x, x^2, x^3 –
are different orders, similarly apart
are modes of knowing, to be grouped
as proper to the senses, reason, heart.

The heart has reasons reason does not know.
In us like rivers. *Rivers are moving roads*
that would take us where we want to go.
Even these torpid among Norfolk's Broads,

their names blunt Anglian, Bure, Yare, Ant, Thurne,
pragmatic villages where life enquires
means, not ends, moves taciturn,
flint churchtowers lacking visionary spires,

this afternoon's gold miles of stubble-field
proposing an accountant's universe
calculable in its yield –
all sense the sea, along which cars disperse.

We pause at Yarmouth: pier, bars, FUNLAND. Chris,
it's thirty years now since we first went to town
on the ideal; half-scared to kiss
real girls, bought for a laugh for half-a-crown

a six-inch rubber Jane Russell from a stall
that, squeezed, grew tits. While Joan, to reach a dance
you'd hitch wild miles through Donegal –
drunk melées in the ballrooms of romance.

You've settled here; your visitor, I live
in Ireland now. Willed quests? or quantum grace-
notes, siftings from some cosmic sieve?
Our species a chance stanza flung on space?

In our perplexities our definition
and essential being. Pascal, great
physicist and mathematician,
inventor of the earliest calculat-

ing machine, gap-leaper, writing to Fermat,
Mathematics? I'd not step a metre for it;
thought's noblest practice; but only that,
having outstripped Europe, you ignore it.

For our true study, man. Until the pain
blossomed in your body, and you died.
The autopsy could not explain
the spiked belt next your skin reproving pride.

You'd scorn the glib ways we've conceptualised
ourselves since, breathing in like fuel-exhaust
narcotic jargons, desensitised
to our emotional truth. And built a vast

diversion-industry. The twig-limbed hosts
of famine gather on our screens, to set
full tables shuddering. Civic boasts
are scabbed with spreading slum graffiti . . . Yet

as now, car parked, we stare – blue flux, curved beach –
a childhood is re-entered. Here I came,
to Corton, magically each
August. Is that ship out there the same

as 1947's? Freedom far
as eye can reach . . . I clamber down, my hand
scrunching soft ochre cliffs; that are
the crumbling verge of smug recessive land.

In Memoriam Reggie Smith
1914–1985

It's like reaching to find no books on the shelf,
or turning with a smile to empty chair.
You trusted life as gift, gave of yourself.
Your postcard tells of projects in the air,
memoirs, a play, the Med. But the phone-call said you're dead.
How can I answer now when nothing's there?

'Pawn to King Four, old mate' . . . But I can't tip
the chess bits from the box to start again,
and hear that irksome ditty on your lip
as you cogitate, set traps, advance your men:
'By and by there'll be pie in the sky when you die.'
Plus, for you, booze, cricket, talk, sex, poets, pen.

Up there, there's very few you'd not let in:
sociologists? cheats? bosses? pedants? – you'll
still separate the sinner from the sin,
living, some carped, by sentimental rule.
'Is there no one Reggie hates?' 'Can't he discriminate?'
You brought our best out, and were no one's fool.

But I won't pretend you'd faith in any more
than human nature, though your own transcends
whatever is innate in any law
of physics . . . I've slipped gear to present tense,
a habit hard to kick – even after you got sick
you'd go anywhere for rugger, book-talk, friends.

Two strangers cast up on an island both
knew you, told your first novelising wife.
From Wight to Perth to Dublin's Hill of Howth
we're all amputees still feeling you post-knife.
Farmers, writers, scientists, that Aussie tramp who turned up pissed
in Derry: 'This fat Pom once saved my life.'

But your epicentre was the BBC.
Bliss was it in that dawn when radio
'Features' bet on creativity,
not output, ratings, costings, admin. So,
Dylan's *Milk Wood*, Louis's *Tower* – and the George. Until sour
compartmentalisers tidied up the show.

You kept that end up through the time you taught
our Coleraine students, scorning hacks who'd wall
poems behind analyses. You thought
teaching your 'privilege' – and taught us all.
As, decades back, meeting classes, helping victims, till the Nazis
drove you from the Balkans at their fall.

Remember King's Cross? – scrambling to miss
a train, we sought the bar. Pints on our knees,
'"The moon shines bright. In such a night as this,"'
you quoted, '"wind did gently kiss the trees . . .
Let the sound of music creep in our ears . . ."' You took a deep
draught, 'Sheer magic, everyone agrees;

but what time-serving academic guff
ignores is – why on earth did Shakespeare pick,
from the play's couples, them for lyric stuff? –
him a ponce and scrounger up to any trick,
her a traitor to her Dad and culture, thief, a bad
lot – delinquents both, ripe for the nick.

So what was going on in Shakespeare's head?
Had he forgotten they were shits? Or just,
wanting some uplift to send folk to bed,
didn't care? No, rather, you can trust
that, attuned to what is real, he knew even shits can feel
in such a night there's more to it than lust.'

I glance out. Crewe. 5 a.m. Right I write
you, mover, on the move; and to my kid;
the boat, this sleeper. You backed my doomed fight
(that drivelling judge) for custody, amid
your illness and tax-hash. Your card ends, *Soon more cash
to help*. Reg, I owe you five hundred quid.

From your start spark-bright in dour depression Brum –
you'd all its ballads; and the Afghan Wars' –
you never lost, however far you'd come,
an axial sense of truth and a just cause.
The world's a smaller place, that can't look up and see your face.
Last week Earth missed a heartbeat: it was yours.

Fresh Start

Tinkling refinement of skill and steel
aseptic in a private ward;
hushed service rendered for a price
'social reasons' can afford;

and what was duly flung away
could muster no dissenting word.
But nurses dawdling from a break,
passing near the sluiceroom heard

it screaming: limbs flailed at thin air,
uncomprehending anguish stared.
After 'the matter was discussed'
a consultant was prepared

to save it. *Baby Tim's New Life!* –
fostered. Spare it growth to the hard
what's-best chicaneries his first
life fluked past, bloody but unscarred.

Lincoln Cathedral

It crowns the city's coil of traffic like
Christ knows how many tons of marzipan.
You pedal round its green verge on your trike
past lunchbreak typists sprawled to catch a tan.

And, inside the great contraption, stare
at stained glass, sculpted masonry, a cool
intricately proportioned scoop of air.
'This building's old, men made it beautiful,'

you say, pre-empting what books amplify;
then at a lit-up aisle depiction of
the Good Samaritan are puzzled why
you can't 'put coins in so the people move'.

Liking the place, you ask me what it's for.
Visitors shuffle, spouting French or Dutch.
Tills ting through the cathedral gift-shop door
dispensing teatowel souvenirs and such.

Part's roped off for a service going on;
you thrill to music from what seem to me
rites legendary as the dying swan,
sideshow to tourism, that cannot be

fitted to what's out there. Yet, petrified,
ritualised, in obsolete ornate
approximations, instincts that confide
our freedom from brute process congregate,

helpless against rebuff as when nailed to
the cross that's why these stones are here. We light
our candle, answer that makes sense to you,
a glow that carries on when out of sight.

To the Island

Instead then, to the island: in this season
let the boat slip from laden mainland –
its supermarket of reason, tangling faces
lapse into cleansing greyness, shrug of water.
Somewhere ahead white cliffs so often seen
shimmering across blue sound in modulations
of prismatic light, the island
fragrant with wildflowers. But that was summer,
was love in different weather. Now it forms
as a mere coalescence; ventured on
is lustreless and monochrome.
Walk up beyond the few poor lights that cling
around Church Bay. Grass stirs,
and reeds chill in unreflecting lake,
innocent of history – old massacre
(Choc na Screedlin means the Hill of Screaming),
this fragment of a fort Drake's guns smashed down,
ruins of abandoned cottages.
See, you can prise from the landscape a handful
of flints – the Stone Age axe factory.
But countless birds for whom today means always
are murmurous as beehives gathered under
headland cliff. And darker than any words
a flock of guillemots rises like thunder.

We Talk to Them

We talk to them, inside our heads, for ever.
Those radiant women resonating on
within us. Though, out there, we know whatever
we took them for they were not, who are gone;

the heart in time like a torn dock-root healing.
But – a remembered gesture, swoop of hair,
whisperings on a pillow . . . Outpoured feeling
pools subterranean, now the hilltop's bare

where turning to me from sea's glitter blue
eyes flowered, the core of light. And such love, when
its object's gone, persisting unconsumed

grows intransitive, speaks on subsumed
to possibilities we still pursue.
Self we would share. Now try my eyes again.

Translations from Rilke

THE CAROUSEL
('Das Karussel')

Within one roof and shadow it revolves
a little while, and carries round its band
of gaily-coloured horses, from the land
that lingers hesitant, till it dissolves.
Though some are yoked to cars fixed to the stand
all have courage moulded in their features,
a fierce red lion goes with other creatures,
and now and then a pure white elephant.

Even a stag, as in the forest, who
however has a saddle strapped on, prances,
clasped to its back a little girl in blue.

And on the lion rides in white a young
boy who clutches with a small hot hand
the savage beast's bared teeth and lolling tongue.

And now and then a pure white elephant.

And also, as the surging throng advances,
a blonde girl soars, who has almost already
outgrown these mimic horses, from their eddy
sending in this direction radiant glances.

And now and then a pure white elephant.

And so it rushes onward until ended,
a circuit turning merely, without aim.
Red and green and grey rotate, suspended,
a little half-formed profile. Like a flame
igniting, now and then a smile, so splendid
in its bliss, so dazzling; expended
squandering on a blind breathless game.

THE UNICORN

(from Die Sonette an Orpheus*)*

Ah, it does not exist, this animal.
Not knowing it, they loved in any case
its bearing, neck, and ceremonious pace;
its mute bright gaze met theirs, reciprocal.

Though it was not. Yet, loved by them, it stirred,
pure animal. They always left a clearing
uncluttered. Effortlessly it occurred
within that sanctuary, lightly rearing

its noble head. They fed it, not with corn,
just with the possibility of being;
which nourishment was able to confer

such strength its brow thrust out a horn. One horn.
The white form strolled towards a virgin seeing
it in a mirror's silver; entered her.

THE RIDER

(from Die Sonette an Orpheus*)*

See in the heavens: is there no constellation
Rider? That image mysteriously impressed
upon our earthly pride. A sublimation
that drives, sustains us, carried through our quest.

Is it not so, as we hunt down, subdue
the sinewy nature of being? The course
and turnings. Something answers pressure. New
vistas. They are one, rider and horse.

Yet are they? Or does shared direction yield
only illusion of united will?
Tacitly they are parted by table, field.

And their stellar union is the stuff
of dreams. Though let us for a while yet thrill
trusting the figure. It is enough.

ENOUGH

('. . . Wann wird, wann wird . . .')

. . . When will, when will, when will it be reckoned
enough, this inveighing and saying? Have not fecund
masters twined human words? Why further endeavour?

Are not, are not, are not we forever
battered by books, as by bells' perpetual noise?
If, between two books, silent sky appears: be joyous . . .
or a strip of commonplace earth in the evening . . .

Louder than gales, louder than oceans the keening
and screaming of humans . . . What a preponderance of silence
must dwell in the cosmic spaces, that through our violence
of clamour the cricket is inaudible to us. That stars
mutely shine to us in the clamoured-at heavens.

If they spoke to us, our remotest and oldest parents!
And we: hearing at last! – the first human listeners.

CAST OUT

('Ausgesetzt auf den Bergen des Herzens . . .')

Cast out on the mountains of the heart. Look, how small there,
look: the last settlement of words, and higher,
although so tiny, a last
farmstead of feeling. You discern it? –
Cast out on the mountains of the heart. Stark rock
under your hands. Here, even so,
something blossoms; from the mute sheerness
an unknowing plant breaks into blossom, singing.
But the initiate? Ah, who began to know
and is silent now, cast out on the mountains of the heart.
Yet many with whole awareness, surely
many mountain creatures roam there secure,
shift pasture, pausing. And the great cherished bird
circles the pure negation of the peaks. – But
uncherished, here on the mountains of the heart . . .

TRANSIENCE

('Verganglichkeit')

Drift-sand of hours. Incessant soft erosion
sparing, so far, the lucky blessed recess.
Always life blows. Already the protrusion
of broken columns, roof gone, purposeless.

But decay: is it sadder than the fountain's return
to its reflection, lustred with what sprays
it? Confront mutability's jaws, that it may learn
fully to comprehend us in its gaze.

from DRAFTS FROM TWO WINTER EVENINGS

(from 'Entwurfe aus zwei Winterabenden')

No other such beauty. I was then too small.
One afternoon. Their sudden urge to dance,
The old carpet rolled back briskly. (Over all
the scene persists a sort of radiance.)

She danced. And one saw her alone, in thrall
yet often losing even her because
her odour had become the world one was
immersed and drowning in. I was too small.

But when I was grown big enough to bring
such fragrance under my control?
Yet from the whole unutterable thing
to plummet, like a stone's sheer fall?

No, through it all, such beauty! Her scent now
blooms in this winter-garden, and that day's.
How intact it is. Cancelled by nothing. How
it is mine. Whom it unfailingly repays.

*

We've this: the chance that happiness may sail
past us. No, it's not that. Not so much
even as chance; but our supposing merely
that summer then, this garden too – that such
music as flying minutes made was really
innocent, when it was pure betrayal.

And you, grown woman then, how do I see
you now? No more as when a dumbstruck child,
but almost as a god would in his bliss.
Were such hours everlasting, life might build
within us edifices made from this
discovered fragrance, luminosity.

Make Believe

A smiling blue toy engine rounds its track.
Creatures compliant to the love you pour
on them, your teddy-bear and horse smile back;
who tucked in bed with you will thrill once more

to the escape of beanstalk-climbing Jack;
share your dreams. World validated through
being purely feigned, its paradisiac
essence must fade to a dead residue

heaped in a box. As lured by the ideal
down ramifying routes you learn that smiling
promises are broken, and the real
giant's torturers dismember Jack.

While still soft dummy visages beguiling
child's play watch trains circle plastic track.

The Parade

Proclaimed by music's brazen certitude
arresting the thronged city-centre, they
paraded through behind the band. We stood
aside, applauding – everyone aligned
like filings to a magnet. An array
of old men, some with sticks, in wheelchairs, blind,
proud under banners, dark suits hung
with decorations from when they were young.

As others on those beaches stay. Eyes-right,
each rank salutes the war-memorial where
the mayor and such stand. Your small claps ignite
on one face answering smiles, as if you bring
alive, incarnate, vague stuff that back there
they'd been told it was for when, scrambling
to boats, shell-shredded, beaten, they
scraped home from hell, to try another day.

Thrilled by pure pageantry you ask, 'What are
Dunkirk Veterans, dad?' So I explain:
'Many years ago there was a war,
those men were in it. I was just a few

days old when . . .' The old tale. 'Did they feel pain?
Or cry?' 'Oh yes. But thought they fought for – you,
the future.' 'But you think fighting's wrong.'
– When suddenly a Spitfire flew along

the High Street, dipped its wings and roared away
past the cathedral, and its huge unzipping
dispersed us back into our shopping day
from a brief exaltation, not of pride
in war, but at an embodiment that stripping
away our squandering decades ratified
yearnings unassuaged still: clear
in all the march-past recollected here.

Transfigurations: a love cycle

WHITE-FLOWERING PLANT

Today as usual feels a waste of life
not being with you. Scribbling lecture-notes,
browsing, trundling the vacuum about,
cooking for only me . . . I could go out,
getting away from myself,
chat-up some woman who's not someone's wife . . .
Stuff that. I flick the telly. On the shelf
beside it that white-flowering pot-plant floats

unreproachingly pictures from the night you brought it,
your blonde hair loose: 'I love it like that,' as
I'd said, who'd liked it thickly plaited till
'He does that for me,' you explained, to kill –
but no, love's Midas-touch
redeems to gold all we are, who'd not sought it.
Nervous, because of which I'd cooked too much,
stood dithering between classical and jazz,

I took your coat, brush-kissed September-chilled
radiance – and heard my voice indifferent
or sharp helplessly, as if I had to prove
this meal no ploy to set up . . . Held aloof,
I thought just, *Christ, I love you.*
And afterwards in sheer relief refilled
my glass more times than . . . Till my jabber drove you
off. I don't remember when you went.

But phoned next morning to apologise.
Cock-up in all ways but the best, that night
remains my ballast to our gorgeous others,
beach, theatre, woods. Perhaps, likewise, your mother's
pained incomprehension,
your children, his 'I'll kick you out', comprise
your negative stabilisers. Whose dimension
ensures us truer course than travelling light.

Towards such candid, all-subsuming white.

NO REASSURANCE NECESSARY

That hollow in a cushion, thread
of blonde hair on the floor,
blue script chaste on an envelope
glissading through my door,

align me in the deserts of
a busy rest-of-life
to its oases: the embrace
of someone-else's wife.

I think her ceaselessly, aware
that nothing in me is
complete until imparted – those
sweet phone-calls during his

office-hours . . . So – marginalised
by things as structured now;
knowing the odds in such terms stacked
against such love; and how

I crave dimensions, breakfasts, chores,
ihre schwäbische Heimat, which
are his and hers; their kids' sporadic
'Mammy's friend' – I'm rich

in hope that what's so good can't fail
to find means to come true;
in your integrity which checks
denial of it in you.

So here, in lieu of flowers I can't
present, nor clothes, nor ring,
accept this compass-needle: trust,
set true, unwavering.

FROHE WEINACHTEN

a letter, Christmas 1988

Aglow in red today in grey Coleraine
you and your children, as we pranced among
dour shoppers, tinselled windows, twitched balloons
under a drizzle of loudspeakered tunes,
beercans rattling. Then you were gone again.

So, Christmas nears. I picture your home hung
with green sprays . . . Well, TV extravaganzas,
crass ritual boozing, all that I can skip,
to dwell on what redeems man's fellowship,
gracing, I know, your family rites. Your tongue

confirms, love, how our meetings link like stanzas,
loose ends picked up, transfigured to a chime.
In peace mere geography can't wrench untrue
I'll ring my son, and wait to hear from you.
Trusting our rhythms to intuit answers

as they gather to the final rhyme.

OUR REALM

Like some deep-rooted overshadowing tree
spread thronged and singing to enfold us when
we pause, at desks, or you with family,
is our green world exhaling oxygen

where seamlessly consort all the terrains
possessing us: those golden strands, our talk
and teasings, plans, guilts, books shared; narrow lanes
of your South German childhood which I walk

who've not yet visited; our love-embrace.
What we inhabit haunts the everyday
it craves, which this cold night insists your place
is elsewhere. Does your husband see you stray

half-lost now in that dripping summer wood,
a twilit mush of leaves beneath our feet?
'*Blumen*,' you uttered, '*Blumen*' – and we could
as readily as a real person meet

among such timeless labyrinthine glades
with Hesse's Goldmund, as his quest winds on
to where he started from, arched colonnades
of the ascetic cloister Mariabronn,

to tell truth's found through images, which bloom
on lust, pain, beauty, want – experience,
hungered for as is what it must entomb:
our first 'nothingness and innocence'.

ON THE BEACH

Dodging off work, I saunter from the train
to find you, since you telephoned and said
you'd be here with your children. My eyes roam
a yellow expanse dotted with red
and blue, swimsuits and summerwear. Again
cries from that undulating fringe of foam

shrill clarified by immensities of space,
balls bounce and arc against a lambent sea
cradling far out above the beach
the usual ship incuriously
passing beyond the headland. Then your face
meets mine, our gazes locking each on each.

Close-up shows glass and beercans on the strand;
dogs scuffle, radios simmer. While we build
a castle with your daughter's spade her small
brother gets the thermos filled
with sand, then flings the stuff about. We wade
ankle-deep; then find a stick and scrawl

our names in gold sift, till – your hands brush mine –
you 'must collect' your husband. And you add,
'Was this not boring for you?' 'Not a bit.'
I shake out towels, simply glad
of what, alone and later, I define:
domesticity camped-out on the infinite;

so all I share of what you waste indoors
on him . . . I watch the sunset's gorgeous drape,
recalling passionate evenings, fade to less
than blankness; emptied benches gape
at what, as ever, supervenes: the shore's
moon-desolated briny wilderness.

DURING YOUR ABSENCE

Your postcard comes to tell me what you do –
you and your marriage gone vacationing.
Dressing-gowned, I gulp your blue
script: *Florence, Botticelli, Dante's grave,*
your *we* . . . *we* . . . *we* . . . machine-gunning
me . . . Again I fight
off swirling jealousies . . . As from a cave
shaking emerge to blink in vacant light.

This is a mere surviving,
your absence in me like a weight, its ache
wrenching out my 'I love you!' cried
aloud an hour back as I came awake
from dream: us in a car, green glens, you driving –
then suddenly gone – I grabbed the wheel, it flew
round uselessly as the car swung wide –
and just before the crash hit, I came to . . .

I go to work, space-out desk-top routine
with coffees, phone a friend – his cat is sick.
The summer University is lazing.
Back home, junk TV . . . Once more, with a click
the kettle's singing ceases . . . Time unspent,
three weeks like this it's been

since in this bed – there flood, half-crazing
me, thoughts of you with him in that distant tent.

And then, your 'Trust me' whispers through my dark,
'You are always in my mind and heart,' you've said.
And I rest here healed and whole,
as if caressed, knowing for me to fail
to give the trust your love's solicited
would be the real betrayal,
that now as ever you are in my soul,
and its authenticating watermark.

OUR MEETINGS

As in the Underground there's no mistaking
the train's approach, it pushes air ahead,
whirls paper, the line sings, a sort-of dread
suffusing longing and my platform shaking –
so it is before our every meeting,
till you arrive. Hear how my heart is beating!

TENTS

Midnight. That moon,
looking lodged in a tree,
you also might glance
through a pane now to see –

in truth a great light
in the skies' high tent over
the world's curve between
us, the white cliffs of Dover,

all France . . . Thus it links
us, and getting undressed
I wish you by the far
Danube sweet rest.

And think how when soon
you come to me, slide
from your clothes, and our flesh
embraces, inside

your sweet motion I'll thrill
to the intimate flare
of your eyes, in the tent
of your long flowing hair.

WHITEPARK BAY

A mile of the broad golden strand
we strolled, and back again,
tentatively hand in hand
knew love beginning then,
sporting by sea surefooted and
our air pure oxygen.

This year, the tide besieging all
came in: love's wavering
course crossed rocks inviting fall,
hands clasped for steadying;
its breath more heartfelt to forestall
all checks the world's ways bring.

THIS ISLAND

At peace, limbs interlaced, we lie and drowse.
On, as it seems, this island we've discovered.
Distantly lapping now all adverse seas
of circumstance. Warmed by your loving vows,
our fluent thrills of sexual embrace,
I pull the quilt so you are covered,
hoping that lulled here in our proper place
we'll sleep, to wake together and at ease.

You think, and stir, slip from the bed, and dress,
bound back to husband, children. 'Yes, the time
will come,' you tell me. When we are downstairs
deliciously your lips browse my nakedness.
A last flash of your face in night. Content,
I hear your car start. Once more I'm
pillowed on your departed body's scent
and impress, where my tongue finds long blonde hairs.

CODA

a version of Heine's Ich stand in dunkeln Träumen

Stood in a dark dream staring
Upon her picture, I've
Seen those dearest lineaments
Come secretly alive.

And on her lips there gathered
A brilliant smile, upon
Her eyes up-brimmed heart-sorrow
In teardrops till they shone.

Also my own tears flowing
Down my cheeks I knew –
And ah, I can't believe it,
That I'm bereft of you.

In the Planetarium

Head tilted under the dome
I gaze at constellations,
star-shifts, the infinite's spume

projected through slow modulations.
Thousands of years ago
runs the voice-over narration,

awe-struck people below
would exalt to the heavens those
whom they'd deify. And so

there Andromeda glows,
and Perseus who saves
her from the sea-monster . . . It throws

a switch in my mind, revives
a distant afternoon
on a sofa, deep in the lives

of Greek gods and heroes . . . Hot stone,
dust, olive groves, vines, a scent
of lemon trees, the unknown

along a white path, and my sense
of an unfolding universe . . .
That primal innocence! –

before stuff about sex and careers
buried it, adult pain,
and the sift of things getting worse –

reading, while lashings of rain
streamed down glass, of Theseus, Hera . . .
Memories fixed like a stain

and growing ever clearer
as they accelerate receding,
and the final dark moves nearer,

this ache my heart now needing
mercy, is it? – or
just diffuse internal bleeding . . .

The life and death of a star.
The sun, for instance, born . . .
to consume itself. *Before*

its reactors all shut down . . .
I close my eyes, and see
that *final perfect dawn.*

Then the death agony,
engulfing this green Earth . . .
Let such extinction be

not mere cold ashes, dearth,
invisible in night,
but that other aftermath:

compressed to essential weight
a pulsar flashing forth
pure lighthouse beams of light.

Christmas 1989

Last month's miracle was young people dancing
on top of the wall dividing a city, hands
from the West reaching for those from the East
until that day shot for such transgression.

The Berlin Wall is History! headlines proclaim –
meaning not just dead, but irrelevant. Likewise
our postwar German friends say: 'Hitler? –
that Nazi stuff's just history . . .'

But history never dies, is the perilous tide
that wave upon wave breaking bubbles carries us onward,
floats once again like broken-up jigsaw
Poland, Hungary, Czechoslovakia.

In the baroque basilica of St Kasimir,
Vilnius, history laughs, is a headscarved woman
clearing out the Museum of Atheism:
'All junk now, the lot wouldn't fetch three kopecks!'

While if, in Romania, this day a tyrant was killed,
history weeps through the imperfect living who bury
his victims; melts down their myriad candles . . .
And also history stares betrayed

from sad eyes knowing Utopia too has died,
the lethal old charmer who led us on, alchemised
the selfless to murderers and their prey. Leaving
the future to crave merely more cars and shopping.

The End of the Pier Show (1995)

Paper Boats

I roam the *Contents* pages, look to see
Who's in, who's out. More women these days. So,
A lot here born a fair while after me,
And some of even these, I notice . . . No,
At least I'm not tagged with a terminal date:
Still *1940–*. The anthology falls
Closed. Though not being dead yet seems no great
Reason for being alive. Then that appals
Me – catching myself thinking what I know
I'd never have thirty, or ten, years ago.

So what's occurred, what changes? Well, it's not
Shrivelling passions or intensities
Or lyric feelings, all intact. But what
Form like a glow, as clear transparencies,
Are pictures: the lit Thames from a midnight train
Grinding across a railbridge; pools of white
Pavement petals hushing footfall; rain
Golden in lamplight past my window; bright
Primary colours strewn on beaches; and
The blare and glitter from a park bandstand.

When Cowdrey drove through mid-off, seaside piers
Had *What the Butler Saw* machines, politics
Was pure crusade to end 'the wasted years' . . .
The potency is more than heady tricks
Of gulped nostalgia. Adrift from schooling, home,
I scribbled novel-drafts, joked how I might

Yet rake in middle-distance golds, or comb
Far space for cosmic secrets, move a knight
To clinch the world chess crown. So much lay before me,
Including the glorious girls – could not ignore me.

Or further back: a fragile glint and dance
Of dragonflies over pond; print on my palm
Of bracken where I'd leant; a morning trance
Absorbing patterns of grain on a chair-arm . . .
Moments our rest-of-life becomes a quest
In some form to transcribe, all sealed away
In past we're exiled from, defines it best –
Now I've *got it made* the world would say . . .
Ahead, the paper boats I and my son
Launch, vanish into tunnel, one by one.

From Two Chapters of an Old Natural History

Above the level of the ocean and
Defended against its irruptions, land,
The rhinoceros is very large
And strong. This quadruped
Has skin insensitive to flies
In thick folds. It is said
Enamelled with flowers, adorned with verdure which
Always renews itself, above all rich
That in old Roman spectacles
It fought elephants. Certainly
The one the French King sent the Pope
Destroyed its ship at sea.
In innumerable species of animals, is a place
Of perfect repose. Upon this good Earth's face
He bears his weapon of offence,
A hard horn, on his nose.
His limbs are massy, his large feet
Each armed with three great toes.
In its delightful habitation, Man
Presides, his destiny to aid the plan

He feeds on grossest herbs and shrubs,
Resists muskets, spears. His brain
Is small. Rash, without sentiment,
He is no use until slain.

Of Nature, over all other beings. He
Alone possesses the capacity

His skin makes leather, and the flesh
Some reckon excellent,
While esteemed remedies are made
From horn, blood, excrement.

For knowledge, dignified in his prime station
By the faculty of admiration.

Two Views of the Whale

1 FROM A MEDIEVAL BESTIARY

Cethegrande is a fish,
Largest in water that there is;
Seeing one, you'd say it must stand
Like an island on the sea-floor's sand.
When this huge fish is hungry, he
Gapes his mouth wide in the sea,
And from his throat comes forth a breath
That is the sweetest thing on earth.
Charmed by it, other fishes swim
Into his mouth, so drawn by him
Float ignorant of his trick, till sucked
Within as the whale's jaws are locked.
This fish dwells down at the sea's ground,
And lives there, ever hale and sound,
Till times when storms stir the whole sea.
When winter strives for victory
With summer, when rising, he floats still
While the weather is so ill.
Ships, scattering as the seas drive,
Fearing death, longing to survive,
Looking around suppose this fish

The island for which they all wish;
So the rejoicing sailors steer
To it, use all their strength, draw near,
Fasten their ships, go up, with tinder
Make a fire blaze on this wonder,
Warm themselves, and eat and drink.
He feels the fire, and starts to sink,
Diving at once to the sea-ground
He kills them with no wounds, all drowned.

Whoever attends the devil's lore
In time shall rue it, that is sure;
Whoever fastens hope on him
Shall follow to hell's regions dim.

2 FROM A MODERN ENCYCLOPEDIA

The order *Cetacea*, large marine
Animals, is divided into two
Groups, those possessing teeth, and the baleen
Whales which eat by straining plankton through

Horny plates inside the mouth. Some dive
For over an hour, to surface spouting air
Through blowholes in their heads. Most types survive,
Though vastly reduced in numbers everywhere.

Social behaviour. Living in schools, the whales
Often move in ballet-like formations.
They help their sick. Grown calves, when something ails
Them, seek their mothers. Seasonal migrations

Cross many latitudes. They like to play,
Leaping and riding waves in aerobatic
Antics, pitchpoling on their flippers, grey
Whales rise to look around them. These aquatic

Creatures have evolved a complex mix
Of sounds, enabling communication
Over huge distances: barks, whistles, clicks;
Use sonar echoes to aid navigation.

Whaling. Guns fire the harpoons, and a fuse
Explodes the charge. The carcass is inflated,
Left to float flag-marked while the ship pursues
Others. Processing is facilitated

By flush-deck openings on factory ships
Which in less that an hour can dispose
Of a 100-ton whale. Machinery strips
The blubber, bone is cut up. Nothing goes

To waste. The flesh we shun makes cattle-feed,
The cooked bone bone-meal; oil yields margarine,
Varnish, soaps, lubricants, things people need
From cosmetics to commercial glycerine.

The Cheetah

So here they are, what above all
  You've longed to see – the cheetahs.
Earth's swiftest beast, its speed exceeds
  One hundred kilometres

An hour. They lope or laze, strong tails
  For turning in mid-chase
Twitch idly. Born to run, they know
  It's pointless in this place.

One briefly scampers at a trot
  To hint what it might do;
From instinct cubs play stalking games
  Though born inside this zoo.

Another pads to the wire-mesh,
  Pauses. Eyes meet. We see
Crisp rippling sandy fur, black spots,
  He views us patiently

Neither as prey, nor threat; has seen
  So often the likes of us.
Our camera clicks, he flicks away.
  And we go for our bus.

When in your sleep's wide plains a gold
  Streak veers, coils, springs, eyes slits,
Is it the cheetah treads your dream,
  Or you who've entered its?

Natural Justice

'I've marshalled you, marsupials,
  For just war! Kangaroos,'
Says the Koala, 'it appals
  You that the humans use
Your skin for making cuddly toys
Of – us!' Tails thump, a thunderous noise.

'And gentle wombats, for their crops'
  Sake, you expire in traps.
This New Year Day oppression stops!'
  Guns pouched, his audience claps.
Bikes rev, they vroom across the brown
Scrubland into the drowsy town.

They zoom through supermarkets wrecking
  Shelves, zap shoppers, batter
Machines, canteens, do wheelies decking
  Cops, rip skirts, shirts, scatter
Cricket from wickets. The mayor's worst fears
Take shape: blob noses, furry ears.

From wallaby wallops, kanga cuffs,
  Folk reel, the hind-feet shocker
Rends ribs; but the most vicious stuff's
  The whopper from the quokka;
While wombats snarling 'Who wants trouble?'
Kick civic statuary to rubble.

'They're stuffed, enough, we've done our duty,
  But shun extermination!'
Horns blaring, bearing looted booty,
  They roar in neat formation,
Singing 'Triumph to the Just!'
To vanish through the summer dust.

'The Beautiful Game'

(Pele)

This summer's drained of vivid promises,
A chill negation of what should have been;
Betrayed from which, I slump among what is,
Watch World Cup football flicker on my screen.
It too falls short, squanders in dreariness,
Fouls, histrionics, chances thrown away,
Unjust results, gifts thwarted, patternless.
Useless in memory glow Pele's sway
Dummying that goalie, ghost-slides of Tostão.
Yet like life too this game will never fail
Us quite, slips leaden days by alchemising
From battle to romance: that through-pass now,
A juggling run, the net shakes, and I'm rising
To beauty opened like a peacock's tail.

1990

Tenby

Free of life's wastage
The name sounded clear:
Tenby, a bell's
Double chime in my ear.

But when we arrived
Tenby fell into place,
Now configured precisely
Within time and space,

Its cliff-garden dropping
To a curve of gold sand,
Small harbour, old watchtower
On a high jut of land.

Ah, Dynbych-y-Pysgod,
'Little fort of the fishes',
The postcards we filled
With holiday wishes

Showed once-guarded town walls
And Pembrokeshire's vast
Hunks of castle where brood
Bloody deeds of the past.

And twice daily the tide
Cut off Goscar Rock,
And nothing could halt
The whirl of the clock . . .

When it slid from our train
I was glad of our few
Days in Tenby, redeemed
From transcendent to true;

Of our walk fluctuating
From forest to cliff,
Our boat to the island,
The jokes we shared. If

My son as you splashed
In the waves all the cries
Arising seemed tiny,
Brief under the sky's

Huge arch as the vanished
Clamour of strife
Among Normans, Welsh, English,
Still through your life

Things you gazed at when perched
On that cannon, or did –
Beach football, rock scrambling –
Will come back, amid

All accretions, erosions;
Ceremonious, immune.
Keynotes. To such, all
Our years reattune.

The Scheme of Things

1 FIRST WORLD

How it enfolds me now, that earliest world
Whispering on against the garden fence:
A leftover stretch of Epping Forest curled
Round our small suburban crescent, in its dense
Thickets and bracken, sun-splashed glades, our play,
Near as my heartbeat still woodpigeons brooding,
Sudden again the blue flash of a jay.
Why should I hesitate, as if intruding?

– Who clinging high in a storm-battered tree
Once sang, 'Eternal Father, strong to save,'
The hymn 'for those in peril on the sea',
Thrilling to know joy won by being brave,
Fears simple then, unstained by guilts or failure.
Boughs creaked. When I grew up, I'd be a sailor.

2 NATURE LESSONS

My forest Eden wasn't unspoilt nature.
Older children, born before the war,
Told which ponds were true ponds, which just bomb-crater.
What were those concrete fangs across it for? –
'To stop the German tanks.' In the night sky
Searchlights, bombers, droning, bangs, V2s,
Since I could remember. Pointless wondering why –
Such things were since it said so on the news.

Cows straying down our road were more amazing:
Loose in the forest, there they were one morning
Nudging at front gates, stood in flowers grazing.
And more sinister to me than air-raid warnings
Was that dank rubber in the ferns, which my friend Nick
Said had been up a girl on some man's prick.

3 INTIMATIONS

Thick autumn leaves shoaled orange, gold and red
Beneath the beech, more precious than all toys.
I gathered up the choicest, pocketed
Them to keep. Next week, 'The rubbish boys,'
Guffawed the barber, as I delved and blushed,
Finding at last my ninepence only after
Disgorging a heap of brittle shreds, brown dust,
'Stuff in their clothes!' I fled the adult laughter.

Annually frogspawn mantled every pond.
I'd scoop up dollops into jamjars, bring
Them home, for weeks watch with anticipation
Tadpoles sprout legs, so few survive beyond,
To make the next green hopping generation;
And feel betrayed by the whole scheme of things.

4 FATHER

Leant back, knees bent, eyes down, hands plunged in pockets,
Dad flipped the ball just right for me to head.
I'd wake to see beside his empty bed
Draped on the chair his office suit, the jacket
Fragrant with pipe tobacco, hear him splashing.
I stole sixpence when the shops first sold
Ice-lollies postwar, tasted a pink cold
Dissolving sweetness, fearful of a thrashing.

Yet thieved again. Until Dad must have known
But, unperturbed, still on our Sunday strolls
Chipped up the ball, named trees. He kept his tools
Gleaming and sharp; and when I asked had shown
Why the spirit-level's jittery little bubble
Should be centred, steadying it upon the table.

5 INDOORS AND OUT

Shelling peas indoors with Mum, I stared
At the line of tree-tops cresting through grey rain
Spattering our garden laurels. When it cleared
I went out to a world washed new again.
The earth released fresh smells. I stood and listened
To thrushes whistling in a hawthorn thicket,
Pressing my palm against wet bark to mark it;
Waterdrops pearled twigs where berries glistened.

Suppose a tree-house on a hidden bough:
I'd pull the rope-ladder up behind me, lose
Myself among leaves' year-long ceremonial.
'Andrew, get up!' they call, 'You're late for school.'
If I could do just anything I chose
I'd build that tree-house, and be in it now.

6 FRIENDS

First kids in our road, then friends met at school.
We vied tree-climbing, running, sometimes fought.
Nick, George Stone, Rodney Baxter, Brian who taught
Me to spell *queueing*, the Fortey twins ('Just two'll
Be quite enough') . . . From ropes above the Ching
We'd swing, let go, land safe on the far side.
Whooping along on bikes and trikes, we'd ride
To Loughton, Ilford, circles widening.

Where are they now? Some grandparents, some dead.
Passing in streets, there'd be no recognising.
In me they live forever bracketed:
Fairisle pullovers, Woolworths' snake-clasp belts,
Plaster on knees. On branches cut to stilts,
Or pedalling homeward as the moon is rising.

7 BREAK-UP

Mum moved with sister and me to the far side
Of London. My nine-years world whirled away.
Dad I heard nothing more of till he died.
Grown-up, I went back, found bits where we'd play
Gone, built over; strange toys lined the sill
Of our old house. But still my favourite beech . . .
I didn't climb, knew things less tangible
Than its low-slung bough were out of reach:

As if through sheets of dripping ice we'd break
From ponds we dangerously slid on when they froze;
Aqueous, refracted. Futile to revisit
What only lives within me. Though why is it
So vivid now? . . . Hands on the oars, Dad rows
A family on summer's trembling lake.

In Ward 27

'All art aspires
To the condition
Of music' . . . Yes,
But what all art utters
Is life aspiring
To solacing structure,
To purification.
So it is life
That craves to be music.

Tell that to the wearied
Brown backs of Brueghel's
Three hunters descending
The snow through stark trees:
Their cold day, the boughs'
Rigid tracery, village
Below, where children
Are sliding, redeemed
Through art's timeless vision.

Also 'words, words, words' –
None knew better than Shakespeare –
Are stuck in the mud
Of our human turmoil.
Mad Ophelia dying,
Betrayals, revenges,
Cry out unaware
Of the form they are shaped to –
Forms never rinsed clear

Of our mortal lot, here
For instance, shuffling
A corridor floor,
Counting the hours
Between cups of tea,
Till wheeled to the surgeon.
In the ophthalmic ward
The vision we crave
Is simple indeed.

Only music inhabits
That ultimate sphere
Purged of life's blemish.
It moves through abstractions.
Past reach? In a sense.
Yet, moved, I find Elgar's
Cello concerto
Proves eyes wrecked for seeing
Still buoyant with tears.

Uncle Bob

'Use your feet, and bring the bat down true
To the line of flight, head down, and Bob's your uncle!'
They said; or maybe, 'Think the problem through,
Tackle it stage by stage, and Bob's your uncle!'

Meaning it will be fine, turn out all right.
Having no Uncle Bob, I'd fantasise
A puissant lordly being out of sight,
Monitoring my every enterprise.

His hands on all the ropes, and never lost
For a solution, supernatural kin,
Concerned, however we felt mauled and tossed
By life, to see us right, through thick and thin.

Years brought wrong choices, people, home to stay.
For others, too. Unsolvable. Had Bob
Lost touch, not known his work fall miles astray,
Or flushed with the high life dozed off on the job?

No – not remotely all we'd cracked him up
To be, just a quixotic simpleton,
Even before he finally cracked up
Under the drift of things, he'd never won

A major title, steered the ship of state,
Or written Tolstoy. Now he's on his uppers,
Outcast, derided, an old reprobate
Scavenging bins for remnants of fish suppers.

Still meaning well, and wishing others joy.
From the corner of a pub he tips a wink,
Seeing again Miss Right meet the wrong boy,
Smiles 'Bob's your uncle!' raising his cadged drink.

Flax Dams in County Derry

Remember? – twilight thrilling
With birdsong as we trod
The scented path that wound
Past gleaming sheets of water
Configured as if a timeless natural feature
To the slopes; and glad,
Our welling hearts attuned.

Wherein a slow fermenting –
As when green flax in sheaves
Weighted by stones is sunk
Until the outer woody
Husk is loosened – had through weeks already
Disclosed the core, and love's
Unstinting urge to thank.

Fish set the surface trembling;
Along a plank we balanced
Over the sluice, then down.
To find numb petrifaction:
The linen factory's stark dereliction;
Stilled waterwheel, sheds silenced;
Tramlines half-overgrown.

Not living, yet not buried.
As circumstance, claims, fear,
Which from the shadows mutter
Would leave what in each other's
Arms we know. That may, transfiguring either's
Pasts, bring us once more
Unwearied to moving water.

Dora, Dick, Nip and Fluff

Here is Dora. Here is Dick. And here
Is Nip. And here is Fluff. The sun shines clear
From a blue sky. See Nip and Fluff at play.
Nip is black and white. Fluff's fur is grey.
'Woof,' says Nip. Fluff jumps up on the wall.
Here comes Dora with a bouncy ball.
How Nip romps [new word] with it. But now
Dora throws the red ball high. 'Mee-ow,'
Says Fluff, 'I think that this is meant for me.'
And look, the ball is stuck up in a tree.
'Go after it,' says Dora. See Fluff climb
To a high limb [which only looks a rhyme].
'Mee-ow,' says Fluff, 'I cannot get the ball.'
'Come down,' says Dora. 'But I think I'll fall,'
Says Fluff, 'Mee-ow, mee-ow, I can't get down.'
'Oh, poor Fluff,' says Dora with a frown
[New word]. 'Woof, woof,' says Nip, 'let us fetch Dick.'
They go indoors, tell Dick. Dick gets a stick.
Dick runs into the garden. 'I can get
Fluff down and the ball too,' he says. 'Poor pet,'
Says Dora. Dick climbs up the tree and takes
Fluff in his arms, pokes with his stick and shakes
Until the ball drops bouncing. Soon he's got
Himself and Fluff down. Dora is so glad. 'What
Shall we play now?' she chuckles, 'Games are fun.'
They chase [new word] each other. See Nip run.
'Dick, your chum Hamie's here, for tea,' calls Mum.

But Shakespeare [new word] knew there's more to come.

I that please some, try all, both joy and terror
Of good and bad; that makes and unfolds error,
Now take upon me, in the name of Time,
To use my wings. Impute it not a crime
To me, or my swift passage, that I glide
O'er sixteen years, and leave the growth untried . . .

See Dick, flat out on a soiled mattress, clutch
His head. He has the shakes. Dick drinks too much.
Divorce [new word and new experience]
Has fouled Dick up. 'Thank God I had the sense
Not to have kids,' Dick says. Dick's lost his job.
He puts off girls he chases. Dick's a slob.
He swigs his bedside Scotch. 'I'll make the door.'
Dick trips on something smelly on the floor.
'Grr.' Yes, it's Nip. Poor Nip can hardly stand.
Nip has the runs. He cannot understand
The new words 'stomach tumour'. Soon he'll die
[New experience], not knowing why.

See Baby Tim clap hands in Dora's face,
Not knowing he's classed as a high-risk case
At Social Services. Tim's still too dumb
To ask why Granny's younger than his Mum.
'It's Dad's remarriage to that teenage bitch
Who paints her toenails green,' says Dora, 'which
Made me quit college.' Dora's on the game.
And heroin [no, this word's not the same
As heroine]. Prone as often as her brother,
But under some man, each just like another,
'Go after it,' says Dora, to their shoving
Buttocks. She tells Dick, 'I'm just fun-loving.'
See Baby drop his toy car. He says, 'Fuck'
[New word], copying Mummy when, her luck
Out, she drops a pan. Tim smiles. All's well.
Mummy doesn't. Some hope. Time will tell.

That's life. Dick's old chum Hamlet's off his head,
Finding his uncle's killed his dad to bed
His mum. See Dick fall down in his own sick.

I've not forgotten Fluff, even if Dick
And Dora have. Cats have nine lives, but how
Each flashes past. Fluff would be dead by now.
But sixteen years ago, in fact one day
Later, Fluff met a fox. She tried to play.
'Mee-o' was mown short. See Fluff's flying fur.
It didn't feel so quick a death to her.

For Dick and Dora, still what, if they knew it
Was coming at them, neither would go through it.
They do not see yet cancer, madness, heart
Disease; past cure [new experience]; each fresh start
Mocked by its outcome; then the vortex fear
Of age; still worse, what dulls that, close and near.

No fun. Meanwhile, see Dick gazing down
Into the river where the summer town
Is mirrored, houses, shop-fronts, trees, intact,
Inverted and at peace. Waters refract
To purity the spoiled, soured lives we've got.
Dick knows he'd drown there. Wishes he did not.
He thrashes it with a stick, and sets it shaking,
Until the globe of the lost world falls, breaking.

Angels of Mercy

on reading the Eastern Daily Press, *January 1993*

'Outperforming their patient-care quota',
The nurses of Norfolk have been saving lives,
Not letting them croak for the sake of the rota;
So Hospital Management sharpens its knives.

It's closing wards, freezing appointment of staff.
Miss Florence Nightingale's come to apply?
'We've to be cost-effective, so don't make us laugh;
Our budget's no symbol for people who die.'

Flying High

French-windows and a sort of patio,
Our glasses stood on flagstones half-neglected
By talk of how we fear the world will go.
'Eliot' – someone waving his *Collected* –
'Was wrong, it's bang, not whimper.' Ban the Bomb.
South Africa. The issues are all clear
This summer night, as trad jazz flickers from
Inside to lap the lights and darks of beer.
Love, love, O careless love . . .
Whose party is it? This rock-firm house scaled
To more capacious days, crowned high above
With green dome, parapet, a little railed
Platform from which, I imagine, some
Stargazing Victorian *paterfamilias*
Stared and saw all clear . . . A couple strum
Guitars, and insects glimmer as they pass
Among leaf-muffled light. And, 'It's a classic
Post-colonial mess, the Congo. Hell.'
'Our generation'll clear out that jurassic
Crowd who've fucked the world up.' Time will tell.
The mag I've picked up flops apart at where,
Stripped to a loincloth, bound, Patrice Lumumba
The Congo's first elected premier,
Cowers towards his murder. 'Another number?' –
Delia gone, one more round, Delia gone . . .
Then I go, helmetless upon the pillion
Of someone's motor-scooter, roaring on
With whistling in my ears as a million
Streetlamps like an exploding supernova
Swoop past, a sense of destiny: I know
I'll write poems fit to kick their tables over.
Flying high. Over thirty years ago.

Annie's Cats

You don't want to think of them too
soppily – or take them too lightly.
Gavin Ewart

'Misty' because it was after that misty day
On our visit to Lincoln, trees like iron hung
With waterdrops that did not drop, you chose
  Her, and her long fur was grey;
Her sister, runt of the litter, was black: 'poor Mel'.
Eighteen months ago, and I would tell
  Of your cats, who died so young,
Appropriately, indeed not scanting those
Small lives, nor mawkishly embalming them
In large words they can't fit. Yet I would cherish them.

For memory is mother of the Muses, and
The impulse to preserve root of all art,
Which though it cannot make amends for what
  Life voids, by troubling to understand
How it was, what happened, taking pains
Composes what through shapeliness sustains
  Truths that every bleeding heart
Hungers homeward to, so let me not
Fear relaxing to fidelity, to sprawl
Languorous, humdrum, attentive, as cats relaxing sprawl.

Romping together, Misty and Mel would rise
Like porpoises, turn hairpin bends in chase,
Climb curtains, wallpaper, then flaked-out flop
  Together, paws entwined, shut eyes,
Upon the fireside rug or kitchen floor.
And your huge garden all theirs to explore.
  It seemed they owned the place.
Bold Misty scrambled trees, patrolled atop
The roof. It was poor Mel could not get down –
You'd fetch the ladder . . . They pranced at snowflakes fluttering down.

But if cats have nine lives, as spring came on
These seemed to flicker past. It was Misty fell
Into your brook, discovered she could swim.
  But the black kitten was set upon

By something in the night which gouged her lip;
Dragged when you slammed your car door shut to clip
   Her tail. Always poor Mel,
Who had no purr, seemed risking life and limb.
But it was her sister who disappeared.
One May evening Misty simply disappeared.

Run over? Stolen for her chocolate-box
Feline good looks? Of course, you called and searched,
Asked around neighbouring farms. Mel miaowed, bereft.
   Was Misty cornered by a fox?
You flinched at thought of that. But never heard.
Days became weeks, but neither corpse nor word . . .
   And Mel still moping, perched
On the wall, bewildered only she was left . . .
You kept Mel in at nights now, and she slept
On your bed, sucking your duvet-cover as you slept.

And yet, in time, in truth, it turned out that
Misty's death, her dominant role gone,
And having only you to play with now,
   Turned Mel into a supercat.
They say cats only haunt round one for food –
Mel, you'd swear, was attuned to every mood
   You had; when you were on
The phone would sense your joys and sorrows. How
She loved to hide and seek, crouch, rush and spring
Dabbing your cheeks, claws sheathed . . . So, summer bloomed from spring.

Each night your doorstep call, clear as a bell,
And from the orchard, or from fields away,
You'd hear her *miaow* race nearer, through the grass,
   And leap forth, green eyes luminous – Mel!
Until she didn't. Echoing through the night
Your cries; you scoured the garden at first light,
   Sat helplessly to pray . . .
'Just an animal,' they say, 'your pain will pass.'
You found Mel at the foot of your long drive,
Hit by some unknown person enjoying a late drive.

We guessed she had been coming to your call
Across the Kilrea Road, where she would roam

After field-mice, rabbits (cats kill too).
   Unsquashed, unmarked, she'd managed to crawl
To the verge, put paw to her hurt head, and died.
You clutched her stiff corpse to your breast, and cried.
   And so brought poor Mel home.
A strange thing: her green eyes had turned pure blue.
After which, you vowed to have no cats.
And then decided yes, you would get two more cats.

I must digress, to a cemetery far away
From Mel in your Derry orchard. For her death
Coincided with my own more wrenching grief,
   My father's death. That rainy day
We watched him lowered into earth in Ealing
Mel flashed into my mind, and I stood feeling
   (Dad there, no words, pulse, breath,
My heart half-exiled from the priest's belief),
It wrong to overlap two planes of loss.
Then, no: no prim excluding thoughts belong to loss.

Then something strange again, when as chance brought
Us down a London street that I'd last walked
'Thirty years back,' I told you, still the same
   Big bough-wreathed houses, and I thought
Of Chloe Stallibrass, who'd lived in one,
Pictured her bubbly hair and sense of fun,
   You said (and we'd not talked
Of kittens), 'I know what I'm going to name
One of my cats – Chloe.' Coincidence?
Consider the odds: it seemed more than coincidence.

And there's the fact that I, but only I,
Knew that rare name was flickering in my mind;
And it happened in that street. I can't explain.
   Telepathy? And if so, why?
Things happen, and it's maybe better not
Knowing, before they ambush you, just what . . .
   It didn't take long to find
Chloe and Megan. So, you'd start again.
You brought them round. Tabbyish-grey, and weak,
Chloe's life-adventure had entered its fourth week.

You took her home. She vomited and shook.
You couldn't bring her round from kitten-'flu.
The vet said, 'She's too little to get well.
  Just squeeze her, gently.' But it took
Most of the night. You buried her small frame
Next to Mel. So Chloe left a name
  Into which she never grew
For a successor, little tortoiseshell
Chloe II – you took another chance.
She too fell ill, it looked as if she had no chance.

You spooned in medicine, she couldn't keep
Food down; hour after hour she just lay dazed
On a hot-water bottle . . . Megan would chase
  A pine-cone, climb, or burrow deep
Into your linen-basket. She was black,
Short fur a silken gloss along her back,
  But the white dash that blazed
Upon her throat below the pudgy face
Gave her a clerical air . . . There came the day
Chloe pounced for the cone. And throve after that day.

Soon Chloe was the bigger of the pair,
Ousting timid Megan from your lap.
At my house (not, like yours, a bungalow)
  Chloe would preen on a high stair
Then *mi-mi-miaow* her friend to playful fight.
Fun and games that lasted till the night
  That you felt something flap
Against your car's back wheel as cornering slow
You parked at your front door. You got out, saw it:
Megan, head crushed, eyes bulged. Chloe never saw it.

But in the morning, as you hosed away
The clotted blood, Chloe came, smelt, and howled.
The guilt you felt for what you'd never meant!
  For many weeks Chloe would not stray
From your patio. Those who would have us believe
It sentimental to think dumb beasts can grieve
  Don't think how Chloe yowled
For weeks. Not human loss, but evident
Loss . . . So once more, just one: Chloe (II).
She's made it to six months, is happy again too.

I watch her flicking eyes and winking ears
Beseeching us to play. She trails you round
Each time you dig or weed, in rainstorms too.
   And tentative from your pond's edge peers
At huge fish gorging on frogs' new-laid spawn.
She reposes on your sofa, or at dawn
   The bird-table. You found
She'd hidden bones you gave her in a shoe.
As you caress Chloe's black-white-caramel
Fur, you still assert 'There's no one like poor Mel!'

Cats, as well as humans, can haunt our dreams.
Last night, for instance, after much ado,
A restaurant, us with friends around a table;
   And Misty cavorted, shredding reams
Of paper. And suddenly through the open door
A great white stag swept in, I watched it gore
   The kitten, ripping through
Her stomach . . . She wriggled, best as she was able,
Towards us (you'd not noticed), mortally hurt.
I woke crying 'Annie! Annie! it's Misty, she's so hurt!'

All this, of what's occurred, and how, may seem
For a domestic an eventful tale;
But where's the grand design, or even plot?
   Sheer melodrama with no theme
Except this lesson: that love cannot save
What's colonised its orchard grave by grave;
   That our lives, too, are frail,
Perishable as our pets', and not
Only in newsfilm wars. As now you ring me
To tell of a relative's death, and once more wring me.

*

Two years have passed. Your garden blooms again.
Again two cats at play. Not Chloe, who
Last June lured by night's scents past the road's edge
   Was hit and killed. Again your pain;
Watched by, from the slab which you had laid

Over Chloe, her kitten Marmalade.
Autumn came, cold winds blew,
Piteous, small, insistent, from a hedge
Cries brought you running. And so you discovered
Death-sick, dumped – Lillehammer. By your help he's recovered.

Oasis

Half-past midday. Pints light and dark below
The raftered nicotine ceiling of the Dog
And Partridge slowly empty. 'Art, your throw,'
Nods Knacker Orton. After four hours slog
Barrow-running from the goods van sacks
Of sugar, each a hundredweight, your sweat
Curdling to treacle as you heave up stacks
Ten-high inside the brick shed, when we get
Our break it's ale we need to 'wash us snap
Down'. Fingering my dusty railway cap

I watch black bars irregularly drop
Fluttering the picture, down the TV-screen.
Frank has a kip; dominoes clack on non-stop;
Through wobbly false teeth Jack's jokes grow obscene.
Simo's not here since he fell down the cut.
Bert's fire-grate's bust, he asks, 'Remember this,
Young man?' – writes, *If the B mt put*
: *if the B*. 'Miss
Out on that now they've telly, kids.' I recall
Hours casting shadow silhouettes on the wall

From twined hands: cockerel, rabbit. Gaze at street
Outside, the people loitering; time outspread
Before me like those fields entranced by heat,
Lulling the churchyards of commingled dead
Angle and Dane, at Shearsby, Bruntingthorpe,
Marston Trussell, Willoughby Waterless . . .
Art hurls the wooden 'cheese', and through some warp
In the continuum of time and space

It bursts through skittles and the safety-net
Of thirty years, to hole the pub and hit

Me now, in Ireland. As I watch us drift
Denimed among Leicestershire redbrick gripped
In that far summer, to round off a shift.
The talk's of the far oasis, when ('I ripped
The Iron Cross off' . . . 'Best time of my life,
I had in Cairo' . . . Lootings, souvenirs . . .
'More sex that month than ever since from wife' . . .)
They'd fought for what proved all that their after-years
Never shook off: Launde, Countesthorpe, Mowsley, Croft,
Stonton Wyville, Tugby, Sibbertoft . . .

Note. 'Snap' is a common English East Midlands term for packed food consumed during a work-break. In the East Midlands a form of bar skittles is played wherein the skittles are felled by a heavy wooden object, from its shape called the 'cheese', thrown through the air. A safety-net behind the table prevents damage to the pub. The italicised word-puzzle, uttered aloud, comes out as: 'If the grate be empty put colon; if the grate be full, stop'.

Then and Now

But then the heart of loneliness was light.
An attic patient for the haul I brought
Back to sort beneath the lamp each night:

Office-talk; who's marrying; or been caught
Fiddling the petty cash; the rush and scent
Of girls; upon grey city roofs at dusk

The starlings' melancholy loud descent.
Gathered, like chestnuts rolled from the shed husk,
For my great novel, comic yet heartbreaking.

Till I grew beyond it. Relationships, career,
Things take you out of yourself. Nowadays waking
Alone's sole clouded luminary is fear,

Its skies a pallor as when after snow
Has fallen gives away the blanked terrain
All round. Of what has been and will remain

Untended. Time sifts down, obliterating
Glance and gesture; the live acrid glow
Of jazz once flickering from a Soho grating.

Soap

Steve's taken to the cleaner's by his wife;
Granny Grunge has a suspicious lump;
Round the King's Arms Shirl's warned big trouble's rife;
Dad's live-in girl friend gives young Keith the hump;
And Sandra's *gorra gerrout* of this dump,
She wants to *do things, live a bit, see life.*

No chance she'll vroom off in a heliotrope
Ferrari, make the Cabinet, or Peru;
Mums brat-beset at breakfast brightly cope
Only in ads, where she'd be married too,
And magic powders wash all our dreams true.
Their lot's off-white, week in week out. It's soap.

It shifts the worst stains. Keith won't slash his throat;
The old folk never piss themselves or drivel;
Fists rock pub regulars, but not the boat.
Blacks, gays? Fine, if they come up smiling, civil.
World within world! all problems but no evil.
Poets and murderers reach for the remote.

The range pretended to is given back
Squashed. What they play is never chess or Brahms;
Granny Grunge fights off the cells' attack;
God's social detail, nothing that alarms.
Planning an IRA bomb for the King's Arms
To clear the decks got scriptwriters the sack.

So Wayne and Duane go on both chasing Sharon.
The credits roll, *Devised by* . . . But who cares
Why Tracey slags off Stacey over Darren?
Rinsing off suds we turn to our affairs,
Unscheduled, past containments or repairs;
Gloriously unplottable. Not barren.

Postcards from Norfolk

1 BLAKENEY

Turning, the eye can hardly tease
  Out among all our path is banked to crest
The braided blue-green mutabilities
  Of land, creek, marsh, dune; yet finds rest
Strangely in flux, mud, saltings, rafts
  Of meadow with cattle ravelling;
    And far and wide
      The sailing crafts'
White wings; and fluttering
  Close-up a red admiral that
Rich with light is pirouetting at
  My side.

Thrilling through all, the ceaseless song
  Of high birds; casually punctuated by
Patterings as of a brief shower along
  The grasses as breeze stirs; and by
The time we rise, from open sea
  Flooding the channel comes the tide;
    Brimmed and linked
      Waters from quay
To causeways; and to ride
  At last our ebb to sleep, the slow
Tinklings of mast and halyard, music so
  Distinct.

2 RIVER ANT, TOWARDS HOW HILL

We take to a dawdling path along the margin,
On our other hand marsh sprinkled with wildflowers
And traversed by slow triangles of sail
Round the river's bend. My son stands motionless
As the heron he's recording in his notebook.
Here the impatient heart settles into place,
Like the great stilled windmills.
Nothing moves fast, no slope is difficult,
Languid under huge sky all night,
Ignorant of its salty destiny
Water laps our hull . . . A sudden shiver
Whitens that willow, like mortality.

3 LUDHAM, ST CATHERINE'S CHURCH, THE ROOD SCREEN

For those who gave to make what's here,
Intricate carved wood, tracery,
Pinnacled buttresses, *in the year*
Of ower Lord God MCCCCLXXXXIII,

The middle rail of folded leaf
Is inscribed: *Pray for the sowle*
Of John and Cycyly his wyf
And *alle other* . . . Centuries roll

Over what this hammerbeam
Roof sequesters. Civil fights,
Broad-brims with the zealot's dream
To beat out Popery's stained lights.

Still clear the colouring of those
Depicted on the rood screen's base:
St Edmund, St Walstan, St Ambrose –
And here St Appolonia's face,

Patron of dentists, with drawn tooth
In forceps . . . Perpendicular
Stonework clinches fossil truth
Outflanked by video, motor car.

Empanelled dead saints gather dust,
With faith in means whereby they bless;
Yet swell me to what feels like trust,
Winging unsure of its address.

Anne Frank's House

It is easily overlooked, one in a row
Of narrow elegant houses along a canal;
So we walked past it, as thirty years ago
        Der Militar at nightfall.

But we, sure of what we were looking for,
Asked and retraced our path, so came to stop
As millions now do annually at that door
        Where you hid, off the map.

We paid, climbed narrow stairs, and filtered round
The revolving bookcase, your 'Secret Annexe'. So,
Here you ate, studied, tiptoeing so no sound
        Reached the warehouse below.

Pinned still upon a wall is your 'film-star
Collection'. Valentino, Garbo, smiles
Frozen in time. Like yours on the brochure.
        And your *Diary* tells

How at night your fingers pulled aside
The curtain, past reflections on the pane
You peered into darkness: air-raids, people dead,
        More Jews crammed in the train

Of no return. *One can't get them out of one's mind.*
Yet, *We still have our jokes, and tease each other.*
You, the Van Daans, pompous Dussel, your kind
        Father, prim sister and mother.

Careful. Pencil markings here record
Your growing. For a while. Wherein you muse
Of *when the war is over*. Your heart soared
        To catch joy as it flies.

Then it was over. Abruptly you recede
Into lost millions. How does the spirit gloss
Belsen? *Who but myself will ever read*
        These letters? Anne, your voice

Speaks in all the world's tongues today. Your war
Is never over. In Bosnia, Ireland, though
Again betrayed your words refute all mere
        Power to destroy.

And in each of us is a secret annexe where
Something still part child shelters thus,
Soliloquising, in retreat from what out there
        Has gone dark and dangerous.

The difference is, for you the metaphor
Took literal shape, was claustrophobic too
With others' bickerings; and that you had nowhere
        Else at all to go

But death. So forcing in you that astounding
Maturity, growth to which your diaries give
Us clear-eyed; that had (here's what is so heart-rending)
        No adult life to live.

The Institution

He entered into the spirit of the project;
Served on the first committees, that established
A framework for promoting truth, the object.
        He was an idealist.

There'd be some power-corrupted, others hanging
Onto their forelocks for dear life, he realised;
And muddle's nets to check what we'd send winging.
    He was a realist.

The cat sat on the mat. The Council ruled
It was a dog on a log. There was some protest.
Many who saw differently were killed.
    He was an idealist:

'For Christ's sake, all we promised . . .' He implored.
'I'm not Christ,' said the Captain, unabashed,
'I cut my cloth . . .' He fled the whirling sword –
    He was a realist.

Quinquennial Plans, Personnel Development Schemes,
Bribes, marriage deals – the barbarians are vanquished.
Brilliant towers supplant forgotten dreams.
    He is an idealist.

From mountain caves with other exiles raiding
Wrecked libraries, condemned as terrorist
By those whose tumult is his safest hiding,
    He is a realist.

For Pete's Sake

See him. He's a bluffer. For Pete's sake,
That grimed black dented lump of a thing he drives,
Swilling red wine – godfearing motorists make
For the gutter, veer down turns, scared for their lives.

Pete's field was astrophysics, till he took
Up litigation, for a laugh. He mastered,
And set up judging, all crimes in the book,
Most punitive when manifestly plastered.

'Nil carborundum illegitimi'
He crows, grinding the bastards – me and you.
No earthly mandate for his tyranny,
Just signs and wonders, tricks out of the blue.

We try debate, try pleading, not a word
Comes back – just carnage, heartbreak, wars, disease.
It's no go Einstein, or a trip to Lourdes,
He'll still cut off your balls for his deep freeze.

He's toying with us, winds us up, may wind
Us up the other way as a mistake
He's bored with. Playing God. Out of his mind.
Or ours, whose need dreams him up, for Pete's sake.

At a Hospice

'When we met he'd just one month to live.
He thanked me for telling him. I could relieve
The pain. We were never alone, met in the ward.
Kissed once. Regrets? No, not a single word.'
A sort of luck – that, spared life's disrepair
Of all it piles on, love was breathed only pure.

Might Have Been

Your showpiece garden: sweeps of blossom, flowing
Brook, beguiling vistas. I try scents
You name, and call them lovely – and you, knowing
Me ignorant, think it indifference.

But in my heart from childhood still there burn
Dense purple spikes of lost delphinium;
Vermilion clumps of clustered phlox return
Fragrance like love's pulse to strike me dumb.

And when talk of human gifts and scope prompts thought
Of all within me left uncultivated,
It forms to vivid blooms, wraiths not of what
Took place, but things untended. Or unfated.

In Memoriam Dermot Nolan

1913–1992

Midnight, more falls of rain on deluged ground
Ambush my thoughts with the image of that place
Where you lie cold, the branches' whip and sigh
Comes desolately to me as its trees' sound.
I never called you father to your face,
Father. Adopted at six days old, I
Was forty when we met, your hand thrust in
My own was my first clasp from any kin.

Ex-military, tidy about your flat,
Your boisterous laugh and balding head were mine;
Buoyant you gripped the car-wheel, shirtsleeves rolled;
Leapt from a summer bank we picnicked at
To cleave the Thames. Till round your slow decline
Horizons shrank. Room, corridor, your old
Friends dead, 'must be put up with'. In that plot
Of earth stiff at your sides now void hands rot.

I stood dark-suited in the Abbey where
Candles flickered, tinkling censers swung.
Some of the mourners knew me, from your club;
Others learned with surprise why I was there.
I listened to talk of you when you were young,
Escapades, inventions. At the hub
Of ravelling grave ceremonial,
I watched you sunk as rain began to fall.

Hours sorting papers, photos, medals, books –
You'd willed me everything, unguessed by me.
Emptying your wallet felt almost a theft.
Now views you knew hang from my picture hooks –
Your College, Burma. You'd be glad to see
My son with the binoculars you left.
Your grandchild, Dermot. Still the drenched boughs sob;
But new by sodden roots fresh snowdrops bob.

Shore Lines

'Follow the inner shore-line round the bend,'
  The social worker says, her term denoting
The wall-side of the pavement. I attend
  To 'outdoor mobility' instruction, noting
  That 'slipway' here is a far cry from boating,
Just driveways from house garages. To gaze
  Around me rather makes me feel I'm floating
Far out among suburbs hulking through a haze
I know will never clear through my remaining days.

Coming to in the ward I couldn't see
  Anything, left eye blind for years, a pad
Strapped to the other after surgery.
  I gulped the sweetest tea I've ever had,
  The nurse just voice and guiding arm. When clad
For discharge two days later, 'It's been a novel
  Experience,' I told Sister. 'Not that bad
Surely?' she bridled – hearing it as 'an awful'.
I've to relearn how to live, work, relate to people, travel.

Don't vacuum, carry shopping, wash your hair
  Read the instructions. However, I must feed
Myself, bath, keep at least indoors tidy. So
  I negotiate days slowed to tortoise speed
  Mocked by shelves of books I cannot read,
The only social highlights pub and shopping.
  Teach literature again? My hopes recede.

Dumped in a chair, dawdling the kitchen mopping,
All I can be sure of is this never stopping.

Lying in bed, when I've switched off the light.
  I tune to the Shipping Forecast's poetry:
Dogger . . . Fisher . . . Rockall . . . German Bight . . .
  Trafalgar . . . Malin . . . Visibility
  Poor with mist patches. A long litany
Conjuring, as more rain falls, evocations
  Of little vessels tossed far out at sea.
Then follow *the reports from coastal stations,*
Boomer . . . Dover . . . Mumbles . . . My imagination's

Jumped point-to-point round bays and promontories
  Of our whole shore-line, varying sweeps of sand,
Castle-topped headlands harbouring ancient stories . . .
  Weather reports for inshore waters – and
  Hearing *from Cromer to Dungeness*, I stand
With my son last spring on that eroding cliff,
  The path from Cromer round to Overstrand.
I vow, although all future scares me stiff,
We'll walk that way again, a case of when, not if.

Meanwhile I am hard-pressed to walk the street:
  The town is thronged, the entrance to each store
A social venue where all and sundry meet,
  Hold seminars on the October weather or
  Prices. While it seems I need shinpads for
Protection against kamikaze pushchairs flying
  Towards me. Home, bags unpacked on the floor,
I find the tomatoes I'd thought I was buying
Are onions – they'll serve just as well for breakfast frying.

I'll never take up golf or drive a car;
  The Old Masters are out; so far as I can see
I may no more look for romance than find a star.
  'Perhaps,' I joke, 'I'm qualified to be
  A cricket umpire, football referee.'
I'm told of various retraining courses
  By someone sent from the RNIB,
Closed-circuit TV to read by, other resources.
I sign on, ready for the jumps as any horse is.

While footbound I dodge each day's permutation
  Of scaffold-poles, dug-up paving, heaps of sand,
Concrete troughs of civic vegetation,
  Pavement-parked cars, skips jutting head-high, and
  Vans' side-mirrors. Confident I'd scanned
My familiar home streets tonight, I walked
  Thwack into something soft my clutching hand
Held from falling over as it squawked:
A dark-coated little old dear. 'I'm sorry.' Smiles; we talked.

Fastnet . . . Humber . . . Thames . . . Wight . . . Finisterre . . .
  Disease and disability are like
I've heard, a foreign country. Exiled there,
  I whisper to a cassette recorder mike
  Memories of my native land that spike
All new resolve: landscapes I used to know,
  Where I played tennis, learned to ride a bike,
The country called health, where I can never go.
Malin Head, falling slowly . . . Tiree, continuing snow.

And all night it's the sea, successive dreams
  In which its deepest blues have flooded back.
The cretinous subconscious, bent it seems
  On plundering colour with kleptomaniac
  Avidity, denies I've lost the knack,
Must wake to a drained field of blanks and blotch,
  Each day a misty day . . . However black
The outlook, two things this can never botch:
The music of Beethoven and the taste of a good Scotch.

As always, others are worse off than me:
  Children sightless from traffic accidents,
Or programmed to this by heredity;
  Casualties from our Ulster violence;
  The suicide-attempt who aimed askance,
Condemned to darkened life. Black, brown or pink,
  It's blind to that, wealth, or intelligence –
Like Cupid, as old Greeks supposed. Or drink.
We tread like fogbound walkers, ignorant to the brink.

I'm practising the keyboard skills I'll need,
  No more the old three-finger look-and-poke.
Instead of print exercises I can't read
  I use radio: *Soundtrack, Down Your Way* from Stoke.
  A cookery slot expounds the artichoke.
The social worker thinks I'll pull through fine.
  Thinking of mad Swift gesturing at an oak
Blasted by lightning, I type *Heseltine*
Looks stronger on first ballot, must Thatcher now resign?

She wears checks and bright colours to help clients
  See where she is; discourses on her store
Of gadgetry devised by useful science:
  Bleepers to fit a cup so you don't pour
  Your tea to overbrim on clothes and floor,
Dictaphones, magnifiers, clocks you feel;
  I could hold the whole world in my hands once more
With a Braille globe, or learn to cook a meal
By touch. Aids which confirm a fate they cannot heal.

I've flown the Irish Sea, am in a train
  Jinking across Lincolnshire to my son . . .
We stroll round the cathedral, once again
  Ascend the castle walls; I even run
  For a bus. And his concern for me is fun
As well as touching: he finds things in a shop,
  Now reads me bedtime *William* stories. Un-
derneath all which, he's weighed me up, post-op:
'I think you're managing, Dad. At least your jokes don't stop.'

'If it were only carrots that Kuwait
  Produced, not oil, the West would let Iraq
Stay put,' I argue. Faces remonstrate,
  Blurred gold as I knock the next whiskey back.
  Waking painfully from another black-
out, I wonder how on earth my feet
  Walked me home, finger a bloodied crack
On my forehead, must have fallen in the street.
Right, just Beethoven. My hands are jittering as I eat.

Touch skills now incorporate the top row,
   Numbers, tapping out changes of address
With postcodes soon gets tedious, and so
   Instead I devise what surely must, I guess,
   Be the first ever practical use for chess:
e4 c5; Nf3 d6; d4 . . .
   I play myself blindfold till the wilderness
Of variations halts me at its shore . . .
The news: *Saddam defiant as the Allies gear for war.*

I've taken down my Christmas cards today.
   The count of paces from which as I stroll
To the University I make out that GIVE WAY
   Sign's up – a trick of light. In bed I scroll
   Through last week's English holiday, on parole
From fear, guilt, doubt: the game for me, theatric-
   ally cheering as my son described each goal
Was spot the ball. But our star scored a hat-trick.
Inshore waters . . . Calm . . . from Holyhead to Portpatrick.

Calling, she wields a saw. 'Is that to chop
   Up clients?' No, to shorten a white stick
For a lady she's en route to. 'Can you stop
   For coffee?' 'Yes.' She suddenly leans to pick
   Fluff from my shirt. I'm moved. Impolitic,
She questions my gaze . . . By now each knows the score,
   We fence, then shy love gushes from the quick,
Clasping us to each other on the floor,
Tender, salt, dangerous. As the Gulf slides to war.

Through TV it woos millions, provided
   With armchair spectacles as fireworks pluck
Out evil, and our 'smart bombs', laser-guided,
   Follow along a street, turn corners, duck
   To doff at chosen doors what blows to fuck
Flesh scraped to burial next day in Baghdad.
   'Collateral damage' screens as pure ill-luck
A blown-up school, while back here Mum and Dad
Are told 'friendly fire' means John's mid-air death's not so bad.

White canes, dogs, ghetto-jokes about meals and bruises –
   Among others on this course who've not the choice
I've magnification software. What they use is
   Perfect Percy, a synthetic voice
   That would make Tennyson sound like James Joyce.
Killing the Gulf, high-tech's benign to me:
   Word processing, scanners, printers, audio-toys . . .
Our tanks entomb the dug-in enemy,
Oil wells flame, vast spillage clogs wildlife in dead sea.

I parch for colours that when I was a child
   My paintbox held, vermilion, cobalt blue,
Ochre and purples, as I wait in mild
   Weather past GIVE WAY, the river view
   Spread bleached beneath me. Flickering anew,
As ever, buds on last year's lopped limbs. Craving for
   The primary virtues, beautiful, good, true,
I take the coast bus, stroll along the shore . . .
Land's End to Cape Wrath, fog . . . Still so much to explore.

*

More springs have passed since I talked all that unsorted
   Into a dictaphone, pressing RECORD
Among strange freaks of what seemed then aborted
   Rest-of-life. In vain I sift the hoard
   For pattern – except, there sounds our primal chord:
Go on . . . My son beside me now I crest
   Sea-crumbled Cromer cliffs, knowing restored
What George Herbert trusted in, whatever test
Lies always round the bend: 'the gladness of the best'.

Thickheads

Through millions of years these things evolved
To do what then through millions more
They did as if they'd got life solved:

Natural selection meant what they did best
On the Cretaceous forest floor,
When not pausing for a rest,

Or sex, or to chomp dreary vegetation,
Was head-bang each other on the hop.
Generation on generation

Woke daily to more bouts of knockabout.
Pointless, but they couldn't stop.
Till naturally they died out.

We reckon a career like that would bore us:
I can't face up to that again . . .
Micropachycephalosaurus

We've named them. Fancy title. All that's found
Is thick skulls with scant room for brain
For aeons fossilised underground.

Now academics who can't read or write
Make great literature their terrain
For wielding dense texts in doomed fight.

The Self-Seeing

Blessings emblazoned that day,
Everything glowed with a gleam;
Yet we were looking away.
Thomas Hardy, 'The Self-Unseeing'

What we walked into didn't just begin
When we reached, beyond the edge of town, the windmill, white
Sails motionless; already among the cobbled tight-
packed streets, half-timbered houses painted in

Lime and ginger dozing in the light,
Hollyhocked, something within us was burnished. Leisurely
The incline elevated us to sight of sea
On both sides of the island. At the height

Of the 'Ærø Alps' – as they term seventy
Metres – we ate our picnic, near the standing stone
Commemorating the union under the Danish crown
Of these long grasses, place-names suffixed 'by'.

At Tranderup we checked the map, turned down
Towards the coast. Occasional white farms, thatched or tiled,
Embraced three sides of courts where bales of hay were piled;
Lanes looped round unreaped ryefields rippling brown.

Opening another cola you said, my child,
'I think this is the happiest day of my life.' The thing
Most miss is knowing it while it's still happening –
Not just in hindsight, maybe then beguiled

By tricks of the mind's lens that time's gulfs bring.
Along the strand I watched calm sunlit waters sway:
The Baltic. I just replied, 'It's not yet late in the day.'
So far from home, feeling a homecoming.

How Protestant Ulster Won the World Cup

We faced the whole menagerie, a mix
Of Papists, atheists, other heretics.
The Poles? Chopped. Dutch? Ditched. Cameroons? No hope,
Them darkies couldn't knock snow off a rope.
We played as in the bygone days of yore –
It wasn't sweepers or a flat back four
Won King Billy glory at the Boyne,
But thranness, strike-rate, crunching skull and groin.
Brazil in the quarter-final tried all tricks,
Backheels, swerves, dummies, one-twos, bicycle-kicks;
They'd not last one late night in Newtownards.
The ref was sprouting red and yellow cards.
Bookings, was it? – wee Sam fetched him a skelp
With the Good Book, you should have heard him yelp.
'No artistry, technique, footballing ideals,'
Carped critics, 'No coach, bar that wreck on wheels!'
Aye, we've no truck with such idolatries,
Newfangled texts, quare diets, shrinks, spin-off fees.
Fired up on the Ulster Fries we love,
The only sponsor we need's Him Above.
The semis was Germany. See Fritz's running
Off the ball, us in pursuit! He's cunning:
Dives in the box, greetins and girnins, till
He'd conned a spot-kick, stroked it home: 1-0.
We upped our game. Now they weren't shamming dead.
Their goalie picked up, looked to throw – instead
Was hit by Billy going like a train
Clean through the net, we're back on terms again.
Penalty shoot-out. We'd trained using live
Rounds in the Mournes, no way Fritz could survive.
As the smoke cleared, a staunch voice sounded from
The stand, 'Next time we'll replay at the Somme!'
Again the Press was scunnered, talked of riot.
Face facts – we'd left the ground destroyed with quiet.
The media boys were cracking up, the Pope
Redd out the Vatican for a hank of rope.
Our team, in orange sashes, brave and broad,
Lined up to put the Spaniards to the sword.
The rest is history. Our names resound
From Strabane to Strangford, Erne to Rathlin Sound.

Them dancers pushed the ball round smooth as silk.
Big Willie John turns slower than the milk,
Ach, he's a hallion, but. Wired to the moon.
That's why he's picked. The Dons soon changed their tune,
Saw he'd not give an inch. He dug a trench
(That started up some gulderin from their bench).
See Jim's Jack Russell, Hughie's Kerry Blue,
They'd not be bluffing, took a limb or two.
They slabbered to their saints to save their souls
While we collected a brave wheen o' goals.
We buried the Fenians, then the referee.
And lifted the World Cup in victory:
'Yousuns get back to your fancy hacienda –
What we have we hold, and no surrender!'

He raised it high again, swigged, jack-knifed, boked.
The barman said, 'The eejit's went and choked.'
The great Ref in the sky had blown Offside;
His fantasy exploded as he died.
Yet through Infernal smoke he made out more
Who'd got the worlds they'd once been asking for:
Midas deranged by gold he couldn't spend,
Stalin patrolling gulags without end;
Romeo cursed with Juliet at his throat;
Academics doomed to read the stuff they wrote.
For him, a rain-swept divot, and the thrum
Of bigoted sermonising, Lambeg drum;
Great gales stentorian with ancient malice;
Still dead-weight on his lap the poisoned chalice.

Towards the Light

i.m. Olive Waterman 29 June 1900–4 June 1994

I am told, 'You belong to darkness.'
Perhaps, perhaps, but I walk toward the light.
Pablo Neruda

I was an airflight away –
On the phone they'd said you'd seemed better, drunk tea –
When my sister cradled your head as your breathing
And pulse expired. 'Mum,' she said,
'You didn't make it for the Mozart Players.'
And the matron replied,
'She's with Mozart now.'

Not in your book, you weren't.
Born with the century, one of the last
Victorians, 'ordinary Smiths' moving
In search of greenness, fresh air, light,
Down the Great Eastern Railway line:
Bethnal Green, Cambridge Heath,
London Fields, Hackney Downs,

The names 'a cruel joke'.
For that crowded, gaslit, horsedrawn world
Where the many toiled for a pittance, the few –
Well, you'd recall them, waggling derisive
Cigars at your Mayday parades from affluent
(Doomed, as you thought)
Clubland balconies;

Or how, when one lay ill,
The streets were hushed with straw so that
The ailing plutocrat's repose
Might not be troubled by the traffic
Of ordinary folk. Your gospel
Was socialism in
Its unsullied dawn.

Uncle George inspired you,
Seeker after truth, and lover
Of Dickens, shelterer of roaming
International Workers of the World –
The 'Wobblies'. Out there at Enfield
George also grew
Fine strawberries,

And when, desirous to purchase
With compliments and a fancy basket
The lady came, you waited giggling:
'You people think you can buy *anything* . . .'
She received a sermon on Property as Theft –
And the fruits of Uncle
George's patch free.

Staying there at weekends,
You were woken at five o'clock: 'Are you coming?'
George, with wirecutters. You followed
Rejoicing in their voluptuous snip
Along the public paths of Cuffley,
Keeping a bit
Of England free.

Wearing your Sunday School badge
You told friends in sepulchral tones
Without a blush that its IBRA
(In fact *International Bible Readers' Association*) meant *International*
Brotherhood of
Real Anarchists.

Those passionate meetings, discussions!
Hardie speaking in Trafalgar Square,
Socials at the William Morris Centre,
Larkin's Irish strike, suffragette marches . . .
At political street meetings your role
Was reciting the poems
Of Blake and Shelley.

Drawing a crowd around
(Unthinkable in our electioneering
Today), before making way on the soapbox
For the candidate's plea for a Just Society . . .
'Be good,' they warned, 'or the Kaiser will get you!' –
His moustaches bristled
From newspaper photographs.

And when, in his war, believers
Refusing to slaughter their comrades, hid out
In Epping Forest, you brought them food;
At the party organised for them whirled
Them from arm to arm to the sound of music
Till raiding police
Joined in the dance.

The huge airship enveloped
In searchlights passed above your house northward;
You saw it burst into flames, as fiery
Pieces floated to those fields round Cuffley
And the guns stopped, there was long silence;
You stood in the garden
In a ghost world.

And across the blacked-out valley
At first a scatter of voices singing,
My home in Tennessee, That's where I long to be,
Till the whole suburb was rocking with sound,
And you turned indoors, and thought of the German
Aviators burning
To death in the sky.

Uncle George was killed by the war.
Not in it. By it. 'Never the same'
After the air raid when fetching back tea
For the clippie who sought shelter from
Her abandoned bus met the blast. 'I put her
There,' he'd repeat,
'I put her there.'

Mother, the light you sought
Also meant music, the theatre, poetry.
Talented at the piano, on leaving
School you were told this pointed to
A promising career as a typist,
And sent to work
In a City office.

But acting was liberation,
Toller's *Masses and Man, Singing Jailbirds*
By Upton Sinclair. When, in the office
Of his Globe Theatre Leon M. Lion
Offered professional terms, you declined –
To stay free to perform
'Plays that meant something'.

And working for Gerald Gould,
Poet, critic, editor, socialist
(Though the sea-green carpet in the tall house
That 'looked poured, not laid' abruptly stopped
At the stairs up to the servants' attic),
The light for a while
Seemed within reach.

But then came a second war,
Your life took a different story, adopting
Me as the London pavements shook
From the guns at Dunkirk, and the world became
A different theatre, the old scripts,
Hardie, Shaw, Blatchford,
Forgotten irrelevance.

And where, on motorised highways,
Are the Clarion Cycling Clubs now? There are still
Great actors, musicians, poets; but most
You'd hoped would seek them prefer the *Sun*,
Sleaze, soaps, soccer – only the last
Of which (you supported
Spurs) you could cherish.

In the wider world still darkness,
The Soviet Union, whose birth seemed
A dawn, lies a dismembered ogre;
And names familiar to your childhood
As cockpits of strife, Bosnia, Serbia,
Are back on the map
As that again now.

But the roundabout doesn't merely
Come round again. You lived to see
Nelson Mandela walk from the darkness
Of prison into the light of the Presidency . . .
Fearful things wouldn't shape well, 'Some hope!'
You'd shruggingly say.
Yes, mother: some hope.

And you never gave up. In recent
Years, a regretful agnostic still playing
Piano at services in your Sheltered
Housing, hearing the vicar exhort
Gratitude for a just society
You took him aside
And sermonised thus:

'You ought not to talk like that.
These people are old, they are very gullible.'
Mother, you were the oldest present!
At ninety you spoke of a 'final ambition –
To see Thatcher out of Downing Street'.
The day she resigned
I phoned: 'So what next?'

And always the actual light
And landscapes beneath it. I see you
Here in Ireland on that Antrim cliff-path,
Eagerly naming the wildflowers that
You hadn't 'seen in the Home Counties
Since way back
Before the Great War'.

In the CWS morgue
(Still true to the Co-op) when they drew
The curtain, I meant to affirm what you doubted:
Your life's meaning, diffusive and sure
As falling rain. But your corpse lay
Pale, cold, a waxwork
That wasn't a waxwork.

I hear you on your beloved
Brahms: 'So truthful and brave. In old age
Still at concerts I close my eyes,
And listen, and the music floods me,
I give myself, and feel I've come home.'
Gently I touch
Closed lids in the coffin.

I almost forgot: your gymnastics.
Not in recent years, toting that zimmerframe,
But all those medals won years ago!
And, as you meet whatever it is
We all must surmount at last, I picture you
Vaulting it, looking
Back with a smile.

Freeze that image! But no,
Apt enough for an uplift ending
It is swallowed in the flood of things
Going on, like a sentimental trinket.
I catch myself, as news comes in
Of this or that
In politics,

Or spotting a concert on telly,
Reaching for the phone to tell you,
'What do you think of . . . ?' – 'Don't miss this . . . '
The dialling-tone sings into my ear
Like ripples of eternity . . .
That's all for now.
I'll talk to you again.

The End of the Pier Show

THE LAST RESORT

When I sauntered along here the beach was emptied,
The roundabouts stilled, the lightless helter-skelter
Defrocked of shrills and skirls. Just one last boy
Running in vain to lift his flagging kite

From sand where a billion bubbles broke each instant
In the lacy fringe of an idling tide dissolving
Abandoned ramparts and keeps. It was the hour
When you were all back in your guesthouses and hotels,

Caravans and bars, or the crab restaurants.
And past the pier, low-slung by the cliff the sun
Stood on the sea a great red ball, so beautiful
I turned back for my camera . . . Only by then

It wasn't the same. Well, isn't that always the way?
And a shiver in the wind, but that might be rain . . .
Still, lovely to see so many of you have made it,
Especially the kiddies. This is a family show,

And it's warm in here, balanced above the heartstopping
Swirl underneath. A bit of a last resort?
Lady, d'you think I chose it myself? But nothing
Beats a good laugh. Don't laugh, you'll bring down the house.

BYGONES

The microwaves are pinging in
The sidelanes where our mothers'
Greasy fingers plucked forth chips
From newsprint, while their brothers'
Pennies conjured saucy scenes
From *What the Butler Saw* machines.

Postwar Paradise, they'd cleaned
The barbed-wire off the beaches;
Trawling shoals of seafront girls,

Permed, pencil-skirted peaches.
Golden lads and girls all must
Like Punch and Judy bite the dust.

Swept from the pier the Gypsy Seer,
The Crazy Mirrors Hall
Where Brenda burgeoned to blancmange
And Little Tich walked tall.
In Funland's din a high-tech toy
Chirrups Beethoven's *Ode to Joy*.

Skins then velvet to the touch,
Lips fluttering back when kissed,
Have long worn others to the bone,
But what you've had's not missed.
The show goes on, the lost heart eats a
Machine-tooled burger, plastic pizza.

SOMETHING FOR EVERYONE

Lifers on parole we deck ourselves
In primary colours, lapse to cleansing play;
Radios natter on hot sand that shelves
To ocean spread like harpstrings in the sun;
A cliff path dawdles round to the next bay.
Nothing so right, something for everyone.

Some bob in white at tennis, others steer
Gokarts hurtling round a tarmac *8*;
Boat-trips, teashops, anglers on the pier;
A straggle on the stepped path up the East Hill
To the Smugglers' Caves. Some just contemplate
The goings-on, for once free to stand still.

From a beach kick-around, shirts for goals, the ball
Soars gloriously into a trajectory
That could clear the planet. Children call
Excitedly finding crabs, seeing the boat
Pirouetting. As we do, nonchalantly
By something in the ambience kept afloat,

As by a membrane beyond our discerning
Insects stroll water surfaces at will.
Here at the crazy golf we gauge the turning
Of a miniature windmill's sails that block or free
Path to the hole, knowing it's faith, not skill,
Freaks us through, and on to victory.

A pointless game? Not quite. Of course that ball's
Dropped back to earth for kicking round in vain
Quest for perfection. A toddler's ice-cream falls
Splat on the pavement, and his sobbing rends
Our fragile harmonies – nothing can explain
Things will come right, the world will make amends,

Until the replacement is in his hands; and he
Must learn the further lesson as he grows:
Some things gone wrong have no such remedy.
Yet he'll come back, cliff-walking, bathing, fishing,
Drawn by the place's gift of, we suppose,
Immersion in a mutual well-wishing.

ROUGE ET NOIR

  The music starts, bring on the girls,
With tutus, laundered smiles, leg-kickings, twirls
In synchronised formation, just for you,
  The punters. Taut flesh out of reach
And lovelier than any on the beach.
None of this thrusting groin and breast seems crude
  Transfigured under lights into
  Family fare, an anodyne
    Signalling that life's fine:
You clap and clap in candid gratitude.

  Offstage, she drifts anonymous
Through supermarkets, hesitates from a bus
Between the pub and the swarmed-over sand,
  Indifferent. Inside her head
The awakenings: again a stranger's bed,

Their touching flesh, the glare of a new day,
  As to her cheek he reached a hand
  Her eyes stampeding to blank wall;
    And her mother's words from all
The spent years, *Child, don't wish your youth away.*

DOUBLE TROUBLE

As I walked on the beach this morning the voice
Arrested me, spinning me round.

'It is you!' he said. Lap lap lap went the waves.
Of course I remembered the face, from shaving mirrors,
In the Underground reflected across
The carriage brooding beneath thick hair, those eyes
Now bitter to find me bitter here
Between the dunes and the fluctuating breakers.
So I waited for what he must say, a drift
Of sand creeping over the distance between us.

'You have betrayed me, are what
I vowed never to be, why do you come,
Intruder in my perfect vista?'

'Because it was I was betrayed by you,
Here, or somewhere like here.
Your ideals still spin in my hurt head.'

Divorcé, wage slave, clown,
You should never have been born.'

'You fathered me.'

Or was it this place, or others like it,
Generating hunger for distant brightness
That sears like betrayal now?

'Your worst sin against me is unhappiness.'

'Yours, thinking it only lasting for others.'

So I faced his intolerant virgin stare,
Till a sudden misting parted us – his cry
Inviolable to my stumbling forgiveness.

STATE OF THE NATION

In the very posh School on the headland where they wear
Different ties for Full Colours, Half Colours, Prefects
(Senior and Junior), House, and each year the Combined
Cadet Corps marches to honour the Tudor Founder
Behind the Corps of Drums playing 'Men of Harlech'
And 'Sweet Polly Oliver', now in the chemistry classroom
Dr Dabby is demonstrating. He's Persian,
'Rub-a-dub-dub,' he utters, and 'Hubble-de-bubble,'
According to him talking English, the boys all giggle,
'Abracadabra' – the whole bloody place explodes.
      'We are sorry to lose Dr Dabby,'
Says the Headmaster at end of term assembly.
'We sing now, as always, *"Schola quam amamus"*.'

In the very Grand Clifftop Hotel old Spavin is tickling
The ivories, much as he has for a million years
Since the good old Edwardian days when top-hats and tiaras
Rolled up in carriages, talking of golf, horses, angling.
Now over Chili con Carne and Breaded Scampi,
It's 'globalisation' and 'accessing information',
They think they are talking English, none being aware,
As Spavin forsakes 'Tea for Two' for 'Ain't Misbehavin'',
That Hitchcock upstairs is accessing his PA's bed,
In he plunges – the whole bloody place drops into the sea.
      'We are sorry to lose the Grand Clifftop,'
Says the Mayor, 'But that's how things go with coastal erosion.'
The piano washes ashore at the Muppets' Paddling Pool.

In the very High Court Sir John (Mr Justice) Lately
Is flouting a welfare report by preventing a father
From seeing his son, the mother not wishing such 'contact'.
Not that he gives a bugger, red-carpeted round the circuit,
On huge pay and holidays, it's hardly surprising
His own kids don't see him, and after Court it's not homeward

He toddles, but off to the Club for a nap and a bottle.
In front of him now, one Counsel's asserting, 'It's chalk,'
The other, 'It's cheese,' he savours this till, 'Just look
In the bloody fridge and find out!' – and the dad shoots him dead.
    'We are sorry to lose the old judge,'
Say women he thought fit for nothings but minding the children,
And the one in the brothel who flogged him dressed as a schoolgirl.

On this very old Pier you can fish and eat candy-floss,
Riding the bumper-cars target the girl with huge knockers,
Go boss-eyed at the wheel of road racing simulator
Machines in Funland, or hanging your face through effigies'
Head-holes be photographed as a clown or gorilla;
Or sit writing postcards over your coffee, or saunter
The boards to the end, where our lifeboat is housed – touch it.
Then come to the show. Traditions that run through the town
Story like lettering through rock. Until the Big Storm
Hurls a barge – clean through the ramshackle bloody structure.
    'We are sorry to lose the old Pier,'
The Town Council say, 'But the cost of repair, we must move
With the times, sell it off.' For one pound, or the nearest bidder.

SAUSSURE AND LAWRENCE: IN THE OCEANVIEW LOUNGE

How dare you, sir, whoever you may be?
Though nothing you can say denotes reality.
I'm Bertie Lawrence, I got in my shout
Before you, the barman grasps what that's about.
Language is a matter of interrelations
Working through negative differentiations,
This furry creature on the stool is designated cat
Because the system dictates not dog, snake, bat.
    How dare you, sir, whoever he may be?
    Though nothing he can say denotes reality.

You should dip your toes, you bloodless linguistician,
Into the ocean of our human condition.
In the beginning was the Word,
It's the Book of Life. *Don't be absurd!*
Name-calling cannot touch me, if you believe

Words relate to objects you are merely naïve.
My dad was a miner, when he knocked his head
On a pit-prop 'I can't say it' wasn't what he said.
  He should dip his toe, the bloodless linguistician,
  Into the ocean of our human condition.

And if owt means nowt, you needn't duck or run
On being told this fist's about to dot you one,
Nor put up your own, so just sup your beer
And try differentiating cauliflower ear
From bloodied nose, I'm not so puddled with booze
That I cannot deconstruct you. *Pray excuse*
Me, I've suddenly recalled I've somewhere else to be.
That's seen him off. Now a swim in the sea.
  And if owt means nowt, he needn't duck or run
  On being told this fist's about to dot him one.

THE WHOLE THING

Like cloud-arms on the ocean
The gleaming headlands lie;
Full waters' slumbering motion
Glitters beneath wide sky,
And any sigh
Of air breathes as devotion.

At ease from indecision
A sprinkling of moored hulls,
And muted the derision
Of interweaving gulls,
Nothing annuls
Intactness of the vision.

Never known more purely
Than when encountered first,
Our birthright. Seen maturely
Later, the bubble's burst,
Something dispersed
That was, we sense obscurely,

Within us, not deriving
From seascape still as bright.
And only through reviving
Childhood we shrugged off might
Soul reignite
What irradiates mere surviving.

THE GOOD OLD DAYS

In the days of yore when the grass was greener,
And Britain ruled the waves and there'd never been a
　　Drugging or a mugging,
　　Nor a telephone-bugging,
Life was one long knees-up round a concertina.

Demob heroes of impeccable demeanour
Never lost at football to Brazil or Argentina;
　　A Brisbane sticky wicket
　　Was for Hutton just the ticket;
All was hunky-dory, and glory to the gleaner.

Sauntering pier and esplanade, pavilion or marina,
Arm-in-arm your blarney'd charm barmaid or ballerina,
　　Pre-Aids sex a box
　　Of multiflavoured chocs,
Winnowing willing women like a randy window-cleaner.

But as horizons rolled away the soul of things grew meaner,
You never got to heaven in a Ford Cortina:
　　It proved Cloud-Cuckooland,
　　Half vicious and half bland,
The rich got richer, the graffiti obscener.

As muzak silts the supermarket, mall and mezzanine a
Sense the ship is going down around you becomes keener,
　　The Royal Family crashes,
　　And we never win the Ashes –
No testosterone in the Test arena.

Biggles, Bambi, Mr Toad, Dick Barton, Thumbelina,
Are buried as King Arthur, now blood drips from the screen, a
        Thing from outer space is
        Melting human faces,
And Robin Hood rewritten rapes the village sweet-sixteener.

A fading blaze, the good old days, once lambent and serene, a
Memory-trick of brain or dick as blood gets cold, shanks leaner;
        The writing on the wall
        Speeds your dying fall
To generations long inert beneath where grass grows greener.

INTERVAL

Interval. The bar
Is open. Faces,
Hairdos and glasses,

And glasses filled
With light or dark
Slowly emptied.

Or take a turn
Outside, consider
The lit skein along

The shore, discrete boxes
Where they are saying
'I love you' or

'It's over' over
Laden tables,
Or talking football,

Arched by the stars'
Spindrift. The void.
Listen to it lapping

Beneath you, drop
A coin for luck
Through boards of the pier.

But there is the bell.
Buy some more popcorn;
The show goes on.

ALL AT SEA

Raised above the huddle of the town
It catches us on the turn, a grey tower jutting
As we look back over mudflats wondering
Why we are grown used to not attending,
Bent on our pursuits, gone for a song.

Set on its eminence with intent to crown
Our goings-on, it is enamoured of moonlight,
Awash among stars its freight
Of centuries: rood screen, tombs, the quiet
Dust of old yearnings, the conflict of wrong and right.

That ancient tumult of faith, the smashings-out
Of stained glass, whelming terror of a damnation
Flickering fire through faults in the hill's green,
The chiaroscuro of righteous passion,
Ebbed to a more worldly deformation,

Prosperous, well-dressed, with no self-doubt
Unhinging doors shut tight upon the soul,
What shall I do to be – respectable?
Its only cry, its moral rule
Immune to love or reason as its style

In bonnets. Practical Victorians, who put
The tower to use, employed it as a lighthouse
Sweeping illumination across dark waters
So mariners should navigate safe course.
Till a modern structure was built for the purpose.

Now, clambering the rocks about its foot,
Or cresting the Big Wheel's apogee,
When we notice it at all it is not what we
Have come for: 'Picturesque', we merely say;
But suddenly out of our depth, moved out to sea.

LOVE MAKES THE WORLD GO ROUND

You combed the beach, impetuous for
    The off – and backed a beauty
With all first love, keeping faith more
    From rapture than mere duty.

Alas, among dunes' treachery she
    Veered astray – bribes or dope?
Well, *Plenty more fish in the sea*
    You knew, still young in hope.

Next time out you put your shirt,
    Your house, on – sweet fuck all,
Lashing heels. You watched, deep-hurt,
    Folly's sandcastles fall.

A stayer: 'Often decked,' she says,
    'Still questing on for' – you.
Those others, husbands, hunks, quick lays,
    'All proved untrue.' Untrue? –

As her dud emotional cheque bounces over
    The moon, she's over the moon,
Her final words, 'May you discover
    Someone worthier soon.'

You weighed things. Played the field. You tried
    The thoroughbreds, goers, needy;
The promising proved to have lied,
    The spiritual turned greedy.

But what of other punters who
  Quit with the first race,
Claiming, 'There'll just be always you,'
  And that the answering face

Will equally none other love,
  Swearing they'll not be parted,
When being grown-up, Heavens above!
  Has scarcely yet got started,

Most of its entries not yet met?
  Plainly fucking insane!
As shadows lengthen, see them get
  Scrambled by boredom, pain.

Hubris! – vowing so young to give up
  Falling in love for ever,
Sip to the dregs one cooling cup . . .
  Time shows they've not been clever.

But you, as tides flood in, ebb out,
  Are left now high and drier;
Though annual fresh limbs splash about
  Setting your heart on fire.

Of those in your age-range most by now,
  If not too dire, are hitched
(Unless fouled-up with griping how
  They've been abused and ditched).

What hurts you most on her U-turn
  Back to her married station
Is that she lacks the guts to spurn
  Pride's raft of rationalisation:

Her mind there fragrant as a drain,
  Perspicuous as fudge,
Deliberative as a weather-vane,
  And honest as a judge.

So, given all they say about
   Flogging a dead horse,
Why is it you're still turning out,
   Intent yet on the course?

Ah, no more than dreams can be
   By glaciers erased
Can love's potentiality
   Be ravaged by love's waste

When once, far back, by fragile chance
   Of time and place ensnared,
You caught its virus: a voice; glance;
   That radiance of things shared.

GHOST TRAIN

Read me a story. *Once upon a time . . .*
Is it about a wolf or wicked witch?
Oh yes. Your favourites. Once upon a time . . .

Red Riding Hood came to the cottage, raised the latch,
Entered the cosy room. From the brass bed . . .
I know – big eyes, big ears . . . *But now we reach*

'Granny, what big teeth you have,' she said.
'The better to eat you with!' And with a leap . . .
Etcetera . . . So at last the wolf is dead.

Tell me another. Where the children tip
The witch in her gingerbread oven . . . *There you are,*
All's come right in the end. Now go to sleep . . .

It's different these days. *Less familiar,*
The shapes? The thing that's clumping in the attic?
The Mummy's Curse comes true – he won't flee far.

And look, stood on the dunes with a raised mattock . . .
It's thrilling, but my dreams . . . *And there's no getting*
Off. Being clever, brave or energetic

Cannot halt the skull-faced figure flitting
Through trees towards our hero, or assuage
Its venom . . . Till I put the book down, sweating . . .

All's changed again. *Yes, horror's left the page.*
It hangs like an infection in the air,
And in my heart. *Ah, now you've come of age.*

Famine wraiths. Dead babies. High-tech war.
No use to seek or hide from it. It calls
Wreathed in smiles – you're opening the door.

It's scattering its seed through wedding bells.
Tell me another . . . *Insidiously it kills;*
This is our colonist, our cancer cells . . .

Once you took ghost trains for their phantom thrills,
Jinking past shrieks and skulls, that flashlit ape
Harmlessly roaring, pleasurable chills,

Knowing the ticket returned you in good shape
Into sane light. But once upon a time . . .
You drew another, one way, no escape.

ON THE BEACH

Sand between your toes
Again, as you bend
All's there in a flash,
Spread golden before you

Banking to groyne after groyne,
The hush of waves lapsing,
Trance of cumulus,
All yours.

Behind you, the wooden steps
Down which you've escaped
The cliff-top games
(After winning the egg and spoon race),

The chalets sunning
Along flowerbedded paths.
Each breakfast the summons
O what a beautiful morning

From the Hall's loudspeakers
Beneath the galleon flag,
O what a beautiful day.
It is, it is . . .

Let them get on with the Dads'
Knobbly Knees Competition;
You are no age,
And do not know you are happy,

Crouched at the pool
Where a crab, at your touch,
Buries itself
In the pith of that day

When fleetness of childhood
Vraced feet you'd, as now,
Inch by inch rise from,
Year upon year.

STEPS IN TIME

The Roman skimmed stones on this sea,
  Guarding the Saxon Shore.
England wasn't England then,
  But war was bloody war.
The Empire crumpled in its tide;
  He left, and came no more.

The Normans built their castle high
  To dominate the port.
Sieges came and went. Some tongues
  Were torn out, limbs lopped short.
Still generations passed on charms
  To ripen corn, cure wart.

And fishd and fiddled, pastured herds,
  Mowed lea, played pitch and toss,
Their talk as local as their beer;
  What matter gain or loss
Abroad, to sins here shadowed by
  The Gibbet and the Cross?

The railways came. Then cars. Today
  The Visitors Centre Staff's
Run off its feet; kids smirk astride
  Dead cannons for photographs;
Though skimming stones, arcade machines,
  Beat Heritage junk for laughs.

SAUSSURE AND LAWRENCE: ON THE HELTER-SKELTER

I can't know what's out there, naming it helter-skelter
Means nothing at all about it, thinglessly
Words mean only because not other words
In a self-enclosed system working through negation.
What is it all about? What should I do?

Get out of that chair, off into the great unknown,
Pick up that what for convenience we'll name mat,
And mind the otherness of the steps as you climb.
Then launch yourself away into life's adventure,
Let me know what it feels like, tell me the truth.

But you don't understand. Consider the 8.25
Train from Geneva to Paris: the carriages change,
And the staff, it may not leave until 9, but remains
The 8.25 train, purely because of its place
In a timetable's structure. Likewise words in language.

But it got you to what we'll agree to call Paris.
How were its let's say women? Saussure, you told
All that before you died, if I may so call it,
In 1913 as I launched my book of life
Sons and Lovers. Now push off – or are you frit?

I, I letting go, whoosh and I plunge in chaos
In vortex tumbling now head over heels
Sea over sky whirling both under land
This void and nothing able to tell but words
How can I know what on earth is happening?

He's gone arse over tip, the mardy old loon . . .
You called 'Help!' – well, here I am, you spoke truly, are bruised.
Now come to my house, it is open to you, as language
Is to phenomena, as my poem welcomed
That snake 'Come a guest to drink at my water-trough'.

WE REALLY MUST GO

Disassemble the big dipper, shutter discos and arcades,
Pull a switch and watch the lights dim, listen as the music fades;

Drain the Dolphinarium, box the bandstands, little seafront train,
Fold the pitch-and-putt course up and store it safe from snow and rain;

Headlands, castle, are deflated, sandgrains vacuumed by the ton;
Finally we pull the plug beneath the sea, reel in the sun.

Yes, another season's over, time to pack and say goodbye.
Off you go, some fitter, others fatter, bathing snaps don't lie.

Cleansing swims and lobster dinners, scuba diving, cliff-face thrills,
Vulnerably you came asking simple cures to complex ills.

Love for many: moonlit romance; ties refreshed; that mega-fuck
Causing caravan meltdown. But for other seekers no such luck:

Kev's primeval chat-up gambit's left him reeling from a punch;
At the pier-rail his mate Colin's heaving up his liquid lunch.

Minor keys for major feelings. Bless you all, we do our best,
And next year, when we reopen, you'll return, renew the quest.

Things may not be what they once were, run down, tarted up, the most
Fanciable women jetting off to sun-drenched Spanish coast.

Contents captioned, two quid entry, see his oilskins, boots, pipes, bed,
Harold Blaggs's cottage, lifeboatman supreme, three decades dead.

Captain Flynn's Performing Ducks are still recalled by some old dear,
Also Professor Narwhal's blindfold cycle-dive clean off the pier.

Some of you, before next summer, will have fallen off the twig;
Annually in the Rat and Trumpet shoulders shrug between each swig:

'Poor old Woody, who'd have thought it?' 'He'd that fearsome cough, had
Tom.'
Eyeing a new generation's pushchairs storming down the Prom.

Theirs will be a world of shimmering screens, and no horizons set,
Crouched at keyboards surfing superhighways of the Internet.

Strayed from designer-slaughter movies, cyberspace and leisure-dromes,
Baffled they'll gawp at lacquering, dado, in leftover stately homes.

Once upon a time you heaved aside a massive stone and saw
Creatures scurrying hither, thither, wondered what it was all for;

That's the way we carry on, we haven't got a bloody clue,
Knowledge vaster, travel faster, ignorant why we are, or who.

Whiskered Victorian geologists tapping fossils from these rocks
Thought that *homo* finally was pulling up his sapient socks,

Cracking the code, deciphering the scheme of things entire: one more
Heave and reason would dispatch disease, crime, ignorance, slums, war;

For there'll always be an England: Prussian, Kaffir, Chinee, Turk,
Learning the rules, aspirant, would fall in with Progress's great work;

Playing the game. Like Admiral Wilson, umpiring the submarine's
Advent: 'Underhand, unfair, and damned un-English!' By all means

Laugh if you must, nobody else is. There's too much grief in this farce . . .
Yet the show goes on, each April posts fresh bills up, mows the grass,

Still our unforeseeing congregations stare into the flood
Cresting, breaking; drawn here purely by sweet habit of the blood.

Counting the Cost

Thousands of people gathered, their thousands of candles,
At the fiftieth anniversary of the night
The Florence of the Elbe was cindered to moonscape
Stashed with (some calculate) 40,000 corpses.

Today's Mayor of Dresden says, 'We did it first.'
So it was all right? But that's true too of Auschwitz . . .
The Duke of Kent represents us, with careful words
Confined to 'regrets', not saying 'sorry'.

Which 'would infuriate Bomber Command, who lost
55,000 of 120,000 aircrew'.
I've met them in Lincolnshire, old men, recollecting.
'The Nazis weren't beaten, we felt we were saving our groundtroops

Thousands of lives.' It is hard, computing morality . . .
In the cellar we found, I follow her through subtitles,
My family, the bodies burnt tiny. Just one
I could recognise, I remember crying, 'Aunt Ilse!'

February 1995

Death's Embassies

A stile. Wide light on slaking
  Greenness, silver thread
Of river, a deciduous slope. Heartbreaking
  Peacefulness outspread.

Thirty years ago. And no backtracking
  Could find what's leavened to
Pure image irradiating all that's lacking
  In things passed through.

Like others in me claiming
  Terrain, immunity
From temporal laws, demesnes we flinch from naming,
  This is death's embassy.

The flag proclaims though earthed in our condition
  They represent a power
Beyond it, colonising all cognition
  Each living hour.

New Poems 1995–1999

Obituaries

Reading obits, it's the year
These goners were born I check first;
1907 leaves clear
Space, I've still time for a burst;

But most now are '20s-ish dates,
Some too young to fight in the War;
My childhood's cricketing greats,
This poet, that air commodore.

As when you're stood on a beach,
The gradual tide coming in,
Knowing, though few waves reach
You yet, that your will can't win,

Until suddenly crash! and a shoeful
Sends shiverings through your blood.
1958! – rueful,
Rooted, I wait the flood.

Shop Talk

Anything going on below the bridge
I'd missed, but when I turned into the shop
Billy was saying, 'I passed him on the bridge,
Ten minutes before. He asked me for a light.'
'He wasn't sixty.' And June behind the counter
Intones, 'The Bann claims three lives every year.'
This one has jumped. Listening, I figure out
Who, strain for the features, yes, a quiet
Man over a pint, a nod when you'd encounter
Him up the hill. 'Why would he have?' The shop
Agrees, 'He's not considered his family.' Who
Knew him. Who did not know what is now ended,
So intricate. Once new as this child who
Ignored, frets in a pushchair, won't be quiet.
Outwardly, what's different here is only
Absence of weather talk, or of last night's match;
The shelves of bread, Daz, biscuits, sumptuous plums
And peaches resting a short while unattended.
'He'd crossed it daily all his life.' No more
Than a stone's-throw down the road, in failing light
Police drag the river. 'Three lives every year' –
And even as it is said, how many more
Drops in the ocean, causes no one plumbs?
Carrying on uphill, I'm left with only
Images: the brief flare of a match,
Tobacco; darkness, a huge going out.

The Captive

The great white flanks heave comatose on straw;
Or it clatters the cage, its pelt rubbed bald in places,
Snagging the gross encumbrance on its head.
Nothing to thrill the watching faces;
Its blue eyes lustreless even when it's fed.
No mythic grace or luminosity.
Always we'd hunted it. The credulous saw
Or dreamt it; virgins fantasised it might lope
To suckle from them; we glossed its potency
At healing nature's ills. At last we doubted.
Our megacities sprawled, wastes killed the ocean,
Withered green foliage from the farthest slope;
We levelled mountains to build motorway,
And colonised the inner space we'd left
For it to roam, pure poetry in motion.
Triumphant searchlights swept the dark,
Proving it false. And yet, we felt bereft.

It turned up browsing in a public park,
Drawn by the picnics and the children's play.
The capture made news. What should we do about it?
Therapists drew a blank of course,
They'd quickly sort it were it common horse,
But here's a creature nothing can tame or train.
Its noises make no sense, or it stays dumb.
Not stick nor carrot works. A useless freak?
But now we are conservationists, humane:
We've landscaped an ample paddock – it won't come
Out of the shed. Still, it's unique.
It seems to crave a mate, but the bay mare
Lashed out with hooves, the rhino smashed the bars.

Bored, people drift to drink elsewhere
What daily poisons, untouched by that horn.
– Harrowing them in their tracks, the unicorn
Whinnies immortal song beamed from the stars.

On the Bench

'You've a wee boy?' He'd sat down reeking by me
On the Ealing Common bench. I closed the sportspage.
His bottle was cream sherry, the hand missing
Thumb and forefinger. 'Yes, as a matter of fact.'
'Would he like this?' He rummaged in clothes needing
A blowlamp to get off, then conjured forth
A white rabbit, the meagrest, grubbiest ever,
And bobbed and wagged it. 'Yours for just two poond.'
'Thanks, but,' I lied, 'he's too old for soft toys.'
And dropped my gaze back to my paper, half
Too solicitous, half too nervous, to walk off.
Where was I from? 'From Ireland.' 'I'm half Irish,
My father's from a town called Tandragee,
Which name means in the Irish, "Arse to the wind",
Although the County Armagh, so I am told,
Is a very fine county. I've not been in Ireland.
I've been to America. Those were the good days.
Work and weemin, until' – he raised his hand –
'Took off by a machine. Have some of this . . .
Too early? Aye, you've sense.' He drank. 'I've no sense.
In Scotland I was barred from every bar
For twenty miles. Even the bars you couldn't
Get barred from, unless you walked into the ceiling,
Or *never* swore. But they'd sell from the side-door.
I'd carry gallons up the mountain where
I lived, a house, it was no sort of home,
No fire nor water nor electricity.
But full of friggin suites of furniture,
The Vincent de Paul Society brought stuff there,
So many sofas, chairs, you couldn't fall.
Banjaxed, for days I listened to my hair grow –
None of the rest of me worked, legs, bowels, kidneys.
Next stop, I thought, the asylum. Lock me up
And I'd go mad. They do. So I came south.
So here I am, to meet with Squeaky Joe
And Dublin Johnny. Past the Tube stop, see,
The off-licence opens early. Free as air
Sleeping out this fine May, the noise the leaves make
And haw white in the hedgerows, it's a different
Kettle of fish in winter. Thirteen days

I'm out of St Bernard's, many's the time I'm in there.
To take the cure. Depends upon the weather.
You've to go to meetings, meetings and bastard meetings,
I lost my single room when I refused
To go to more meetings. I discharged myself.
My pension had piled up. I bought Bell's whisky,
And by the time the bus reached Shepherd's Bush
I fell out. But d'you know where I'd my money –
The notes?' I shook my head, and he shook laughing,
'*Doon in my underpants*. An alkie's trick.
For when you're flat out and they try to rob you.
You'd soon perk up when they felt there. I'm wise.
I've robbed. A full beer barrel from a pub once.
The polis nabbed me. So says I in court,
"I'm alcoholic." They made notes, the beak said,
"What are you doing for it?" "Going to meetings."
"So when were you last at one?" "Saturday night."
"It doesn't seem," he said, "it's doing you
Much good, since that night you were apprehended
Wheeling the barrel over the town bridge
On a supermarket trolley, also stolen."
He's his big house, he's sitting on the bench,
Wants my sort tidied from sight. The Social Workers?
This muck-face-made-up blonde gives me the lecture,
Dips in her petty cash, hands nothing over,
But marches me round the corner, buys me cornflakes.
I'd sooner die my way, call it arse-to-the-wind.
Now here comes Squeaky Joe . . .'
                                        I'll take the rabbit
Leaped in my mind, but fell short of my lips.
Nor, looking back, was he I'd left transfigured,
Robed and radiant; still less his companion
Crooked above a stick, a flapping tripod.
They jabbed, swigged, and broke bread with tremulous fingers
Vain to prevent the waste of crumb-showers scattering
Upon the ground, and it seemed that never was so
Reduced whatever there is of Christ in men.
Except, imagining how I might have even
Kept the rabbit, washed it more deformed,
Then at most laid it hidden in a drawer,
I felt the lesser. Clean shirt, tie and jacket
Adrift on what crests yet again as failure.

After the Greenwood

Waking, he brushed off earth, and checked his quiver;
Patiently cropping thistles stood his horse.
They left the boneyard. The wide land looked worse,
Brick-cankered, more distressful to deliver.

Sundry mischances met him on the road,
Dunts from great engines, pukings from their fumes,
Execrations. Churls in tavern rooms
Quaffed fleering at his talk of doing good.

These groaned of swingeing taxes, heinous laws;
Yet when he bid them smash the alien yoke
Rude grapplings flung him forth, such meddling folk
As he, and vagrant, were their burden's cause.

How must the sheriff gloat to have such sheep
Liker to raise their hats than pike or stick!
He spurred apace towards the ulcer's quick,
The city, that fiend's castle with its keep.

Darkness fell, dragons ramped with eyes aflare,
His arrows flew in vain, he leapt the rails
As one alas! broached his poor brute's entrails –
Man's help since Adam now not worth a tare!

Dawn brought him through choked skirts where the unfree
Herded to drudgings; mazed with signs and wonders
He reached palaces cram-full of diverse plunders,
Cloths, gems, gauds, French wines, oils of Araby.

Of old the foe was plainly to be seen,
The mound-set stronghold thick-ribbed against siege
Where spiting a crusading absent liege
Vermin grew fat by fire, rope and rapine.

Footsore he found, come to the fount of sorrows,
The castle ruined, and the miscreant flown
To some seat else; for all betrayed full-blown
The tyrant's mark. But where now point his arrows?

He mused on confrères who'd with him waylaid
Cart-trains and freed bagged gold from mincing thieves,
Feasts on roast boar and deer beneath green leaves.
All forest gone, how more such escapades?

He stove in glass – was straight clashed on the wall
By two helmed hirelings, asked his name, abode.
This was as of yore! He answered: 'Robert Hode,
Most rightful Earl usurped from Locksley Hall.'

The robed judge ranted, minions cringed 'My lord!' –
Often thus snared he'd seen the gallows gape,
And relished anew devising trim escape.
Instead they haled him to some Bedlam ward.

Zanies there probed him of his dreams, filths, mother,
Yet used not rack or chains, nor locked the door . . .
Next he sought out the warrens of the poor.
Alas! misprised, these robbed and knifed each other.

He stepped between, cried 'Hold!' – with many a curse
Assailed and footpad rounded joining forces,
Soon overbore his venerable resources.
One sliced his ear off, the other had his purse.

A troupe of jongleurs scarved in white and red
Fresh from some sporting joust he hailed – misliking
Somewhat his garb viridian they with kicking
Merrily rearranged his noble head.

Spitting out teeth he rose, he liked such odds.
A comely dame restrained his whirling dirk:
'Misrule has scanted these of wits and work.'
They too were victims, their cause one with God's.

A damsel's cries lit his great heart like tinder,
There in an arbour lay she close-molested
By a grim trull, that by his vaunts seemed bested.
The maid said, 'I know how to use your gender.'

She clasped him plying kisses, whispered, 'If
You're Robin Hood, then I'm Lady Godiva!

Lie with me, you have arrows in your quiver.'
With his own sword she lopped his pintle stiff.

He saw aghast her face was Marian's,
Meek helpmate among greenwood outlawries,
Ready alike with broths, thread, bandages –
Sworn sister now with unkind harridans!

I veil worse scathes, entreating your compassion
Attend him as through the realm he much denounced,
Yet in each venture bloodily was trounced,
For antique chivalries are out of fashion.

He traced bold Little John, nimble Will Scarlett,
So apt for wrong's redress stout limbs to risk;
John now fleeced alms-funds by stealths at a desk,
Will waxed trafficking in drugs and harlots.

Scholars and holy men he found deep-sunk
In usuries, graft, and grosser appetites;
A pack of pimps and players now dubbed knights;
What pomps claimed sway null as a headless trunk.

Whence then such woes, coercions? Loons he sounded
Painted new Babel, pointed over seas,
Spoke of outlandish guilds, vile sorceries
Conveying pelf unseen. Hood gaped dumbfounded.

One showed him then a hall of snickering screens
Whereon danced scripts, computings. 'In this wise
They bleed us, that give back mere vanities.'
What pact with Baal had got the leech such means?

He drew his blade, beneath his havocking arm
Heaps of these fell devices tumbled stuck,
When rent his frame was, as by lightning struck,
From bum to chine, that dealt him mortal harm.

With his last strength he raised his horn and blew,
There came no answering flash of Lincoln green.
Yet certain pious dreamers vow they've seen
How from his grave a mighty oak-tree grew.

In the Cobweb Club

How did we get here, where did it all go wrong?
These sheepheads for instance, crimped upon stools or propped,
Glasses aloft or at elbow, a frieze along
The bar spouting garbage, the nicotined lighting moulders,
You picture spiders busy from ankles to shoulders
Enshrouding the lot of them. Hasn't the penny dropped?

I might have become a trombonist, run a scenic
Railway line in the Pennines, gone into marine
Biology, among glimmering sub-oceanic
Corals and fins have stumbled into that rich
Fulfilment of being we sense as our birthright, which
Slipped through the lines we learnt when young and green.

But that's all history; and to have time over
Again knowing what one knows now would not unfold
Some leafy vista yielding a life in clover.
Though I'd cherish the small things more: those crocuses
By my path, ripped out with the hedge, how they used to please
Me thrusting through iron winter their purple and gold.

Meanwhile in the Cobweb Club the stools are jinking
With indignation: cutbacks, shake-ups, it's red
Alert, the tight little ship's in danger of sinking.
Professor Heathcliff flails round the bar in search
Of the pipe in his mouth, old Vlad's dropped off on his perch
Without dropping off; and I'm away in my head.

Audio-visual aids for the next lot to take
Heed what to avoid from? Likelier, where they are tending.
We too had bright prospects, who flinch from a lengthening wake.
Now gin, not genetics, is Dr Medusa's lore,
The Dean's having technical problems with the floor,
O'Toole's done with wives unless deaf, dumb, and rich but low-spending.

How many true stories have a happy ending?

One Week in July

So death came like a whistle in the dark,
Reeling him in to heel, his corpse slumped over
His taxi dashboard in an Armagh road,
Shot by his final fare. Passions are burning
Countrywide, flashpoints triggered by the order
At Portadown to block the Orangemen.

Camped round their Drumcree Church the Orangemen,
Bands playing, numbers massing towards dark,
Assert the ancient traditions of their Order:
Rocks criss-cross RUC plastic bullets over
Barbed wire, above their fields troops' flares are burning,
But they will march down the Garvaghy Road.

Unchecked across towns and townlands loyalist road-
Blocks spread, in Belfast Catholic men and women
Are driven from homes, foodstores and cars are burning.
From my bed I hear a chopper chomping the dark
Above Coleraine, where vehicles are skewed over
River bridges and entry roads in order

To shut the town. It's stranglehold disorder.
We'll walk with dignity the Garvaghy Road.
And others, *This'll get worse before it's over.*
And churchmen mediate, and all *amen*
Is drowned by a Lambeg drum that sets the dark
Throbbing. Tension mounts, the fuse is burning

Towards the Twelfth, tomorrow, both sides spurning
Compromise. Then comes the countermanding order:
Catholics battered aside so that the dark
Suited sashed ones parade along their road
Behind one drum, escorted by RUC men . . .
And nationalist firebombs flare the province over.

How lately peace, our fools' gold, glamoured over
This country, like June's whin. Towns, cities are burning
Now that government, caving in to men
Of violence, signals violence, terror, murder
Win. A Derryman's mashed on the road
As petrol bombs, bullets, whistle through the dark.

Death comes like a 'Hey you!' across a road;
Whistling in the dark, or with tears burning,
We rage for order, for nightmare to be over.
1996

A Monody for Christmas

1

Tonight we turn the clocks back: Summer Time,
Sickly for weeks and gagging rain, expires,
Its bare-limbed barbecue-browsing paradigm
Of bliss shut off as we close blinds, light fires.
As dusks scythe in on us like Poe's pendulum
        Our unappeased desires
Turn towards gift-wrapped pandemonium
Whelming an antique voice: *And has Christ come?*

For some the answer rings clear of all doubt.
Among the tat and tinsel celebration,
Shopping-and-pub glissade, flings, fallings-out,
Till gorged from Christmas dinner half the nation
Snores slumped before a TV show or quiz,
        Some find fresh confirmation
Of faith they've grown within's huge edifice,
Its theme park of signs, wonders, sorceries.

Come loop the loop with God and see life whole!
The music's hypnotic, the ghost-train won't hurt you;
There's a cot-to-grave assault course for your soul,
A snakes-and-ladders board of vice and virtue.
What shocks me's how routinely millions pour
        Weekly, their minds inert, to
Cross what all my spirit's hungering for
Transcendence cannot get me through – that door.

I'm touched by friends who've prayed for me, my plight
Could use a miracle; most lives are a mess.
But Bob's-your-uncle, trust-and-all-comes-right
Notions of the divine won't coalesce
With gassed Jews, tortured children. It's no answer
    To cite quirks of redress
As proofs – it casts God as a bloody chancer
If each Lourdes cure costs millions dead from cancer.

Rescreened, my own case looks a panorama
Of slaughtered hopes, wincing guilts, misguided drives;
A magical mystery tour among banana-
skins; *lachrimae rerum* flooding what survives.
I can't turn back that clock, or file away
    In fusty old archives
Memories incandescent to this day . . .
Still heedless boys and girls come out to play,

Sealed in the cling-film of what, if no starry
Eden, yet holds joys, sorrows, fears and dreams
Intact. Till it's stripped away. Our outcomes vary,
But however singular our motifs, themes,
Ample the scoring, whatever we're broken-hearted
    Over, at bottom seems
A re-enactment of the wrench that parted
Us from that given world in which we started.

We bear its pattern like a watermark:
Layout of rooms, that garden, ponds where we'd gather
Frogspawn, a mesh of streets inlaid with park.
What once meant 'home' and kept the self together.
If only you'd stayed . . . That too brings orphanhood,
    Not just from mother, father,
But from the heart's landscape: brick engulfs a wood,
Skylines warp alien, cars din where cows stood.

Waking for Christmas, 1946
Or '47, at my bed's foot hung
The bulging pillowcase's thrilling mix:
The pen and paintbox I'd so craved among
Slighter delights – a cache of chocolate money
    In gilt foil; tube of strong

Peppermints; marbles, metal puzzles, funny
Mask. At the bottom gleamed a bright new penny.

We walked the frosty mile to Uncle Alf's
And Aunt Maud's for Christmas dinner – always goose.
High sepia rooms, clocks ticking, plate on shelves,
All musty-cold. Fob-watched, at seventy-plus
Coaxed to retire as a solicitor,
        Alf 'had a screw loose',
Had brought home all his office furniture,
Sat lonely upstairs brooding on the law.

Perhaps all rest-of-life's a sort of vain
Pursuit of what imperfectly once held us.
Where among highways, hedge, is that lost lane
Back to our own completion? Like our elders,
We in turn find the world has grown a stranger.
        Still annually that Child is
Through sleight-of-heart recycled to a manger,
Frail pulse of hope against despair and danger.

2

I'm writing this in Durham, in my head,
In a hotel room near the River Wear;
My son lies fast asleep in the next bed.
He says he's fond of autumn: autumn's here,
Leaves squidge beneath our feet; mist-muffled street
        Buildings disappear
In a dissolving world – though not yet quite
The great cathedral, on its wooded height.

It's been here almost a millennium,
Massive and yet not ponderous to the top
Of its three towers. To step inside's to come
Within our species's most audacious trope,
Passionate stonework flung like a great net
        On wheeling time, a scoop
Of the eternal, filigreed with light,
Seasoned to withstand encircling night.

And yet the mighty pillars of the nave,
Rib-vaulted ceiling high above, carved screen,
Chantries, triforium, transepts, the whole brave
And sumptuous contraption, has long been
Bypassed, moves us now through obsoleteness,
        The fossil of a dream
Our forebears had of harmony, completeness,
Approximate then, marooned now in remoteness.

Out in the street, gone haywire, faith these days is
Palmistry, star-signs, New Age hocus-pocus,
Creationists, witchcraft – hordes of rampant crazies;
Or else jumps tracks to a material focus:
Lottery-junkies mumble their crass *credo*:
        Gimme a windfall! – the *locus*
Operandi for a festering libido
Thus magicked to the Med, from Luton Lido.

Well, as we walk the river's loop light gleams
Silkily on it through wet trunks, leaves falling;
I halt on dank track as eleven chimes.
'You're always doing that, Dad – like a car stalling.'
I explain the date. Two minutes in sobered mood
        We ponder war's appalling
Carnage; that hulk on the far bank more odd
Than ever, as human feat, or work of God.

3

Tweaking the drift of things to shape and rhyme,
Coffee at hand, there's things I'd have it out with,
Ground to be dug, dykes cleared, viewpoints to climb.
I'm planting arbours, thickets of knockabout with
Topical topiary, interlaced
        Fruit and thorn to flirt with;
Suddenly on a woodland stroll a grassed
Glade opens flashback vistas to the past.

In1960 I clerked in at a bank
In London, where towards Christmas it got freezing.
My bedsittingroom was draughty, cramped and dank;

The Underground pestilent with coughing, sneezing;
I'd no coat – given in summer to a tramp.
When I'd paid for my season-
Ticket and rent, bought food, financial cramp
Kept me indoors beneath the reading-lamp.

By Christmas Day, screaming to pull the plug
On all that, round at Marco's I got tight,
Woke among blankets huddled on a rug
To find the world outside the window white:
Through more pints at the Woodman, we evolved
Our plan to ring birds' feet,
Covering England (till the snow dissolved)
With CND symbols – we'd world conflict solved!

The globe reeled from one crisis to another
Then: like brain-damaged bruisers the US
And Soviets brandished warheads at each other,
Blustering on the brink, each primed to press
The button ending things with a big bang.
The churches sang *God rest*
Ye merry gentlemen . . . As their bells rang,
What swept us was more waves of *Sturm und Drang*.

I'd gone at Him like a terrier at a bone,
Been flummoxed as a frog trapped in a blender;
Tried communal tuning-in, prayer on my own –
(Worse than a letter marked *Return to sender*,
Nothing came back). On blank sheets headed CREDO
I'd scribbled my agenda,
The Problem of Evil, Free Will . . . What did He do?
Played dumb; sent neither tip-off nor torpedo.

Still touting their Supremo of all Shits
Holy-rollers discovering Design
Through history from Attila to Auschwitz
Lock horns with zealots equally malign
Insisting what certain human lives attest,
St Francis, Bach, Einstein,
Is just a spume off physics, all the best
Of thought mere printout, not a palimpsest.

But now, *Hypnosis makes you fuller-breasted*
I read: we've Health and Beauty for morality.
Where pie-in-the-sky pilots at least suggested
That doing good for others was the key,
We learn from gurus of gels, jogging, gym,
    To *do this all for me* . . .
Vast as cathedrals fitness centres brim
With souls for whom Life Eternal's staying slim.

'You have to learn to love yourself,' I hear.
They've ringed targets, halved the drinks bills, squared the wife,
Got their kids on track and revamped a career . . .
Somehow self's truanted, it's just a life-
style they cosset. Yet my own pursuit
    Of wholeness, self-belief,
Has warped awry and brought forth bitter fruit.
My own fault? – or this Age's, rank with doubt?

Times past, my raised hand wouldn't have been missed,
I could have been a worthy country vicar,
Connubial, solacing, a keen naturalist.
Yes, but another claimant, puce with liquor,
A shit in a plumed hat whose life's the Raj,
    Bawls my name too . . . The flicker
Of inner need yearns childlike to enlarge,
But ramps amok without soul-anchorage.

Some of our maestros transfer to God's squad:
Eliot grew nun-struck; thought-crime made Gogol
Burn his book; John Donne, once Jack-the-lad
Coaxing court crumpet, turned coat to enrol
As His team coach, squealing 'God, ravish me!'
    To save a sex-stained soul.
They scrambled to hunch gibbering up His tree,
Between the devil and the deep blue sea.

God's team has talents: Milton played a blinder,
Kant and Pascal were tough defensive cloggers,
George Herbert's juggling runs, Blake's dead-ball bender
Can stun us. But the hearties, choirboy-huggers
And death's-heads selling His programme are distracting:
    And how can one hear the *logos*

When wincing at the vocables it's packed in? –
Like actors acting amateur actors acting.

Shadows lengthen in life's last-chance saloon.
One ends with pottering round the park, the terrors
Of superstores. Till that's too much. And soon
The dark. What underwrites our quests, what fear or
Promise? God is too difficult, hints of grace
        Denied by the world's horror –
Yet to say that's as if were I to gaze
In a mirror I could not see my own face.

As when tide floods in on a fractured shore
Seaweed rises on it, tremulous,
Nourished and erect, that has before
Lain parched and flat, likewise it is with us,
Souls at the mercy of some cosmic flow,
        Grateful for its embrace,
And helpless at its ebb; the waters go,
We shrivel back to stoniness below.

4

How patiently most wait, as baggage is
Spewed random from the chute to thump pell-mell.
The lucky move on. Among my images
(I've scads, though shots at heaven's stay blank) for hell
Is of unclaimed belongings circling on
        An airport carousel,
Sent miles astray, or just the owner gone . . .
I'm home from another flight to see my son.

Pudgy snowmen leer down from store façades;
Loudspeakered carols drizzle on vortices
Of shoppers clutching their good-cause Christmas cards,
Gift-wrapped perfumes, hampers, chocolates, cheese.
Crackers crammed with trinkets and trite mottoes.
        While, crazed with promises,
Toddlers blurt to beery Santas *sotto*
Voce demands for heaven now in his grotto.

Thus it is in Coleraine, and everywhere:
In London, New York, Munich, Budapest,
Mammon carpet-bombs us, Vanity Fair
Is lit up. And not only in the West:
Good Lord, they're cashing in in Tokyo
    Where it's some Alpine *fest*
Kurisumasu's sleighs, bells, plastic firs, fake snow,
Denote, not mystery of long ago.

And yet, *A Child is born* . . . We pause, recalling
Our childhood's picture of the Christmas scene
We wished for everyone: real snowflakes falling
Past laden eaves, lit window; looking in,
A family deep in chairs drawn to the fire,
    Gift-spangled tree, and green
Holly. We learnt for most that scene's a mere
Fiction – unpack it, cans of worms appear.

A child is born . . . Our impulse is to bless,
Whether it's in a palace or a manger,
So rich in possibilities. Unless
in Delhi or Dacca, where there is some danger
The newborn hand may be lopped off, or legs
    Crippled by a stranger
So that it more profitably begs
For those enslaving it to rags and dregs.

Our great cathedrals, like some ducal trove
Of monogrammed, invaluable plate,
Rear in official sumptuousness above
The roofs of spoiled lives in the erring street.
Yet how many of the pious have forsaken,
    Like Him they celebrate,
This world, its institutions, been outspoken?
For which He was nailed on their cross, and broken.

The sort of Church I need has been expounded
By our Anglican Archbishop Carey:
Papua New Guinea where he found it,

A curiously designed cathedral where, he
Relates, there are no walls, just a huge roof,
        It stands open, light, and airy.
He takes this building as an image of
How the Church might best express Christ's love:

'A church of blurred edges, somewhere people can
Ask the hard questions without condemnation,
And share their deepest fears . . .' I am the man
You'd see stray in and out the congregation,
Now try a hymn, now heckle, boo, or crack
        A joke; and on occasion
Stroll out for sun, or sin, or just a snack;
Dubious, but always coming back.

This Christmas, I'll sit in, reflect, perform
Small tasks, hear radio carols; try to feel
Sweet music at the heart of life's great storm.
My son, we need, to find course through the real,
Poor donkeys, dangled carrots; so jog on,
        Though never catch that meal.
As for heaven – we all cry for the moon.
My gift to you's a flight in a balloon.

Of that old tale of manger, angels, surely not
Plain truth yet haunting us still, I only know
What the ancient fabulists forgot,
That other awestruck shepherd, who although
He glimpsed the star, lost it in cloud, and missed
        The way in blinding snow.
And rose again, and carried on his quest.
Because it's there. The spirit's Everest.

Out of His Mind

So God yawned, and out flowed Time
Scattering galaxies. Zillions of stars
Doing their thing in a sublime
Dance on darkness. But the *longeurs*

Of twirlings, mergings, spin-off filaments
Fracturing to planets, bored Him stiff.
After a while, knowing the elements
Backward, God dozed off, and dreamed Life.

One speck in the void, for aeons shuffling
Ocean and land, went into labour,
Twitched its mountains, and discreetly muffling
The deed gave birth to an amoeba.

Good God! God woke, and blinked; so missed
The ammonite, huge swamp-wallowers dying,
The fatuous slowness of the quest
Through which some limped from falls to flying.

When sudden spires and minarets
Poked through the clouds, God smiled: *I see,*
Like Beethoven's string quartets
That's how they try to talk to me.

But human angsts and antics soon
Snapped patience. *Why on earth do you climb*
again to stare? He asked the Moon,
It's fouled up, all a waste of time.

But barren Moon adores the show,
Flower-foam, plumage bright in branches;
Delicate crystals dropping as snow
To mass to smashing avalanches.

Fin de Siècle

The heavens fall, deluging darkened garden,
Spattering off laurel leaves; indoors
Rolled on the hearthrug, my new conkers glisten;
Over the mantel, deep in Alpine flowers
Forever, *Herta Zuckermann, 13*;
And, dishes washed and dried,
Mum switches on the radiogram. I listen
To piano quibbling against descending
Rain's orchestrations, sudden
Drumbursts on a pane,
Arpeggios dropping from a leaky gutter.
Rain falls in lamplit puddles, on bombed gaps
Among the houses, clogged with weeds and litter,
And shivering down through foliage drips
From horse-chestnuts where this afternoon we shied
Sticks at soft-spiked burrs that split on landing,
Yielding our trophies round and shining.

So when, piano ceased, the wireless voice
Spoke of wonders, things to come, *each home*
Its housework robot, in the cities tiers
Of travelling pavement, even the ocean
Harnessed, present-day postwar girls and boys
Will live into a new millennium,
Briefly, as through a seaside telescope,
I saw, far out, great spaceships moving,
Then let it drop back into blankness;
Content by a coal fire's
Blaze, amid the seasons' slow procession,
Rain that would pass, nights drawn up close round Christmas,
Skies hardening and ponds iced for dangerous sliding,
Until again chestnut chandeliers
Lit with blossom along the driveway leading
To the big house deep in forest where
The Colonel stumped in 'shoes you'd see your face in'.
Too old for Hitler's war,
He'd drilled the Home Guard to beat off invasion.
His balustraded gravel, perfect roses,
Servants for everything.
'For shaping,' Mum said, 'napkins into swans,'

Sealed in a sphere remote from ours, yet proving
Our sense of ineluctable ordinance
Wherein God saved the King,
And screaming spreadarmed in dive-bomb swoop,
Storming the Oak Hill pillbox, shooting air,
We made-believe, safe as houses.

Autumn again, and the bowling greens are closed;
Stuttering metal of a gust-whipped can
Along a kerb; and on the cusp
Of the millennium now, the tarnished husk
Of a world rolled beyond our grasp
As circles widened, landmarks were erased,
And our débris litters space.
Among our lying jargons, botched
Cities, the heirs of boys who came
From football, pit-heads, childhood lanes, old thatched
Rectories, at the nation's call, to cleave
To what bands blared, till pitched beyond belief
Into the shellholes of the Somme,
Know and believe in nothing that's not on
A screen. The Colonel's game
Is up, even the booziest
Old monster sunk, guns blazing and gills puce.
Generations of dinner-gongs struck dumb.
Gone too the collier's tin bath with its dream
Of New Jerusalem, shining halls
Of social justice. History's worked-out seam.
A mass-trash culture, druggies, faddies, foodies,
Is ruled by packs of dunces, crooks and toadies;
The Sunday faithful flock to car-boot sales.

I put on Muddy Waters's bluesiest
Track, *I Feel Like Going Home*,
Sepia vocal, bass, and picked guitar,
Strut and filigree, plangencies of sound
Recorded when childhood held me:
The hollowed oak leant cradling a pond,
Among its knotted roots through blue unbroken
Unschooled hours I watched
Dragonflies glittering above still water.

Late on in the evening I feel like going home . . .

And that was not, the older children told me,
'Real pond', just filled-up bomb-crater.
From when the heavens fell and earth was shaken.

Mother used to say two wars
Took her youth and middle years.
Between them, her one foreign holiday,
The Bavarian Alps, gentian and edelweiss
She brought back home to press
In the leather-bound Browning I've inherited,
'And the children marched with sticks and shouted *Heils*,
Alone of all the guests we *would not* say
It back at breakfast in the hotels
When the waiter stopped at your table clicking heels
'Heil, Hitler!' – and they did get shirty, tried
To stare us down. We travelled on, the snow
High up so clean. So long ago.'

Still flickering wars, despoiled by what invention
Has curdled to, stripped forest, ozone layer,
Gene therapy, things to come now our nightmare,
A blue-green planet
Bowls on; we startle into being like
These raindrops pulsing on my window-glass,
That run and wriggle, pause to gather mass,
Then off again, merge, divert, each seeming
Sinuously unique, steered by intention,
Where only gravity compels
Downward swift course to dissolution;
And still more coming.
The earth receives us, and we make or break;
And seasonal as that bird-flock that now rises
To huge migration on it,
Children hurl sticks and watch the conker-falls,
And gather up new shining prizes.

A Nice Day

'Oh no they won't,' growls Old Scrot, as shop-girls coo
'Have a nice day!' – not that young twerp rejected
In love who'll go home to hang himself; not you
You old bat, in for worse news than you expected
At the hospital. He hasn't gone through however
Many world wars it was (the memory's not
What it used to be) for the likes of them, and never
Mind the filth who barging past shout
'Sad old loser!', 'Plonker!', 'Wanker!'
Each of which is true, the first and last
Since Mrs Scrotum slipped anchor.
'No kids,' she'd agreed, 'just a bleedin waste.'

Lunch at the British Home Stores, plastic-chicken roll,
'Enjoy your meal!' More bloody orders. Adhering
To the It-All-Goes-Down-The-Same-Hole
School of Cuisine, Scrot wolfs it. Swivels, hearing
A baby bawling: 'While you still can, stick to slumber,
It'll get worse, work, love – sole hope as you plod
Into twilight you'll get too gaga to remember.
Enjoy your life!' That calmed the little sod.

Scrot telephones: 'Lynne here, how may I help you?'
Unless you're a blonde with long legs and huge tits,
Who'll slake my lusts, and not trailing some whelp, 'You
Can't. Just transfer me to Benefits.'
Who summon him in, it seems there's 'something amiss',
He's led to a separate office. When the hoyden
Goes off with his claim to query 'discrepancies'
Scrot grabs the desk phone, rings his brother in Croydon,
Queensland: 'Don't hang up, leave this running!'
And runs; past 'Have a nice day!' from the front-desk tart,
As if it wasn't already decayed to raining
Twilight; as if she gave a fart.

But wait, he spots a nice slimy layer
Of leaves on the Council's path – a quick plummet,
Footballer-writhing, then Scrot hops off to his lawyer:
'Negligence! Sue the bastards off the planet!'

Safe indoors, he borrows a cup of sugar,
Which he will punctiliously return,
In a smaller cup, from his neighbour. 'Ooh yer bugger,
Yer socks dun arf pong,' she screeches. Turn
Them inside-out, they'll do (the sense of smell
Is not what it was) for another week. TV,
The News bad, wars, rapes, murders – living hell.
God's been having a pretty nice century
If you go by the body-count, His Eternal Lifework
Being the cull of souls. Next, open-heart
Surgery, plenty of close-up knifework:
'Should've gimme a triple bypass at the start,
Round the whole bloody boiling,' Scrot guffaws.

Tomorrow Old Scrot will go fishing on the heath.
Why pay the supermarket? He knows
The trout go ape for maggots, a five-minute seethe
And he's emptied the pond. Scrot knows, having in his time
Been a bailiff, that this is illegal: many a supper
He's had from evidence seized of a poacher's crime
(It won't keep till Court). A very proper
And moral employ, confronting the disasters
Of others – watching toffs' fat faces grieve
As he carted off their pianos, plate, Old Masters.

Nice days; long flown. But still tricks up his sleeve.

Wintersong

Each day the sun rose sullenly and late,
Clung low round vague horizon and then dipped
From sight again, as if earth's tilt had slipped.
The snow lay dirtying, till another spate

Of blizzard blanched the streets and rigid park.
Such traffic as there was crawled headlights-on
Through days not reaching day's pitch before gone;
When gales blew up and rummaged through the dark.

Outdoors eyelashes froze to spikes of ice;
Across the land the power cuts got more
And longer; ice came down the North Sea shore,
Even the seabirds vanished from the skies:

Pierbound fishermen missed the weave of gulls
Crying above the water; saw on floes
The scatter of birds that where they landed froze,
And mourned the fallen realm of lost friends' souls.

It seemed the seasons' cyclings had broken
From time's axle, skewed to final stasis.
Oblivious that soon through snow's last traces
Daffodils would thrust, earth's gold awoken,

As annually through the decades since – unlinked
To our interior weather-shifts, where lapse
To winter may calm to a freeze perhaps
Killing down through the soil till all's extinct,

And circulating on the crust above
The ghosts of broken hopes bear up, make light
Of cuts and shortages, face the cold; at night
Weep for all unrenewing greenness; love.

The Ascent

Hillary and Tenzing

Above the great Icefall, the sudden
Crevasses, the sheer verticals ascended,
Beyond all the knowhow and backup, in that cold
And rarefied air even the plants and creatures
Cherished by the heights cannot inhabit,
It was something purely human took them on up.

Those who waved them off from the highest camp
Watched them vanish – the one who had been to college,
The other illiterate, of a servant kind

Scarcely admitted down here, yet a natural
On these heights, none had gone higher.

A slow chipping of steps, eyes inches from
Iceface, and when they could look up along
The windscoured ridge with its killer drops,
The peak uncertain in the lie of the land.

At the summit, one most properly shook hands,
The other in rapture made offerings
To his gods, burying in snow some biscuits, chocolate.

They came back, weakening, still roped together.
To those who met them from the tents questioning
The first said (the other barely spoke our language),
'We knocked the bastard off.'

So Beethoven, having finished the Ninth Symphony,
Very likely, being a pious man in his way,
Flung down on his knees in gratitude;
And a stubborn one, muttered, 'I've knocked the bastard off.'

And so for most who, though never approaching
These heights, see at all the point of scaling,
Tracking what supports them to its vanishing
In cosmos, it takes what is most like that pairing
Within them; driven by fear of failing.

Haydn and the Fish

Brilliant slivers, how strange to us these fish
In their element beyond glass, some speckled gold
So adroit, others mere blobs in their lacy mesh
Of fins and tail; these red-and-white hooped hold
Briefly formation like notes on a stave, then scatter.
A serrated sail-like thing as if cut from black
Crêpe paper hangs. How evolved, every organ intact,
This pulse of gills and feeding in quivering water.

And I think of bees' hives, the hexagonal symmetry
Of the cells, the myriad larvae. I've no inkling
What goes on in the brain of a single bee,
If you call it brain, or in their world speak of singling.
And all the way from Africa flocks of birds
Are winging overhead, as every year
Finding again the great cathedral tower.
And what raised that but instinct for what's past words?

Now it's with science we probe, our telescopes
So sophisticated they catch light travelling
Across ten billion years, ghosting the shapes
Of the galaxies forming, matter unravelling
From the Big Bang – where Einstein's maths and Hubble's
Scrutiny founder. *A universe can expand*
From something far smaller than an atom: mind,
Stars, empires; outlandish fish; love, and its bluebells.

Or it might be such a universe as when
Our nearly empty train ascending into
The foothills of the Alps stopped, and we ran
Across the carriage and flung up the window
And all was sunlit greenness and a stillness
That brimmed with millions of grasshoppers singing,
And we turned to one another, our hearts singing.
But the train moves frittering on, we lose that wholeness.

I wake early these summer mornings, birds are singing,
Our corporate monkey wheels are stilled, the covers
On keyboards, streets ungridlocked, roofslates shining;
From shore to shore pale feet jut from humped duvets.
Sampans drift past crumbling gilt pagodas;
Sinuous lizards ripple green jungle floor.
I listen to time sing: of the more stars than are
Sandgrains on Earth's beaches. Of loves, and murders.

And music issues from my radio,
From far beyond it – how strangely come about,
Commissioned from a placeman long ago
At a Hungarian princeling's mincing court,
For flunkeys to scrape. We foist upon it crude
Pictures, storms, lovers, wars and emperors,

Half-comprehending thrill as from a source
More elemental heart's truth is renewed.

The footballer Danny Blanchflower knew it, what
The great composer teaches: *Most think the game*
Is about winning. It's not. It is about
Glory . . . What houses this aquarium
Was once a madhouse. Mooching up to the glass
A huge phosphorescent blue fish flicks edge-on
And vanishes; then flashes reversed, sinks down
To its lair. A wink from unfathomable space.

Sixth Sense

After the years of wine and roses, women and song,
Have dinned and dented our five human senses dimmer
One begins to wonder and hanker after what most have a glimmer
Of in us somewhere we fancy, though never for long
And we can't locate or control it, or rely on it for directives,
A sixth sense. And I don't mean seeing ghosts or psychic tricks,
But the sort many animals have for specific objectives.

The rattlesnake for instance has two other cavities
Below its eyes, but each of this pair packed
With cells so sensitive to heat that they can detect
Across metres variations to fractions of degrees;
So in the dark it need not see or hear to get a fix
On a mouse or any mammal, that registers on its brain
As a fuzzy blob, like a blip on a radar screen,
And the snake glides in for the kill. Or in the marine
Wonderworld the dogfish mooching above the floor of the ocean
Equipped to pick up the tiniest electrical emission
So finding creatures buried in sand and slime.

But senses not only for prey. Most inscrutable and sublime
Are the migrations of birds; how does the swallow
Returning from Africa find so exactly again
The English village church spire where it nested last year?

It is the sun and stars, so theory said, that they follow;
Which given our northern cloud-cover seems absurd.
But now, although they can find no organ in the bird
For this, it's by detecting the magnetic pole they steer.
And does that throw light on their flights? Not a scrap,
What earthly use is a compass without a map?

We make no more sense of it than could the Roman long
Ago, who certainly knew of the fish because
It's on frescoes, but hadn't a clue what electricity was,
When touching a ray he found himself flung on his back.
The thing hadn't bitten him, not moved, by what means of attack
Had it knocked him clean out of his senses? When they crawled back
He pondered awhile the derided Christians, known to revere
A fish; before crawling thankfully back to the here-
and-now they abjured, wine, women and song.

Lamb Lore

Lambs born to wind and sleet
Have no reason to surmise,
Staggering to their feet,
That sodden ground, grey skies

In months will be transformed
To sumptuousness and ease,
The rush of grass, sun-warmed
Luxuriance, shade of trees.

And nothing will betray
Their bleakness, who themselves
Lie wrapped as meat by May
On supermarket shelves.

But their siblings who remain
To be annually fleeced
Must learn a crueller pain,
Suffering unreleased

That cycle nothing alters,
As again green bliss deceives,
Turns rank, and shreds and falters
To blanched cold, fallen leaves.

Another Life

Already summer is memory. This sun
Lifts late, and nothing you'd call day's begun
From its low trawl through bare boughs in the park,
Before it sinks. A quilt against the dark
The town's loudspeakered carols, that suborn
The awe at miracle that with time we mourn
As our lost childhood, to this seasonal
Bland lure to striplit high-street shops and mall.
Come buy! Come buy! Thronged greeds, wants, pushchairs plied
To carve a track to get at what's inside
This door, stacked on that counter. A small fist
Protrudes to thieve, the mother whacks its wrist:
'Do that again, *I'll break your fucking neck!*'
Dad joins her, hung with bottles; off they trek
To stuff their booty in the boot of a car
Parked in sodium-flare that kills Christ's star.
Grilles crash, the streets are left to blown cans, a ruck
Of gulls fled inland. And I feel guilt pluck
At my heartsickness over what, if flawed, still lifts
Most to a daze of warmth and colour, gifts
For kids . . . My son's grown now; I have no wife.
I've taken the pension for my rest-of-life.
A bird jinks buffeted past, trying for flight,
Reels, rises choppily, is gone in night.

I jumped at the Institution's pay-off bargain,
The place's soul long sold for lying jargon
Filthy with weasel words that start with *C*:
Costs, Corporate, Counselling, Community.
Though at the *Talking Retirement* seminar
The speaker's uplift stuff began to jar:

Another life, all dreams fulfilled . . . The ending
Great literature attests is ills past mending.
She quoted Picasso claiming, at eighty-odd,
His life had never been happier. Lucky sod –.
Of course, by that decade of his long fame
He only had to autograph a game
Of noughts and crosses, and people wrote huge cheques,
And as for women, treeloads offering sex.
Most lives aren't thus. Next, Diet: nothing sweet,
Not much of anything one likes to eat.
I slipped outside to light my pipe, evade
The anti-smoking fact-pack and tirade,
Returning with the tea-trolley: 'Have a biscuit . . .'
The rest was all downhill. The Finance whizz-kid
Unrolled his make-your-lump-sum-grow-fast spreadsheets;
Questions gathered round life shrunk to bedsheets:
'If I need residential care, can they
To pay the bills just take my house away?'
And Living Wills – things whereby you direct
Doctors to pull the plug when you look wrecked.
Most not yet sixty, darkening the skies
Like vultures flocking to their own demise.
Senility? Suicide? I can't be carted
Off, I've lives to live I've not yet started.

Back when they'd nag *What do you want to do?*
Meaning *career.* I'd shrug. Although I knew
A few things that I'd not mind ending up
As: Wimbledon champion, star of our World Cup
Team; living on a boat; the man who found
Our sun's tenth planet. None got off the ground.
Sheer lack of talent. But, too, time forces choices
That overlook supplicating inner voices
Not all crass, fanciful. Wintry now, and near,
Ending up flash-floods *what to do* with fear,
So nor more wishing on a lucky star,
I'm not Jack Hobbs, the Jack of Hearts, Jack Tar
Sailing the seven seas, rebel Jack Cade,
Jack the Giant-killer, Jack of every trade
Owning nothing except my right of way
Across the land. Pipe-dreams of yesterday.

I must be practical. I'll buy a flat
In Norfolk, on the coast. I'll keep a cat;
Join clubs, societies, enrol for courses
On plumbing, the fugue, Italian. I've resources,
Freedom, already have stood where as a boy
My emotions thrilled, on the ruined walls of Troy
And pictured Hector slain . . . I'll cruise the Nile;
In Riga I'll be spellbound by the smile
Of gorgeous Latvian women, as they glance
With green eyes pitying my ignorance
Of the deep onrolling of their vast
Forests, their centuries of terrible past.
I could disappear. Like Alice in free-fall
To wonderland; through the green door in a wall
To the garden where all are beautiful and kind.
Ah, to roll over this world's edge and find
Myself in a parallel one, but fresh and whole,
A different tale . . .

No bolthole for the soul
Nowadays even in our children's stories.
The White Rabbit won't lead Alice to the glories
Of logic-crazed Hare and Hatter, Caucus Race,
Live playing-cards, the disembodied face
Of the Cheshire Cat. Let loose from its cramped hutch
It's kicked to death by Dad who's drunk too much.
If Dad's not long cleared off. Mum's in no shape
To cope, picks men up. Alice tries escape,
But to a squat. At first it seems all right,
The folk there strum guitars, stay up all night,
Keep warm by burning stuff lifted from a skip,
Tilting the bottle, taking an acid trip.
It sours: injections, knife-fights, vomitings, waking
Beside some stranger. Something within her breaking,
The death of hope for love. Her best friend trades
Sex for cash for drugs, will die of Aids.
Today kids' stories have a moral theme:
It's dangerous to fantasise and dream.

This country should know it, where I've lived so long,
Green contours blemished with too much gone wrong,
'There's something magical about Ireland,' said

My visiting son. Its legendary dead,
One-eyed Balor of the Mighty Blows,
Fionn MacCumhaill, who everywhere one goes
Has scooped and shaped the land, one giant heft
Of his spade flung out the Isle of Man and left
The hole Lough Neagh fills. But you'll find lakes here
On tops of mountains, lakes that disappear
Unreasonably then come back like Loughareema,
Isle-studded lakes for the hermit and the dreamer.
Mountains kneeling down in purple dress
To water mirroring their loveliness.
'Of course,' they say here, 'we're impossible.'
Their features have some grimmer facts to tell:
Ringforts and castles, broken Celtic towers,
Roofless cottages carpeted with wildflowers
Whose peace is born of famine and eviction.
Streets bombed and homes burnt-out from pure conviction.
The past ferments to myth gridlocking hates
That kill on lonely farms, Belfast estates.

Leaving leaves too the rosebed in the park
Here in Coleraine. Shyly, as it grew dark
Three years ago, afraid of challenge, I stooped
Down with a trowel to the soil and scooped
A hole, and from the plastic bag let slide
My mother's ashes. It seemed a good place. I'd
Daily pass the rose gardens on my walk
To work, would sit and think there. Sort of talk.
I seldom paused to do so. And now I'm aching
With what feels almost guilt that I'm forsaking
The dust-remnants of an empty frame's cremation
That rain has long dissolved beyond location
In earth that was not hers. Strange ending-up,
I'm swept by a crazy urge to fill a cup
With earth, take something back to where I should
Have laid her first, among a bluebell wood
In London's Epping Forest fringe, the place
Where from her youth she found peace, beauty, space,
Among the oaks and beech, and where she knew
All flowers, but loved the most those that are blue.

Again this solstice sun lifts late and weak,
Low over rooftops dribbling a bleak
Light on the here-and-now I walk among
This season when a hijacked Christ is sung
To millions on a retail-shopping spree;
Children rage for trash toys spawned by TV;
While in the pub, 'I don't mind if I do,'
Croaks yet again the raddled old dear who
Sits in the corner, never any trouble,
'Well, as it's Christmas, then I'll have a double,'
Not knowing that by next year she'll be gone.
And still our froth of misplaced wants swirls on.
Skirts will get longer, then short, then again
Longer; people give up sex, meat, or caffeine;
Change partners, jobs or cars; and riffle through
The supplements on *Style, Wine, Living, You.*
Liberating choices? Like beasts caged
We pace them, turn, recoil; still unassuaged
The howl at the heart of things. In our extreme
Emotions, fear, love, pain, we shout and scream.
So what chance retirement's odyssey,
This vessel holed, unfit to put to sea?
Still on my front path I'll erect FOR SALE,
Shred my store loyalty cards, and hit the trail.

On Norfolk's bluff cliffs, when the tide is full
I'll hear after each wave has crashed the pull
Of shingle-drag, its suck-back to the past.
And what does one remember at the last?
A voice, twigs tapping on a pane, a glance,
Bits of views, a tune from a lost dance.
Some freeze-framed shaming moments that appal.
But happiness? stabs the mirror on the wall.
Not missed, exactly. *No, but never tried*
Wholeheartedly, protected as it cried
Out for, so lost in muddle, spilt. The time
Was never right, or if it was, your crime
Was that you didn't cleave to it, distracted,'
Well, that's how it goes. And my refracted
Double in the mirror twists his knife:
As people say, 'Perhaps in another life . . .'

Four Bagatelles: Moralities for the 1990s

1 THE GOOD GERMAN

(after 'The Vicar of Bray')

In Kaiser Wilhelm's golden days,
When Empire was no defect,
A furious monarchist I was,
And so became class-prefect.
Our King, to schoolmates I'd insist,
Is God's anointed icon;
Then I marched on nations who'd resist
In a helmet with a spike on.
And this is law, I will maintain
To doubters all my sermon,
That whatsoever power shall reign
I will be a Good German.

When Weimar scrapped the shattered Crown
World peace became the fashion,
All pomp and brag I hooted down,
Upheld the League of Nations.
Democracy I found would fit
Full well my constitution,
And I had prospered under it
But for new Revolution.
And this is law, etc.

When Adolf our deliverer came
To heal the nation's grievance,
I turned the cat in pan again,
And swore to him allegiance:
I sang round healthy camp-fire smoke,
I loved our Alpine gentian,
Vowed riddance to the Jewish yoke
And death to *Untermenschen*.
And this is law, etc.

When Ulbricht, Honecker, ran our show
Pure Communist, my Nazi
Faith and deeds dissolved like snow,
I flourished with the Stasi,

Imprisoning all dissenters base
  And loathing liberal courses.
Utopia in danger was
  From Western market forces.
    And this is law, etc.

Mein Gott! the Berlin wall now falls!
  Kohl comes to end our schism, Sir.
Once more I'll change my principles,
  Espousing Capitalism, Sir.
And thus preferment I'll secure
  From *ein Volk*'s great defender;
Elected *Ratsherr*, I abjure
  Karl Marx, the old pretender.
    And this is law, etc.

The illustrious Bonn Chancellor
  And CDU succession,
To these I heartily will swear
  Whilst they can keep possession:
For in my faith and loyalty
  I never once will alter,
May Kohl *mein Führer* always be,
  Except the times should alter.
    And this is law, etc.

1990

2 MORALITY PLAYERS

The Fifth Duke of Newcastle, Gladstone's Oxford friend, in 1850 divorced his wife for eloping with her lover to Italy. Necessary evidence was procured from a villa near Lake Como, from none other than Gladstone himself, 'disguised as a guitarist'.

The Times, 6 January 1994

When Bismarck put the boot about
  And Tsars were vilely Tsarist
Our Premier Gladstone chose to spout
  Morality; a purist,
He streetwalked to save whores from hell,
And ditched the adulterer Parnell,
And volunteered to act as tout
  Disguised a a guitarist.

Founts of morality today
  May be more hypocritical,
Putting you in the family way
  For motives unpolitical
Won't stop a Secretary of State
Rising to Party cheers to prate
Of hallowed values. Do such clay
Feet skulk at your front-garden gate
  Strumming airs operatical?

Beware: he's not what you take him for.
  On benefits? – you'd better
Sneak lovers out through the back door
  Or else you'll get a letter:
As a Cabinet Minister I must
Discountenance unlicensed lust.
Your money's stopped. Be chaste if poor.
While Catholics on the Pill are bust
  When Love dons a biretta.

Soon even tabloid ratpack hacks
  May tremble, whisky-waverier,
And, biters bitten, watch their backs,
  And even their behaviour,
In case, when any such regales
The punters with royal phone-taps, tales
Of titled sex, some tramp unpacks
A horsewhip: 'I'm the Prince of Wales,
  And thrash you as your saviour!'

And you, whose party's going strong,
  Awash with booze, outrageous
Carnal couplings, filthy song,
  Building to a rampage as
Garish as any ancient Rome
Contrived for show, but in your home
So doing society no wrong
You think? – unbeard that garden gnome,
  The face you'll meet's John Major's.

And bishops burbling sanctities,
  Top Brass, that judge who bellows
'Law and Order!', industry's
  Knights – henceforth, shun bordellos,
Don't 'hello!' sailors, dress up in drag,
Stop luring teenagers to shag;
A swarm of thespian MPs
Will scoop you into their moral bag –
  Plus half their Commons fellows.

1994

3 THE CELEBRITY'S LOVE SONG

So I'm a footballer, rock singer, minister;
Doing my bit at it's been quite rewarding:
Delicate darlings drop all for a tennis star,
Go-go girls gag for it, lie back applauding.

Pulling a cracker or buggering duchesses,
I've done my bit, just another statistic
Notched on my crotch, and *Thanks very much* is as
Much as they sought. Now they all go ballistic.

Boomerang bimbo, chuck it it circles
The *Sun* selling sex, the sophisticate Sundays,
Zaps you (that knighthood will need bloody miracles
Now) with *He Sucked My Toes . . . He Wore My Undies . . .*

I am a chat-show host, great actor, bishop,
Done with sex – straight, sado-mach, cunninlingus,
The persons attached won't get me to a teashop –
Fooled in bed now only by my own fingers.

1996

4 CHARACTER IN SEARCH OF AN AUTHOR

I'm a fat black hunchbacked lesbian battered wife.
Seeking employment in a play or novel.
Authors I go to cry, 'Not on your life!'
Or, 'I've my sales to think of.' I don't grovel,
I knee them in the groin, or pull a knife.
My problem getting work is that I'm evil.

I do robberies, drugs, and murders, lie and cheat,
Sell my body, torture kittens for a joke.
Pay me extra, and I'll bomb a shopping-street.
I've a violent temper. And of course I smoke.
And since Jane Austen good reads aren't complete
Without that stuff. The book trade would go broke.

'If you were white, male, straight, less fouled-up looking,'
They shrug arms spread, 'we'd use you, we agree.
You're proficient over a wide range, hard-working,
Can turn your hand to movies and TV.
But as it is . . .' I never get a booking,
While those bastards get rich. And it's not just me.

Gay, crippled, female, black? – don't be a blackguard:
Caliban, Regan, Genet's freaks, Blind Pew –
All on the dole, with spearmen Rider Haggard
Gave honest work; in China Fu-Man-Chu
Frets biting his long fingernails quite ragged.
And you say you're fighting prejudice? Stuff you!

So I trudge round agents, publishers, in vain:
'These days, your type in fiction must be *nice*.'
I've five kids to feed, we're homeless. 'Well, retrain,'
I'm told. 'Get marketable skills, quit vice.'
I'm too old for that. But I've a fertile brain,
And when I strike, they'll find they've met my price.

1998

Love's Admonitions

I YOUR WORD

More justice had I taken you at your word
When you told me I deserved better, not as fishing
For contradiction; but part-kind, more not wishing
To risk the famishing half-loaf, I demurred,
Praised what I truly could and left unmentioned
Your keeping love hole-and-corner for the sake

Of mere charade, your marriage's hollow fake,
Your thralldom to gossipings of the ill-intentioned.
And how could you think concealment's desert a basis –
You the cherishing gardener who know
That living plants need nourishing soil to grow –
Not bound to mass sands smothering our oasis,
Corrosions making love thwart and volatile?
Your *Let's stick by each other through thick and thin*,
Words to which, eager to be taken in,
My heart soared, proved sincerities only while
You voiced them. You lacked the courage of love's convictions,
That rose within our shyness when we first
Embraced, and we trusted as the floodgates burst.
But you shrank back to dry land's safety-fictions,
Who never had known and told so much truth
Of all you are and your emotions needed
As in our earliest love. Then overlaid it
With pedantries, checks, fits and starts, fear's froth.
Yet I too gave love less than it merited,
Who should have claimed its due, so maybe swept
You off your feet, but faltered in inept
Conciliation of your terms instead
For fear of losing what was thereby lost.
We each fell short, through different counts of cost.

II YOUR FEARS

You feared 'all that old stuff in books' I read;
   Feared also, wrongly, that I held cheap
The 'practical' tasks and deeds you chose instead:
Wallpapering, digging, slipping needle on thread.
   These things in you made my heart leap.

And no matter you could not articulate
   Why your garden's beauty made you weep.
A pity, though, that didn't intimate
To you, whose toil had brought it to that state,
   That 'practical' isn't at odds with 'deep'.

And Shakespeare, Blake, George Eliot, at least might
  Have helped you recognise your confusion,
Shown you how pain can, though it may not, sleight
Into enlarged new wholeness; but never by flight
  To bitterness and disillusion.

III WHAT MATTER

We totted up lacks and failings, the list covers
More than enough to cope with, you'd say. So what
Matter? – whenever did hurts and gaps one jot
Diminish love's unchosen hold on lovers?

IV THE PRICE

Your final betrayal: pretending
  From the start it was bound to end so.
Could never have worked out, amending
  Love's case for mere ease of mind. No.

And I'm glad I still cry out in day for
  What's over, its words, gazes, acts;
Mutilation's the price souls pay for
  Extirpating their facts.

Nor can you: however complacent,
  Intact, your quotidian shell,
The essence of things persists patient:
  Vows, minglings you'd blacken and quell

Will erupt in full sweetness to haunt you
  When you waken some night in your bed,
All they promised igniting to taunt you,
  Your hollow elsewhere and instead.

Ghosts? – yes, of life you let perish,
  Not phantoms false from the start;
That you cannot turn back now and cherish,
  Nor cravenly gouge from your heart.

V PORTGLENONE

From southward this warm spring air blown
Expels thought other than
The bluebells are out in Portglenone
Beside the River Bann.

Beneath the trees they pool and heap;
My mind's gaze holds you, dressed
In darker blue still knelt waist-deep
In shoaled blue that, possessed

By us, was leaven in trust that rose
Through all we did that day,
Lingering where the water flows
Bearing its earth away.

Once more, as if awaiting us,
Bluebells. As if they cared.
Fancies you'd mock: the luminous
Plenitude we shared

Springs ignorant of any lover,
Promiscuous to all,
And paths and hollows blooms recover
Throng annually to their fall.

And so today in Portglenone,
In bluebells by the Bann,
It may well be you walk, alone
Or with another man.

We failed truth we engrossed them to.
So Portglenone, blue-gowned,
Brimming me with unchanging blue,
Is my forbidden ground.

Moving On

I looked over my shoulder, and it was still there.
After all. Then I woke to sunshine streaming
On left-out bedroom toys, to calm my screaming.

Then Love. That slippery word. Naïve, aware,
We use it to wrench facts to its aspiration,
Or fend off fear of their disintegration;

And though by nature promising happiness
So often love comes to pain. We clear the mess.
And looking over one's shoulder, it's still there.

So we move on. From park-splashed suburb where
It started, shifts through townscapes, accent-changes,
Mine became Ireland's griefs and mountain ranges;

Till doubling back now, Norfolk; what two cases
Once held swelled to a houseful. Changing places,
But always, over my shoulder, it's still there.

Like prints on snow (that melts to leave earth bare)
My words wrung from what's been. Are they motivated
By notions it's thus outstripped or placated?

No. It's just that keeping going's the only
Choice. And when light fades on road grown lonely
I'll need no backward look to know it's there.

Sylvanshine

When the road enters a wood and your headlights catch
The innumerable moisture-droplets that trees save,
Like a great lit cathedral shines and glimmers
What you are speeding into, conifers
Vaulted above, with transept spans, the march
Of tall boles each side pillaring a nave
Receding to infinity . .
Sylvanshine
It's called. We didn't invent it or construct it,
Nor were we searching for it like cold stars
Only long-wave spectroscopy brings to light,
Or the life-secrets coded in our genes.
It's always been there for finding in the night.
It was latent in the great primeval forests,
Through aeons held in bark and leaf unseen
By stegosaur and Shakespeare, till in time's merest
Tip our technology by chance unlocked it
With the angle of the beam from lights on cars.

The suddenness of the illumination
Meets with us and envelopes as does love,
And carries along, a radiant lure ahead
As if into its heart of revelation.
And then we're through and out, on either side
The dreary flat expanse, black void above.

But rather than metaphor for such specifics
Of the spirit's quest, accept it just as what
It is, pure gift fluked from the laws of physics,
Explaining nothing.
Still it answers something,
This spectacle of form and light – our ache
For object matched to the sheer gladness that
Most things we've thought to lavish it on mar.
At least in the inner journeys we all make,
Where fitful love and faith daze routes we travel,
And maps disintegrate as the years unravel
Nor anyhow tell where sylvan miracles are.

Play That Thing

Soon I'd no need to play it, though I'd often
Put it on, it anyway would happen
Inside my head, and everywhere I'd listen.

It seemed the city's pulse, the groan and strum
Of escalators, and tunnels as trains came
Pushing its fizz down the live rail before them.

I walked out to the bypass, windscreens flashed
Staccato riffs of sun as cars streamed past,
And every way for miles still rooflines, vast

Chains of tarmac, brick and concrete bound
The suffocated hills; the music mourned
And sizzled, syncopated and profound.

A last road studded with rich mansions lifted
Me to the top, some stars; but when I looked at
The valley beyond, more drifts of suburb choked it.

Then round night's ridge, first kindled threads and slivers,
Then merged to flame, in which trumpet's bravura
Scarlets, indigo trombone slidings, silver

Clarinet filigree blazed to what black dots
Swarming staves could never replicate:
Like lava it crescendoed, and as hot.

And what I saw was not old Storyville's
Distant demolished brothels, drinking-halls,
Nor Mississippi-churning paddle-wheels,

Just black faces bent to instruments, the offspring
Of slaves, if now called free yet still possessing
Nothing, pouring forth heart's hurts and blessings

Under a huge full moon, the blue expansion
Of plain around lit by bright constellations
That met it with no visible horizon.

Train Journey Across County Antrim

'Thon's brave spring weather,' he slammed the door, 'the haw's
Thick in the hedges and braes roond Cullybackey.'
I grin, though no pun lurks for him because
He'd say 'hures'. Lulled by wheels rapping track he
Dozes opposite and, once we are clear
Of ribboning Belfast brick, proves right enough:
Sumptuously eddying all along the line,
Through halts where schoolkids get on and get off,
Ballinderry and Glenavy, on to Crumlin
(*Town of the oakgrove, dwarf's church, crooked glen*),
Thick clusterings of may, and sprawled and tumbling
Over green sunlit landscape everywhere.

I'm flung back to my father, showing me, as we strolled
The glades our suburbs meshed, the small round red
Berries of hawthorn, and the brighter red
And fleshy ellipsoid hips. How, as he told,
Next spring pink-flowering dog rose, while the slopes
Bore smotherings of white haw. We children clung
To highest boughs, swung over streams on ropes,
Dropping our aitches and our coats among
Long grass. Or rode to Walthamstow, not for its High
Street shops, but Hoe Street market where we'd buy
Marbles and cigarette-cards (I'd asked mother
Why there were 'High Streets' but not 'Hoe' in other
Places, they seemed half-missing); then pedalling home
We'd detour half-empty postwar roads to roam
Snaresbrook, Wanstead, Hackney, Buckhurst Hill
('Stead' *place*, 'hurst *wood*, 'ey' *island*), and the white
Scented hawthorn brimming in overspill.

Now we're through Cullybackey, as I watch
The escorting blossom its profusions catch
Rattling the window, the man opposite
Rouses: 'A'm leein asleep, an next stap's hame,
Forby twa mile. Me fether wud ha came
Hadnae he dinged the car fornenst oor dure.
A'll thole the walk.' He stands as the brakes grip
And Ballymoney (*peat town*) rooftops slip
Alongside. And he's gone.

Now there are fewer
White splodges. This upsurge of Walthamstow's
Childhood of *'ips* and *'aws* and *'ighs* and *'oes*,
Me farver 'oo . . . did not, when next year Mum,
My sister and I moved across London, come,
And not for decades and him dead, explanation –
Nostalgia merely? No, more like implosion
As today's blossom annihilates all between –
Moves, jobs, relationships, parenthood, what's been
For me the world and shaping me now blown
Out like a matchflame. And I sit alone,
Today my birthday, in a railway train
Rocking me on and homeward to Coleraine.
Saturated, as fifty years ago,
With haw's perennial white, that melts like snow.

28 May 1998

Caught

i.m. Bill Speake, 1909–1998

They've called it *a good innings.*
  According to what came
You drove, cut, glanced, defended.
  And always played the game.

So when some quirk of pitch
  Or spin (you hadn't blundered)
Caught out what seemed unfinished,
  While the spectators wondered

And some hope to cheat the touch
  You'd felt, you didn't linger,
  Through shadow falling longer
Reached the boundary-rope as
  The umpire raised his finger.

A Letter from Taormina

to Francesca Colosi and Liliana Cucinotta

From the wide railed lip of Piazza Nove Aprile
   Blue falls to sea too far below
For audible murmur. Shirtsleeved in late October
   I sip coffee at the same table as eighteen months ago
When here with my son, who was off buying postcards.
   As our train had glided southward from Naples, when we named
To the man who spoke English our destination,
   The Land where is always summer! he exclaimed.
Whereas in Ireland one day can have all four seasons.
   But Francesca, back home in Palermo from years
Enduring Milan's frigid bustle which shadowed your letters
   With loneliness and fears,
And Lili along the coast from here in Messina,
   Working as English-language guide to your tall
Norman cathedral (that unlike Humpty Dumpty,
   Has been put together after each fall
In earthquakes, in the Second World War's bombardment),
   Again being here brims my head with a sense of how much
Our islands at opposite ends of Europe
   Have in common: centuries in the clutch
Of alien rule, and its residual silt of resentments;
   The cancer of secrecies, behindbacks spite,
And the people killing each other;
   The grovelling to priests, the despairing flight
Of the young who yet come back to be buried.
   Through my dreams the Mournes, the Reeks, Fair Head, Benlettery
Surface like whales; and of your island D.H. Lawrence noted,
   Every outline is like pure memory.

In Coleraine for a year, you both read the Victorians, chose
   For your coursework to write on Emily Brontë,
That novel of passions, vendettas, hauntings, woes.
   Have you been to Yorkshire? I asked. You'd not. *But the Brontës*,
I explained, *were half-Irish*, their father from County Down.
   And you have your own Bronte,
Not a novelist but the lava-stone town
   On Etna. Nelson was made the Duke of Bronte
By Ferdinand of the Two Sicilies when he knocked on the head
   The Naples revolt as the Queen Maria Carolina

Via Emma Hamilton said,
  Like an Irish town (in which, Napper Tandy's *most distressful country*,
The gibbets were creaking after the failed rising of 'Ninety-Eight),
  With summary hangings.
And Bronte being the giant who made, so the myths relate,
  Zeus's bolts, Emma called Nelson *My Lord of Thunder*.

In Ireland, putting on layers of sweaters,
  You took off round glens, loughs, castles, mountain and coast,
The pace of things to your taste, acquiring a taste for Guinness.
  Francesca, you talk of the beauty; while Lili one of your most
Insistent memories is the dazzle and chirrup
  Of the Portrush Amusements each night as you walked back
To your room from the train. And the day you were driving
  Somewhere far west, off the beaten track
In Mayo or Galway in field-level cloud and driving
  Rain, *soft weather* we say, and you passed
A crossroads sign, in Irish you couldn't interpret,
  And drove on for an hour and at last
Crossroads again and you saw it was the same signpost . . .
  But what did you make of the pain
Of troubled Ulster, the shootings,
  The bomb that November that shattered the heart of Coleraine?

Lili, you held your new-born daughter when my son and I
  At the end of our travels met you last year in Messina –
Much knocked about since Odysseus passed by
  Through the tidal swirls that Homer transformed to Charybdis,
Gulper of ships. You were glad we had been impressed:
  Those who come and don't like us we send back in boxes.
There's many a true word spoken in jest.
  We'd loved it. In Syracuse's huge stone-stepped Greek theatre
I sat brooding alone
  (Rory was roaming above round the sweep of its skyline)
On the thousands of routed Athenians thrown
  In the quarries behind me to die; but more on the old glories,
Archimedes at work on sand circles, Aeschylus here staging plays,
  Inventing drama two thousand years before Shakespeare . . .
When suddenly down beside me, black eyes ablaze,
  Quick as her shadow was young Electra.
In jeans. *I'm from Ireland,* I replied.
  That's cool. She was Josephine *frrom Agrrigento,*

Had I been there? *Tomorrow*. Then swarming from every side
  Her friends, a flutter of hands: was I *marri-ed?* what was my *jobba?*
Ah, Shakaspeara – 'To be, or notta to be . . .'
  Was I *cattolico?* Then I was *protestante?*
It's all a bit complex, the problem for me . . .
  Piano, piano! they laughed. Had I a *girla-frienda?*
Ah Josephine! your hands flying and vibrant rippling voice
  And slang picked up, you said, *in Rrichmond, Virrginia . . .*
Rory had watched: *Amazing, all touching you, even the boys –*
  Like you'd come from space. It couldn't happen in England . . .

Which now is *back home* again, after thirty years in Ireland.
  Cromer perched on its cliff, with its lofty church tower,
Lifeboat, End-of-the-Pier Show, putting greens, narrow sidestreets
  With fish-and-chip bars for dodging a shower
And walls of nubbly flintstone.
  And twice a day for kids on the sand the game
Is up as the tide floods in to crash against shingle.
  Across the county pubs proclaim
The Victory, The Admiral, The Trafalgar, The Norfolk Hero.
  Scarcely foreseen by the boy who learned to sail
On the shallows of Barton Broad among reeds and sedges,
  Nor the hazardous battle-travail
That would find him doubly ennobled signing his letters
  (But with the other hand)
Nelson and Bronte; no sailor more honoured
  Since storm-tossed Odysseus put out from land.

Aged eighteen, Nelson swore
  To be a hero and brave every danger.
Yet he too hoped for a final berth connubially ashore:
  This campaign will bring us peace, then we'll set off for Bronte.
He wrote Emma as the fleet
  Sailed for the Baltic, where when retreat was signalled
He famously clapped the glass to his blind eye, and turned defeat
  Into victory. But nor could he then see Trafalgar.
Had he lived to come to his Etna estate
  He'd have encountered a landscape that puts in perspective
All human vaunts and heroics: beneath the great
  Ever-smouldering crater last week again I marvelled
At the interweave of swathes of snow
  With black ash hot to the touch and issuing

Vapours from Hades. A solidified lava-flow
  Protrudes rooftops, a church steeple.

Among olive and almond trees still stand the temples of Agrigento.
  Here is the Temple of Heracles,
Here the Temple of Hera. Or partly stand, for their time-scale
  Is not the tourist's, negligent centuries
Have turned their backs on Greek Akragas, the roofs are fallen,
  Columns rear broken, are gone. A loose
Jumble of rubble the size of a football-pitch
  Was the gargantuan Temple of Zeus,
The largest ever, started in celebration
  After the total defeat
Of Carthage at Himera in 480 BC.
  And it was still incomplete
When seven decades later it was burnt by the Carthaginians.
  And the Romans came and looted, and the Vandals, then a quake
Left the temple to serve Spanish rulers as a quarry.
  The well-kept path we take
Back to the coach-park and postcards skirts a few remnants
  Of the wall of Pindar's *most beautiful city known*
To mortals; where the tyrant Phalaris roasted
  His foes in a brazen bull, to hear it bellow and groan.

At Segesta the temple stands intact in a wide
  Valley, *In gracious grandiosity proof of people who mastered*
Civilisation, reads the English guide.
  At its rival Selinunte, sacked after bitter warfare,
They've excavated nine temples. I lean
  On a fallen capital for a snap; from within Doric columns
Nothing but vacant green
  Undulates to my gaze in every direction.

The ancient cities go down, only fragments
  Of all they matured and intended persist,
Pop-up picturesque on a coach-tour landscape,
  Adrift from their world that bequeathed great names we twist
To cryptic-crossword-clues for urban commuters
  To hazard a lunch-hour guess –
Old sage in bathtub he mad cries Eureka;
  In a lather on water? Suds, o yes!
That lived by plough and oar, pasture and sword, sacrificing

To capricious gods, and more were slaves than free,
On olives and fish and figs and goat's cheese, and were slaughtered
Often enough, or drowned in the wine-dark sea.
Then came Rome and Byzantium, Arabs, Normans and Swabians;
Long neglect under Spain that turned from the heart
Of the old for a new world to plunder across the Atlantic.
Bitter bread for the body, the spirit inert;
Speaking a dialect that is your history's
Oral palimpsest,
Hoarding and interweaving the many-tongued voices
Of the serially dispossessed.
Still the great cone, the Pedestal of Heaven
The Greeks supposed, twists up its tawny coil
Of incense, giving and taking,
Whelming farms with what time makes fertile soil.

Verga depicts the heirs
Of squandered fortunes, ancestral halls dishevelled
To storage-barns, carved bedsteads, sedan-chairs
Heaped as lumber. And the great nobles over the water
In Naples adorning the Bourbon court.
Like Ireland's grandees parading themselves in London
While shreds-and-patches squirelings shivered over the port
In peeling mansions back home, still condescending
To a tenantry mashing spuds to a bowl of champ,
And fleeing to sell their slave-born accents
In the USA or an English navvy-camp,
Still calling down saints and blessings.

That chime between our volcanic novelist and your town
On Etna's wuthering heights has its ironic
Resonance: when Patrick Brunty from County Down,
Having hauled himself up from the cottage in Ballydrumroney
To Cambridge in 1802 amended his name
As he did, it wasn't for any
Cachet poor Sicily could bestow, but to claim
Some kindlings from the lustre of England's hero.
And when the Brontë sisters forty-odd years
On made their literary name soon after his last elevation
In stone on a column above mortal peers,
London rumoured, *They're kinsfolk of Nelson.*

The public gardens, sunlight winking among the greenery,
People stretched along benches; and the pure
Sound from the tennis courts of children's voices
Calling the score.
Yesterday, Lili, when I took *il pullman* up to Messina
On your day off, you gave
Me the tour of your cathedral, and the space and the splendour
Of pillar and aisle and nave
Transcended time's vicissitudes, and my mocking
Spirit was stilled.
And when you turned at the door as we departed
And bobbed, and crossed yourself, it looked not willed
Or ingrained bondage but, if habit,
One natural as to breathe or sing.
Yet so too for the Greeks the carnage of their altars
And smoke of beasts mass-burnt in offering.
Your Giuli had stayed outside in sunlight with her father –
Not yet her sort of toy,
Or whatever more than toy they stand for, the contraptions
Of human faith. Not joy
Of that simple sort one craves less for oneself than one's children.
Watching yours recalled Rory when that old,
As trusting and eager, reaching to cherish lawn dandelions
As earth's precious gift of gold.

And I see them again, their unspoilt
Faces in rows in the paper,
The teenaged lives that were spilt
When the bomb exploded in Omagh
At a carnival Saturday's heart;
Smiling for friendly cameras,
Smiles that foreshadow no hurt,
Now in its aftermath pleading
For the all-still-before-them lost.
I turned over pages of newsprint
Depicting what evil unloosed:
A crumpled pram jutting from debris;
Cars dismembered; an anguished dad.
And I thought of what tact left unpictured.
Twenty-nine people dead,
A hospital-load of the wounded.
And newly removed to uncomprehending England, I longed

To be back home in grieving Ireland,
Rent by the hydra-headed spawn of a past by which it was wronged.
And where, as Sicily has *omerta*,
Whatever you say, say nothing, they say,
Stick to your personal decencies, mind your own business,
Keep fingers crossed and hope for a better day.
And history drives us round in circles.
Ulster is at the crossroads again, in mist
And the signpost as before and the right direction
There to be yet again missed,
Unless the hatreds are buried in the beautiful landscape.

Orange groves prosper across the Plain of Catania,
Here everything's out in the sun,
It gleams on the stone of old temples, new concrete of roadworks,
Eating and drinking are done
Outdoors, on pavement or patio.
Your novelist Leonardo Sciascia said,
Ideologies have never had any
Success here. The Black and the Red,
Mussolini's Fascists and Communism,
Took little root.
As if the sun burnt out all such infection:
The Mafia bomb and shoot
For profit. Is it Ireland's shrouding cloud and rainfall
Ferment romantic dreams? –
So pure faith pulls the trigger, sets the detonator,
And filters out the screams . . .

But such notions engender their own rebuke.
It's armchair fancy to blame a climate for evil's textures,
And its symbolism's an arty fluke;
Torsos in bin-bags demand we look deeper than whether their killers
Came from a sun or a soak.
And the Mafia like the Irish thing began as a cause of the people;
And England too had its Norman yoke,
The iron of alien laws, but there it faded
Into a family quarrel and castle and court
Were repossessed by the native tongue, and outlawry
Was sanitised into the myth of a forest sport,
Treasure hunts with archery stunts, Robin Hood in the greenwood.

Simpering lovelies chirrup out winning lottery numbers
On my hotel bedroom TV,
There are ads for consumer fads, all our trinkets of status,
And inviting you and me
To *SEXY SHOP LA MOON a Palermo . . .*
Where the Norman monuments, the cupolas and domes
Float on a cauldron of traffic garnished with palmtrees,
Above the old kings in their porphyry tombs,
Courtyards scented with jasmine, grim alleys breeding child-labour.
And there in the restaurant, Francesca, you raised
English eyebrows when, one of them having ventured
That you were happy to be back here from Milan, you blazed
Ah, how is one to be happy? – that is the question.
How can one have happiness without love?
But that's true. And as one gets older
One realises more acutely it is above
All the impulse to share, which transfigures a landscape,
Its every grassblade, gives rain in a lamplit street
Firework-gold glamour; makes life incandescent
That denied it finds the great things incomplete.
And it seems only yesterday I aimed for the stars
On the park swing, thrusting higher and higher, clear of the rooftops,
The earthbound procession of cars.
And it all, with love, seemed a birthright.

Nelson kept his aim clear, like the old Greek heroes
His slogan: *To glory we steer.*
He watered the fleet at the fountain of mythical Arethusa
In Syracuse before sailing to Aboukir
Bay to trounce the French; and chose the ancient idiom,
I will return either crowned with laurel or
Covered with cypress. All that's out of fashion
As we near the end of our bloodiest century, and war
Now mostly a matter of pressing a button
To annihilate thousands out of sight.
And serious aspiration, since Eliot, Freud and Kafka,
Seeks not worldly but inner light.

Time destroys, disguises or blends. Last week I strolled
The luxuriant floor, with oleander, wild celery, tropical fruit-trees,
Of the largest of Syracuse's old
Quarries, now the Latomia del Paradiso –

Where once those Athenian captives died.
  Their hugeness attests the greatness of the ancient city.
And the Romans' attack was defied
  By Archimedes, devising catapults that projected
Rocks on their ships, and death-rays – focusing sun from concave
  Mirrors of polished bronze – so the Romans thought they were being
Assailed by the gods. But it didn't save
  The city, nor Archimedes, slain at his studies.
But also in Syracuse stands,
  In its island-heart with that freshwater fountain by the harbour
That first lured Greek colonist bands,
  The cathedral, Santa Maria delle Colonne,
Part Byzantine, partly Norman, and when part fell in the shock
  Of 1693 they reconstructed
The façade in splendidly columned Baroque.
  But columns far older form part of this building:
The nave and one of the aisles incorporate
  Those of the Doric Temple of Athena,
Built to give thanks and in triumph after the great
  Victory at Himera,
That prompted at Akragas the massive Temple of Zeus.
  And one time made mock of and rubbished,
While this other is still in use,
  In a harmony of the styles of well over two millennia
And the spirit and mind
  That informed their creation. A composite symbol
Of what allows hope for our kind,
  Despite the worse tricks we've conjured-up since Phalaris.

I've threaded all the narrow winding lanes of Taormina,
  Edging fly-on-the-wall
Past scooters that zip and weave and stop aslant abruptly
  Spotting a friend or to call
In a shop; I've climbed thousands of steps, down to the pebbly
  Beach with the Isola Bella and hotel's pool,
And up the old stepped mule-track to the Saracen castle –
  Which taught me respect for the mule.
Tomorrow the plane will lob me back to a rainy English November,
  Its palette of vivid shires
Scattered with blight and litter, theme-parks and old cathedrals
  Lifting their towers and spires,
That can seem as marooned by history's onrush as the temples

Put up by the ancient Greeks
At the dawn of our civilisation; for every age, being time-bound,
Clothes the ineffable it senses and seeks
In approximate shapes: a bearded Zeus wielding lightning,
A burning bush, Handel's *Messiah*, angels with wings,
These glorious buildings that yet collect merely an echo
Of the pulse at the heart of things.
Tonight I dined late, by the time I reached coffee
Only one couple remained, an American pair
Exchanging counts of their own and their children's divorces,
Like rival bids. I pushed back my chair,
Then she said in an altered cadence,
If you have enough guts, you get smashed. And only the folly of youth
And of hubris don't know it. For Aeschylus in the *Orestia*
It was Zeus's law: *We must suffer into truth.*
That's our ironic destiny. So leaving
Again your lovely island, my wish for you my friends,
Humorous sensitive Lili and questing Francesca
(The quest never ends
Until we do, but I hope you continue resisting
The money-tongued coercions lying about the real,
Urging shop till you drop, get the trappings,
You can't eat or show-off the ideal),
Is *con amore* that you may count your blessings
And catch your luck while you can; and be gifted with the clear
Vision we need to recognise when it is offered.
As on that day when I walked back last year
From Piazza Nove Aprile along the Corso,
And from a table his voice, *Hey, Dad!*
Two huge pizzas before him overhung with thick topping;
And we laughed, full of all we had seen, knowing this moment glad.

The Millennium Letter

1

An aeroplane is droning in the sky
  Off-screen above another game of tennis,
Delayed to let the Centre Court grass dry,
  A blonde from Kansas, a brunette from Venice
  Striking a furry ball with grunts and menace,
Forsaking all else at each break in the rain I am
  Entranced as any devotee of Zen is:
A world that's learnt to end itself with plutonium
Cheers the last Wimbledon of the millennium.

2

A Circuit judge is in the news today,
  Having postponed a serious case explaining
That he has tickets for this fortnight's play;
  In Sydney, up all night, they miss work feigning
  Sickness; bank-robbers, lovers, are abstaining
(At least, until the end of the next set).
  Last time round, when Ethelred was reigning,
And America and Europe never met,
People braced themselves in a cold sweat:

3

A thousand years since Christ, they scanned the sky
  For portents, shooting-stars, eclipse of comet,
Sure then their end (but from outside) was nigh,
Earth would be whelmed like a dead leaf, and from it
  All folk plucked up to a celestial summit
For Judgement, sins transparent: if God's ire
  Cast them from His radiance, doomed to plummet
To the Abyss – itinerary pretty dire
For souls who'd never seen their neighbour shire.

4

Their food, clothes, couplings, all of the one village,
  Nothing impinging from beyond but, now
And then, civil mayhem, axe and sword and pillage.
  We see them stuck behind some ox-drawn plough
  On tapestries, shoving their lives away, clenched brow
And scowling visage skewed towards the sempstress.
  Except the handful perched on the top bough
In gold and furs, whom cat-and-mouse the temptress,
Fortune toys with as King, Pope, or Empress.

5

No chips, phones, care agencies; and no source mentions
  What they did for dentistry or loo-paper.
Stealing honey carried the death-sentence.
  No fun, except some booze-and-sweat-swamped caper
  Subsiding to a floor with unlit taper
(That's still our clubbers' paradigm of mirth).
  No social concepts bubbling to escape a
Routine of tilth, filth, feuds, diseases, dearth,
Fearing hellfire, living hell on earth.

6

But so, to you, might look the way that we
  Live here and now – you're certainly a screen-watcher
Wherever you are because, my addressee,
  I've made my mind up that you're in the future.
  I was tempted first – it's only human nature
To gloat with hindsight at boasts sunk like lead,
  With Shelley to Ozymandias cry 'Gotcha!' –
To pick someone (there's so much to be said)
From *last* millennium's roll-call of the dead.

7

Rulers and empire-builders obviously;
  A host of savants, Locke, Rousseau, Marx, Freud;
Jefferson, whose script for liberty
  Ignored his slaves; the countless paranoid

Puritans stifling art, sex, thought, life, buoyed
By zeal's complacency. Some I'd not care to
Tackle except by mailing: when annoyed
Henry VIII and Stalin didn't spare too
Many who cavilled – till none were left who'd dare to.

8

I'd like to tell Luther how it all shook out;
And Columbus; or Galileo whom they made
Recant, by torture threats, his truth about
Our Earth, *It moves*. Or there's the First Crusade,
Massacring stormed Jerusalem to wade
Calf-deep in blood and sing hymns for God's sake.
Hitler's 'thousand-year Reich'? – *he saw* it flayed.
But not all's *schadenfreude*: I would shake
Gratefully the hands of Blake, Burke, Drake.

9

Milton would seem too lofty, frown at jokes;
In front of Shakespeare I'd feel quite transparent;
Churchill and Pitt were both inveterate soaks –
In one the genius like a raging torrent,
Now inspirational, now run aberrant;
The other good at balancing the books
But cold to passion, whether history's current
Of change, the arts, or women . . . Famous spooks –
Most well worth scribbling to, even the crooks.

10

At Wimbledon, again out come the covers
(Outside my window mellow light assuages
Brickwork, birds volley song at blue above) as
Scooping their gear up, off stalk the teenagers,
Our modern icons, one known for outrageous
Tantrums, smashing rackets, the other's sole
Pastime shopping; they've stormed the tabloid pages.
Their tour-stats, pushy dads, fads – we can scroll
Their websites. Two kids in a goldfish-bowl.

11

Thus fame's devalued since Wren built St Paul's.
  And chivalry? I watched Sir Richard Hadlee
In his last Test Match, firing down lethal balls,
  England as usual batting very badly.
  Leather struck pad: *'HUZZAAAAAT!!??'* – he swivelled, madly
Prancing and pointing, with a glare to blight
  All umpire-doubt. And shaking her head sadly
My German friend said, 'How is he a *knight*?'
White-charger Grail-quest pros were more polite.

12

But, to the future: I don't know who you are,
  For you don't yet exist, and can't unravel
Your ins-and-outs of habitat, what you wear,
  Your politics, recreations, how you travel.
  One's better off just gazing at one's navel
Than concocting detailed drafts and panoramas
  Of things to come. Though sci-fi merchants cavil,
With u- or dys-topias, I'm no Nostradamus.
Tomorrow's weather? – don't ask me, ask farmers.

13

I have decided, though, that you're a poet:
  So *sui generis* square peg in round hole,
Taking pains. Someone I can talk to at
  Ease, a focus and a fellow-soul
  For things we might both care about. Not the whole
Shebang: this sheaf of sketches and reflections
  I flight your way can't cover pole to pole
How Earth fares now, you've your own time's dissections
Of that – though histories are mostly fictions.

14

But when, in your millennium, to place you?
  Better, for communication, soon
Than centuries ahead, for in that case you
  Might be, with gene and surgical science gone

Berserk, a life-form I could not attune
To, wired-up brain-in-a-bottle, concatenation
Of others' parts. Or living on the Moon –
Where poetry's old themes won't find their occasion,
Or must at least be dressed in different fashion.

15

No *season of mists and mellow fruitfulness*;
Lovers, looking up in night's non-air,
Instead of *Moon-June-tune* would have, I guess,
To rhyme on *Earth-girth-birth*. And who would dare
Paint drooping steps of melancholy where
Each floats the sufferer metres off the ground?
Moon *has not anything to show more fair*
Than Wordsworth's London, as you look around
Its sealed communes; and – no atmosphere, no sound.

16

I aim this, then, not over-far ahead,
To someone I should recognise, who may
Among unstoppable subtopian spread
And strangling coils of five-tiered motorway,
Still know the sights and sounds we like today:
Woods and moorland, if shorn back, not missing;
Sandcastles on a seaside holiday;
Kew Gardens, Tower Bridge, trawlermen reminiscing;
On rain-soaked June roads bicycle-wheels hissing.

17

No doubt they would not let me light my pipe up
Where you live – or at least I'd have to sneak,
On cloudy moonless nights when time was ripe, up
A distant godforsaken Pennine peak,
Or play some irksome game of hide-and-seek
To dodge your Anti-Smoking-Squad police.
It's getting that way now – although last week
Lost in Castle Mall, seeking advice,
Lighting-up conjured up staff in a trice.

18

But still, in your time, not too many years
  Distant, I am justified I think
In trusting you'll possess, despite our fears
  (But others' hopes, alas) that printers' ink
  Will be usurped by screens that beep and wink,
Plenty of books still – purely as technology
  The book, that cannot 'crash', go on the blink,
Is pocket-portable, needs no apology;
And is much friendlier to Earth's ecology.

19

Will you still use this sort of old-style stanza,
  Rhymed, metrical? It's filched from Spenser's fine
Allegorical extravaganza
  The Faerie Queene, except that this of mine
  Omits one foot of his long final line
Which makes his verse move statelier, more solemn
  Than suits my mix – chat, skits, yarns, in a brine
Of more astringent flavouring, like alum –
Or my course, zigzag like a ski-slalom.

20

Our 'poetry scene' now's ripe for a post-mortem:
  I take, to hang the corpse on, the kerfuffle
About the Laureateship, since late last autumn
  Ted Hughes died. The media picked names to shuffle;
  Plenty more, pigs rooting for a truffle,
Snuffled around – and all the usual host
  Of ideologues carpet-bombed the theme with waffle –
We must have next a black, a woman. Most
Demanded redefinition of the post.

21

Democracy, now teetering on the brink
  Of your millennium, looks back and demurs
At Tennyson knuckling down with quill and ink
  When Queen Victoria commanded verse

In memory of her mother (he did no *worse*
Than *Long as the heart beats life* etcetera, deeming
Laureateship more an honour than a curse) –
Such flunkeying today, beyond just seeming
Anachronistic, sets our levellers screaming.

22

The lyre as emblematic instrument
Of the poet's artistry and flair has
Long been junked; and now it's evident
What's clangorously replaced it everywhere – as
This year our Prime Minister Tony Blair has
Told, the device he'd put (no doubt with hectic
Sound) to represent ours to future eras
In the Millennium Dome is an electric
Guitar. I wish his tastes were more eclectic.

23

And there rose clamour for a 'People's Poet' . . .
Since sad Diana's death the epithet
Fixed then to *Princess* has been one to throw at
All issues: House of Lords reform? – we get
Demands for a People's Peerage; tabloids fret
For a People's Budget . . . I've my admirations
For many people; but the word when met
In populist cant has bleak associations,
As when used by the old Soviet-bloc nations.

24

Some poets are superior? – 'That's *élitist*,'
Bay or bleat the cultural-relativist mob.
Here Tabloid Man is not fooled in the slightest –
Would hound Sir Alex from his Man. U. job
If by signing to turn out for the club
One-legged Sikhs, single-mothers – poets – he
Had on such principles contrived to rob
The fans of this year's fairy-tale victory
Over the Old German Enemy.

25

Of true worth, with some others, we have Seamus,
  Whose deep imaginative excavations
Turn up verse-nuggets that have made him famous;
  He upholds, too, art's noblest aspirations.
  Though some of his cherishings prompt my reservations –
On home utensils. What next? – *The Toilet-Brush*,
  Curve and balance apt for deft bowl-lustrations,
Snug round-the-bend probes, a rapt syllabic hush
Swelling to hymn the chill cathartic flush?

26

But Heaney's so hedged round his verse with Green,
  Not Red-White-and-Blue, as to ensure he
Wouldn't run for a Court post from the Queen.
  Other big fish, Derek Walcott and Les Murray,
  Swim half the world away . . . And so the flurry
Fixings, faxings, fallings-out of old chums,
  Found rest in Motion, like pig-waste in slurry.
At least we're spared a nose-ringed-jerking-thumbs–
Performance-poet backing herself on drums.

27

But (blasting history's heavy-bloomed espalier)
  The post's been lopped from lifelong to ten years.
The sole point of such heritage paraphernalia
  Is its dotty charm, like Beefeaters,
  Enhanced here by the fact these balladeers
Are Royal nomineees. Did the Queen peruse
  Over her cornflakes famous lines of verse
From the early volumes of Ted Hughes? –
My manners are tearing off heads . . . What were her views?

28

Alas, she and her forebears all score zero
  For literary passion, excepting for
Henry VIII, who like the Roman Nero
  Affected arts of peace as well as war,

Strummed, hummed, pranced and scribbled – and before
It had become not quite the thing to knock
Off heads, despatched the poet Surrey, our
First English sonneteer, to the axe, a shock
Non-metaphorical case of writer's block.

29

Though Henry's judgement there was not aesthetic
But *raison d'état*, his is not now our way;
We've poets soporific or emetic,
But live and let live, let them out to play;
Yet where among the host who sport today
Are Yeats's vision, Auden's hawk's-eye detailing
This island now, MacNeice's craft? Passé
Too Hardy's heartrendingness. They pack these failings
In rhythms flat as sticks trailed down park railings.

30

For Laureateship, true, talent has been quite
Irrelevant, most who've held the post were sheep:
Cibber, Pope's Dunce supreme; Tate, whose rewrite
Making *Lear* happy would make Shakespeare weep;
Southey, a Monarchy's Uriah Heep;
Shadwell, whom Dryden crowned for folly's reign
(*His tragic Muse gives smiles, his comic sleep*);
Lately Day Lewis drivelling to sustain
A 1960s I'M BACKING BRITAIN campaign.

31

Nor can there be objection in the slightest
To an incumbent living on until
Too gaga to complete even the tritest
Quatrain, tell the time, or sign his will:
As with Beefeaters whose lot is to fill
A gaudy costume tourists like to view
And no one calls on to draw swords and kill
Insurgents at the Tower, the Laureate too
Has as his proper role to be, not do.

32

But Motion's declared he will 'be an Ambassador
  For Poetry' – not just one more wine-drenched sleeper.
Could there be any aspiration flaccider?
  A poet should be poacher, not gamekeeper,
  In football parlance striker not a sweeper.
Too many now are committee operators,
  Apparatchiks, fixing, shuffling paper –
Not Shelley's *unacknowledged legislators*
Of mankind, but rubber-stamped arts curators.

33

They scramble for the golden eggs that goose
  The State might lay, with councils, residencies
And 'outreach' projects, aim to mass-produce
  (Never mind quality) what gloriously's
  The last of our old cottage industries,
Where mind, life, language, seek their true connection
  In solitude. Now creativity's
Hired for 'placements': in firms' staff-selection,
Banks, parks; here in Norfolk, waste collection.

34

'Poetry Places' . . . Art's nurturing location
  Lies within; cliff, alley, valley, slum,
That travel with us when we're on vacation
  And brim the silence of a room at home.
For those who think by entry-fee to come
Upon that landscape, one of Motion's peers
  Is briefed to set up shop inside that Dome –
Though if for a fixed-term one thousand years
I fear he'll find it pulled down round his ears.

35

And thick upon the ground mapped by the planner
  For parcelling into paddocks for the soul
Are those who spin their lines behind the banner
  POETRY IS THE NEW ROCK-AND-ROLL:

On-the-hoof anecdotalists cajole
Pub-punters, doggerel rap is all the rage;
Narcissists, nutters, and the merely null
Swarm to strut their stuff upon a stage.
And never mind it reads dead on the page:

36

There is a style of nudge-nudge-wink-wink trick
Some poets use for face-to-face rapport:
Lines tell their author has got drunk, been sick,
Had technical problems with a restaurant floor;
That he or she's been a porn addict, or
Not known who they're in bed with – which all flatters
The fans, *I've done that, been there, know the score,*
They gurgle, *this guy's relevant, he matters . . .*
Pope, Milton, Burns, for them unsought backwaters.

37

Bad poetry's always with us – mediocrity
Eighteenth-century style would bow and twirl
For lordly patrons, scribbling with alacrity
Toadying panegyrics to an earl;
Victorian verse, in sentimental swirl,
To top-hats and starched shirts and morals cried
Lawks-a-mercy, sir, I'm a good girl!
(So Jekyll, secretly dissatisfied,
Sallied forth nightly after whores, as Hyde).

38

Well, time will tell, and by yours you'll know whether
The trash promoted by Arts bureaucrats
That seems worse and more of it altogether
Than in the past, when even half-schooled brats
Knew metrics, and could tune their sharps and flats,
Is come to stay, or just a passing blip.
Meanwhile, the thought of placepersons, fat cats,
Decennially scrabbling for the Laureateship
Might drive the Muse hence on a one-way trip.

39

The most striking verses penned not by but *to*
  A Laureate are Byron's, to kick-start
Don Juan; and (though likely quite untrue
  Of our new incumbent) their satiric dart
  Flies so direct and aptly to the heart
Of that most proper subject for a Laureate
  Our Premier, and the course he's seemed to chart
Checking dissent as with a cowboy's lariat,
The lines I think are worth my while to quarry out.

40

Bob Southey! You're a poet – Poet Laureate,
  And representative of all the race;
Although 'tis true that you turned out a Tory at
  Last, yours has lately been a common case;
  And now, my Epic Renegade . . . Replace
Southey with Blair, all's true – I know the old
  Socialist dream of justice nowadays
Is a vote loser, dead; but being told
All good's in market forces leaves me cold.

41

Byron, no friend to kings and cant, so far
  From Laureateship, was hounded from our coast.
Though, gifted, radical and popular,
  He'd have been the best-ever in the post –
  Although the sort of Beefeater who'd ghost
The Crown Jewels out, to spend on tarts and malkins,
  Augment his house-menagerie, that host
Of quarrelling dogs, cranes, monkeys, peacocks, falcons;
Or given how he died, to help the Balkans.

42

We've still the Balkans – as for centuries
  Prior to Byron's Missolonghi trip:
A peninsula of nationalities
  Who will not live in peace and fellowship;

Where fear, mistrust, and wrongs remembered chip
Reason's veneer off to let murder through;
Jigsaw pieces neither statesmanship
Nor war can puzzle the solution to.
I'm pretty sure you'll have that problem too.

43

That is if – and I wonder – you're still there,
In a world tooled-up for self-immolation,
Where a lone terrorist can go nuclear
And take out cities for their liberation,
Not to speak of the whole population.
In our Cold War days, when the only hard-and-fast
Rule was, in case of Great Power confrontation,
You'll have four minutes, dig shelters in your garden fast,
Things were clear-cut – time just to beg God's pardon fast.

44

The present century that is just ending
Has been the bloodiest of humankind's,
And makes one wonder whither things are tending:
For peace as well as war our know-how finds
Technologies that far outstrip our mind's
Small static wisdom. So we overreach,
Our wastes pollute the planetary winds,
Setting sea-levels rising – yes, I preach,
But half Earth's major cities are on the beach.

45

But, as I've noted, speculation's vanity
Directed at the shape of things to come:
Put pictures on it, that way lies insanity,
It's wiser on that topic to stay dumb;
Yet were it possible to post you some
Gift, you'd choose (if instincts aren't deceivers)
A lifeline back to this millennium
As most precious – we say our present's grievous
But, knowing yours, I doubt if you'll believe us.

46

But – *you'll still have the Balkan problem.* That's
   This century triggered our most pointless war,
1914–18: tit-for-tat's
   Been how it's gone, each group when having power
   Seeking to wipe the others out before
They can do it back. So it's gone to and fro,
   Each spate of slaughtering begetting more.
Red with each other's blood, all parties know
Themselves as pure as winter's mountain snow.

47

These past years, conflict's shifted from Croatia
   Through Bosnia, and now in Kosovo,
Where Nato's powers found a *prima facie*
   Cause for 'just war' upon the Serbs, although
   Only from aeroplanes flown not so low
As to risk loss. Americans get frantic
   When wars they fight in countries they don't know
Bring body-bags back over the Atlantic –
Which to both friends and foes seems unromantic.

48

So lads used just to costly training-flights
   Skimming the Norfolk Broads and Cromer Pier
(Or in one case in Italy's Alpine heights
   Dare-devilling too recklessly, to shear
   A cable-car wire, as occurred last year),
Were posted out to smash Serb factories
   And bridges – which for weeks did not appear
Much help to Kosovo's stricken refugees
Fleeing Serb 'ethnic cleansing' policies.

49

'Ethnic cleansing' – our time's slimy phrase
   Coined by those *doing* it for genocidal
Slaughter, and setting villages ablaze
   (Though the Albanians too have not been idle

In such purifying zeal when history's tidal
Ebb and flow has tipped their way that favour).
And those surviving all those who have died'll
Foster revenge on grief – for a mass grave or
Wrecked home's not apt to make one love one's neighbour.

50

We give what happens to us much mental sieving;
According to that fount of wisdom Plato
The unconsidered life is not worth living.
But what has such philosophy to say to
Those wondering where they'll get their next potato,
Caught between Serbian ethnic cleansing squads
And the high-altitude bomb-strafes of Nato? –
Consideration, weighing-up the odds,
May find life thus the sport of cruel gods.

51

But – Serbia in the end capitulated:
We've ground forces in Kosovo at last;
Most refugees are now repatriated,
Some making Nato's soldiers quite aghast
By starting vengeance violently and fast
Against the Serbs . . . 'The end'? We may have won
The war, but how the peace? – all troops amassed
Can do is keep a faulty lid half-on
Such feudings till such time as they are gone.

52

They've opened files on war crimes, stack and stock them up
At the Court of Justice at The Hague;
But how to catch the criminals to lock them up?
On this, our politicians remain vague.
I hope they persevere, and don't renege,
I wish we could enisle Milosovic
Napoleon-style on Pitcairn, Ailsa Craig,
Where all that he can stamp on is a beach;
But he still rules in Belgrade, out of reach.

53

For thirty years from 1968
  I have witnessed ethnic cleansing. No,
Not *scores* of thousands killed at quite the rate
  Of Rwanda, Bosnia and Kosovo:
  The Ulster tribal-murder-rate's been slow;
But there ground forces came in at the start
  In colossal numbers, as a ratio,
And built and manned great walls to keep apart
Those none could coax into a change of heart.

54

An army, as such apt to shoot its rifles,
  Becomes part of the problem it was sent
To solve, adds near as much as it half-stifles.
  Meanwhile, shops, bars, restaurants were rent
  With bombs and bullets; and the innocent,
As ever, suffered most. From their workplaces
  People dragged and shot – their monument
Newsprint snaps of their once smiling faces,
Black flags to mark the spot; the bullets' traces.

55

By the mid-1970s, in Belfast
  Alone, 60,000 *families* had been –
By threats, incendiarism, guns, bomb-blast –
  Driven from their homes: Orange and Green,
  Estates were cleansed till their shade was pristine.
While Protestants who farm too near the Border
  Were shot or forced away. What Ulster's seen
Hasn't been *full-blown* pogrom – just mass-murder
Mitigated thanks to law and order.

56

I cast my vote, before I left last year,
  For the Assembly that might draw a red line
Under the carnage, let the parties share
  Power . . . They've not agreed yet, rows instead line

Front pages below the old familiar headline
ULSTER IS AT THE CROSSROADS. Blair's not balking,
There in Belfast, but two days past his 'deadline'
The bad news is the parties are still talking;
The good news also is that they're still talking.

57

I know a rural crossroads in Mid-Derry,
Among green fields (though only some are Green);
Two houses either side, and I knew very
Well a woman in one – but what's between
Us, how what was and might-have-been
Still haunt my dreams, are not my theme today . . .
Cross Keys they call this crossroads, and the scene
All round should soothe ungentle thoughts away,
Bleated arpeggios, hedgerows foaming may.

58

A mile along the main road, Upperlands –
Blink as your car flips through, and you could miss it,
Though on summer nights you might hear loyalist bands –
Slopes up. No need for words' analysis, it
Just *looks* as staunch as Ian Paisley'd wish it:
One gable-end is blazoned NO POPE HERE
(He isn't, nor is likelier to visit),
Kerbstones are red-white-blue, small gardens flare
Orange lilies in the balmy air.

59

Return to Cross Keys and turn left (the house
Tucked in that corner's Catholic) – no feature
Of field and farmstead ravelling sheep and cows
Signals the fact to the bypassing watcher,
But you've crossed a border that's unknown to nature.
Three miles (you'll hardly pass one car or van)
Along that rural backroad, and you reach a
One-street village, Swatragh, where they're 'thran'
The other way – deep-dyed Republican.

60

At Upperlands the flax dams and old mill –
There over two hundred years, no longer making
Linen, the great water-wheel is still
At the beetling shed, the sluice-gates leaking,
But still a profitable undertaking
In modern fabrics – are (as well I know,
The beauty of the waters is heartbreaking)
Where in fine weather loving couples go,
To walk the paths; and some to fish, or row.

61

But idylls of such harmless sort are set
Aside when each July brings drums and marches:
The local youth mount guard against the threat
That Swatragh bikers armed with flaming torches
Will zap through to burn down the Orange arches
They've rigged across the road showing King Billy
And other icons. Each vigilante clutches
A stone . . . Performed thus, each cause seems just silly –
Why can't they all stop in and watch the telly?

62

The countryside's a place of violent habits:
Those lambs are bred for slaughter; every night
Foxes roam – you hear the shriek of rabbits;
And the owl's hunting-cry before it's light.
A heron from the flax dams lifts in flight
To find another fishpond where he can –
Across in Swatragh, anywhere in sight
Between the Sperrins and the River Bann.
But none of all this mayhem's *partisan*.

63

Along that three-mile backroad from Cross Keys
That twists and dips (so when it has been raining
Your car-wheels splash up water over trees
And hedge and roadside bank and sheugh, and craning

Through windscreen-wipers whopping into waning
Evening light you slow and take more care)
To Swatragh, if appearances had meaning
The Troubles would be worlds off, no affair
Of the just five lonely houses you pass there.

64

From which, in the 'quieter' two years preceding
The IRA ceasefire of '94.
Two people hit by bullets were left bleeding
To death, and separately a couple more
Charged, convicted and imprisoned for
Bombings and murders . . . Locals not 'involved',
Who've done nothing, know who's done things, know the score . . .
More news: the Talks have failed, nothing's resolved,
The power-sharing Executive is shelved . . .

65

Back to the tennis . . . The topics congregated
Within this bundle I cast upon time's stream
If disparate, are not so unrelated
As to your first perusal they might seem:
Pindar took sporting prowess as art's theme;
And it's a safe bet that, however far
Into the future, fans will cheer their team.
From the Greeks on, sport, poetry and war
Show us profoundly who and what we are.

66

Each has its codes, heroics, flukes, reversals;
And loneliness; in each the style's the man;
And failure's not pre-empted by rehearsals.
What better speaks our human nature than
Our childlike impulses since life began
To leap high through thin air or win a race,
To create some form beyond ourselves that can
Transcend mortality through its lucid grace,
And alas! to hate a different sort of face?

67

In football foreigners are simply hated
    By the English; but our tennis crowds are much
More appreciative and sophisticated:
    They're cast as *fiery Latins, doughty Dutch,*
    Moody Slavs; the French girls smash with such
Sang-froid; those Swedes, true, seem a bit laconic . . .
    But above everything, fans love to clutch
To heart those whom when young were thought demonic –
Now seasoned to History from mere histrionic.

68

Becker, who in his teens got up our noses
    Rampaging round the Centre Court to win
(And *German* too), now gets applause and roses;
    And Agassi, who committed every sin
    Abusing umpires, rackets, playing in
Weird garb. While Graf, who always had nice legs
    And grace, is now the crowd's pure heroine.
Her mixed-doubles partner too – still on his pegs,
McEnroe, who called Wimbledon the dregs.

69

More often boasted of than seen in action,
    This is the English spirit of fair play –
Or is it just one gets more satisfaction,
    Because one's getting older day by day,
    Seeing sportspersons half one's age dismay
Others half theirs . . . *I* might win it yet,
    Should I get round to it . . . But from the way
Things tend it's easy to extrapolate
The final you'll see: *Young Brat v. Old Vet*:

70

Brat skateboards out, bronzed, muscular and handsome,
    Dangling high-tension rackets by the score;
Just nine years old, he stands two metres and some;
    He was inducted into the game before

Birth, his parents having the womb-floor
Wired for soundtracks: great games of the past,
Coaching masterclasses, all the lore
And technical stuff their data-base amassed.
He's won five Grand Slams, still improving fast.

71

Brat breakfasts on twelve pizzas each match-day;
His serve's timed faster than the speed of sound;
Warming-up, he puts a few away –
A ballboy's stretchered-off with a head-wound.
'Zapped!' yells Brat. A genteel murmur round
The court tells him the English don't like bragging;
He thrusts his racket-head between his browned
Thighs and swivels at them, handle wagging
(An ancient Connors ploy): 'You jerks want shagging!'

72

Across the net a starkly different figure
Droops and shambles. Vet is twenty-eight.
A dozen years ago, when faster, bigger,
He did everything fans love to hate:
Stormed off, hurled rackets, kicked the turf . . . Of late
He's blossomed to the darling they adore –
Those injuries – they had to amputate
A foot, fillet his spine, he's like a war
Victim, bravely coming back for more.

73

Game on. Ball bounced twelve times, Brat coils to serve.
Vet never sees it. Soon it's four straight aces.
Vet's turn: his first two curlers don't deserve
Such blistering returns that leave scorch-traces
Right on the baseline. As he vainly chases
The next, he sprawls flat-out. Fans call advice.
Stooping to retie his one shoe's laces,
Vet thinks . . . Serves underarm with wicked slice –
His first point, but you can't pull that trick twice.

74

So it goes on, no contest, Vet just crashes;
  Brat's game's all peaks, his own abysmal troughs.
His cunning lobs receive heart-holing smashes;
  Brat's dead-ball thumpings, obscenities and scoffs
  Earn boos from – as he calls them – 'Limey toffs'.
Vet's wily, moves like a swimmer under water
  Between points, buys time with convulsive coughs,
Calls on the physio, takes breaks off the court – a
Good repertoire, but can't fend off the slaughter.

75

6-0, 6-0, 5-0 and 40-0 –
  Brat's serve, with three match-points. The crowd is hushed,
Except for one lone voice from high above,
  'You can still do it, Vet!' . . . He won't be rushed,
  His body's wrecked, but spirit still uncrushed.
He hobbles to his chair, starts rummaging
  (Brat's chewing gum, he isn't even flushed) –
Another racket-change? The antique thing
Vet picks is wooden-framed, has just one string:

76

A joke . . . Brat tosses the ball high, eyes narrow,
  Whole body a steel spring; he pivots, hits
– The deck, between his ribs a juddering arrow . . .
  He never saw it; nor did the umpire: it's
  Game, set and match to Vet, the crowd's in fits
Of adulation, even the Duke's unbending
  (He's always a soft spot for old favourites).
Vet shrugs: 'A shame about the default-ending,
I'd his game sussed . . . Yes, I'll be back defending.'

77

Of course, by your time virtual-reality
  Will be your natural habitat: you can hit
Or kick balls with stars of the highest quality,
  White-water raft or climb Everest while you sit

In your living-room; or feel you're having it
Off with some sex-goddess, like Marlowe's Faustus
With Helen (but he'd to face the Devil's writ).
I'm sure in gadgetry you've far surpassed us –
But *one* we're crazed with will, I fear, outlast us:

78

It shrills again! – the dark suit opposite
Plucks from his pocket the snub abomination.
Why must he bray so loudly into it?
Yet more why these things *here* cause such vexation
Compared with all surrounding conversation
Is hearing drab facts we already know:
'I'm in a train. No, it's still in the station.
It's late. We should have left some time ago . . .'
One day I'll grab the instrument and throw . . .

79

But, no, you can't these days, our modern carriages
Have windows that don't open. Mutely cursing
His phone, I hope what this sounds like, his marriage, is
On the skids, that while he is disbursing
This stuff about reaching London she's rehearsing
Lies as she strokes the lover at her side . . .
But whistles blow, and I relax back nursing
My take-away coffee dregs, as now we glide
Out into sun, and glittering rails divide.

80

Motor vehicles and aeroplanes
Have practical uses, but without a doubt
I like best travelling in boats and trains.
It's not just that one's free to stroll about,
It's also more rewarding looking out,
Even from boats encircled by the sea –
So much water briefly cresting, mass without
Definition, invokes eternity,
Prompts thoughts of what whelms our small odyssey.

81

But best are trains: the Swiss Glacier Express
  Ascends round Alpine bends above quite scary
Drops; Sicily's Circumetnea gives access
  To lava-built villages; the Danes have very
  Smooth trains that glide on and off a ferry.
But scenic as any is the line that teeters
  Round the coast from Castlerock to Derry,
Between strand and mountain, till land almost peters
Out beneath the wheels in Lough Foyle's waters

82

Of lifetime feats, in memory the merriest –
  More than any to do with work, or pretty
Women, or getting printed, or the beeriest
  Student nights when everyone seemed witty –
  Is when I drove the Manchester intercity
To London: every small boy's dream come true,
  A fantasy outdoing Walter Mitty.
I got the chance at forty, when I knew
Scotch Bill – in charge of the 8.32.

83

His 'Come up front,' the night before when drinking
  A slow pint in the pub, meant 'for the ride'
Only . . . Fine: the metal cab-seat bone-jinking,
  Landscape whacking head-on . . . When I tried
  'You are going to let me – do this thing?' Bill eyed
Me: 'After Rugby.' Two great levers – brake
  And overhead power. Bill stood poised beside
Me ready to pounce on any crass mistake.
'I've got it figured, it's a piece of cake!'

84

Numbers on posts meant curves, and if you failed
  To slow to the *80* or whatever, then
You'd have the half-mile-long express derailed
  In cows or cornfields. Orange specks were men

Maintaining the track, it was pure oxygen
To blow them away with klaxon-riffs. 'Er, Bill,
At Euston there'll be buffers, won't there, when
We need to stop? . . .' 'Laddie, I think I will
Do that bit.' 'Fair enough.' I'd had my thrill.

85

Snatches of summer in suburban park,
Featureless tower-blocks, scabrous streets, and grim
Old works and warehouses flash past, then dark
Walls blot view . . . Before your time, they'll skim
It all off. But however it may hymn
Its hi-tech marvels, your age will be a dullard
If it's not kept, and the lore to keep in trim
For runs, steam-powered, streamlined and blue-coloured,
The loveliest machine we've made, the *Mallard*.

86

A few stops on the Tube . . . In sultry heat
Filthy with traffic, I pace in unavailing
Quest for books I want. In Gower Street,
Pausing a while against an area railing,
Petrol-fumes and drifts of waste assailing
The senses, I look pityingly at the row
Of Georgian terracing, now blotched and ailing;
Used anyhow, stripped of glories long ago
When Regency London put on its great show.

87

All night long, carriage-wheels pouring like Niagara;
Bucks, fops, swells, strutted, drank, danced, wenched and swore;
Their sport to seize and dunk some drunken staggerer
In a horse-trough. Lord Alvaney spent more
On a breakfast's strawberries than would keep three poor
Families for a year. Beaus vandalised,
Aristocratic ladies played the whore.
Profligate, arrogant, they gourmandised,
– Thus the society Byron scandalised.

88

For in its outskirts, gathering mass and gravity,
Were attitudes soon to become Victorian,
Branding all licentiousness as depravity;
Church and State proclaiming in stentorian
Tones the basis of our national glory an
Upright respectability (parenthetical
Underclasses told a different story) – an
Ethos licensing many hypocritical
Deeds, marital, commercial and political.

89

The moral pendulum swings, swings back again.
My youth's good causes won their victories –
Race, sex, for women equal rights with men –
And now can seem repressive orthodoxies,
As, spreading from the USA, PC's
Got humour by the throat, made parents shrink on
Finding old books where girls do not climb trees.
Though the last American leader I can think on
Who *was* politically correct is Lincoln.

90

Whatever may be your age's moral code –
Have you still marriage? Bishops? Gay TV?
Do Orangemen march down the Garvaghy Road
While smiling Catholics bring them cups of tea?
(I doubt that.) Is your public transport free,
And private cars more anti-social than
Wearing furs, beating children, or VD? –
Still people will find some way where they can
Round what gauleiters advocate and ban.

91

You may lash young offenders with the cat;
Sterilise adulterers; lock up all not working . . .
The Pill and Net alone should stop all that –
Yet fundamentalism's always lurking –

In every culture, just when things are perking
Up a bit, up pop costive ideologues
Laying down law: *Jump to our tune, no shirking*
Or it's quick-march to a life-stretch chopping logs
Sunny Jim, up north in snows and fogs.

92

I pass through Charing Cross Station: *Hither Green, Lee,*
Mottingham, New Eltham . . . A departing train
Announced . . . Forty years ago that used to be
My line – and, flung back, I see again
High in that big old house masked by a skein
Of foliage, my matchbox-sized bedsitter,
Sloping ceiling with an Africa-shaped damp-stain,
Where snared in London's rush and roar and glitter
I wrote three novels – long since dumped as litter.

93

The rush-hour round me now throngs thick as ever,
Shirtsleeved in this heat-wave. I slip down
Villiers Street and stroll along the River
(Oh-so-familiar the creak and groan
Of trains over Hungerford Bridge – this still my town,
An *A to Z* of bitter-sweet memories
Carried through decades far from where these brown
Waters flow beneath Embankment trees),
To a poetry party at the Cheshire Cheese.

94

A launch for a new anthology – a raft
Of poets now so youthful one or two
May be around still practising their craft
When the time comes to pass the torch to you.
Later, on my train home, I glance through
Some of their verse, and much seems talented.
Pimped-on by arts-spivs, dress ripped, wreath askew,
The Muse outwits our gloomings – the sick-bed
Proves empty each time we'd pronounce her dead.

95

Hale, at a new address, she keeps us writing –
  I trust you'll call it that still, even when
The manual part's as obsolete as gas-lighting
  And children sweeping chimneys. Will you then,
  Instead of anything I'd call a pen,
Make print blossom from voice-recognition? –
  Just *think* a sonnet onto screen? . . . But men
And women will still need creative vision
To keep the spirit upright and on-mission.

96

So I get up again; and our strange world . . .
  Or rather, those upon this longitudinal
Segment of what time sends spinning, hurled
  Towards your era like a crazy fruit, in all
  Parts, as I pursue my day's matutinal
Tasks here, others, at lunch, in bed, in planes,
  Work, pray, love, kill; yearnings half-understood in all
Ignite to music, jump in front of trains;
Superstars thrash each other with turquoise chains.

97

You'll have all that, and worse. And less: for glancing
  At our films and photographs you'll see
Who's paid the price for humankind's advancing –
  Rhinoceros, tiger, eagle, manatee
  (Unless some novel strain of killer bee
Has turned the tables), may to you be mythical
  As unicorns and mermaids are to me.
Yet, walking this shore where wildlife's still prolific, all
I see I hope for you too may be typical.

98

Seals, seabirds, lobsters, crabs . . . And tumbling from
  Car or station eagerly to crane
At water holidaying children come
  Certain of their Promised Land – terrain

Our rest-of-life pursues elsewhere in vain.
Yet hints still gleam for adults, as they steer
Pushchairs, fly kites, chase balls; don't complain
Through patient waits for drizzling skies to clear:
Let's all go for a choc-ice on the Pier . . .

99

I like to think your time will still have leisure
(I know, you have a million different and
Electronic forms of fun) to know the pleasure
Of days at seasides doing things unplanned;
Watching (as I've watched mine) your child just stand
Squirming bare toes at the sea's edge for hours
To lose his feet but for the clasp of sand;
Or roam marsh burnished by rain-waves, sunshowers,
Between grass head-high flecked with purple flowers.

100

A hundred stanzas seems the point to stop.
But how to send this? Wells's Time Machine
Stays fantasy . . . Fax? – e-mail? – or just drop
It in our postal system, which has been
Known sometimes to deliver mail umpteen
Years later – even several generations.
But no: however much has changed between
Us in infrastructure, habits, fashions,
A book's the best route to unknown locations.

And You, If You

And You, if You, through life I've tried prayer: nothing back,
Not even like letters marked *Return to Sender*.

The laws of our physics swirl down black holes
Into *cosmic foam*. For You too we find metaphor:
Heavenly Father, Great Watchmaker, Dove Descending . . .

We impute to You deeds that insult our brain. You are Purpose?

The refugees pour from Kosovo, children robbed of their childhood.

Reason fails dumb at our human black holes,
We listen to Beethoven who means nothing and everything:
Can he be mere spume off blind genes?

On the Cross You are love, not power.

Sunlit lawn: 'That whirl of midges, what are they *for*?
Science says, "Part of the food-chain", but *what for*?'
He is jocular. I reel in Your vortex.

Through twenty centuries heaped with gorgeous fossils,
York Minster, the *Hymn Book*, the Sistine Chapel ceiling,
Your Gospel shines new as the penny my childhood found
In each Christmas stocking, mint-fresh for next year.

We drift the world on bright threads we spin,
Art, memory. You are the dream we cannot give up,
Still vibrant with our cries.

Index of Titles

Index of First Lines